THE WAY OF PERFECTION

St. Teresa of Jesus
1515-1582

THE WAY OF PERFECTION

By

St. Teresa of Avila

Translated from the Autograph of St. Teresa of Jesus, including All the Variants from the Escorial and Valladolid Editions, by

The Benedictines of Stanbrook

Revised, with Notes and an Introduction, by the

Very Rev. Fr. Benedict Zimmerman, O.C.D.
PRIOR

TAN BOOKS AND PUBLISHERS, INC.
Rockford, Illinois 61105

Nihil Obstat: Dom Michael Barrett, O.S.B.
Censor Deputatus 1919

Re-Imprimatur: ✠ Michael Francis
Bishop of Flaviopolitanus
Vicar General
February 19, 1925

This translation first published in approximately 1911. This edition published in 1997 by TAN Books and Publishers, Inc. by arrangement with the Benedictines of Stanbrook, being photographically reproduced from the Third Impression which was published by Thomas Baker, London, in 1925.

Library of Congress Catalog Card No.: 97-60907

ISBN 0-89555-602-2

Cover illustration: Contemporary portrait of St. Teresa of Avila by Fray Juan de la Miseria, Discalced Carmelites, Seville.

Printed and bound in the United States of America.

TAN BOOKS AND PUBLISHERS, INC.
P.O. Box 424
Rockford, Illinois 61105
1997

Misericordias Domini in aeternum cantabo.
"The mercies of the Lord I will sing forever."

—Motto of St. Teresa of Avila
(*Psalm* 88:2)

The Benedictines of Stanbrook desire to express their gratitude to the V.R. Prior Benedict Zimmerman for his kindness in revising the 'Way of Perfection', and also for the notes and Introduction which he has added to it.

Stanbrook Abbey, Worcester.

PREFACE OF THE FIRST EDITION

THEOTONIO DE BRAGANZA, ARCHBISHOP OF EVORA, IN PORTUGAL (HOWEVER UNWORTHY) TO THE PIOUS AND DEVOUT MOTHERS, THE NUNS OF THE PRIMITIVE RULE OF OUR LADY OF MOUNT CARMEL. HEALTH IN OUR LORD JESUS CHRIST!

AMONG many favours I have received from our Lord, not the least was my intimate acquaintance with the Very Reverend Mother Teresa of Jesus, now in glory, because in her I have witnessed the splendour of the gifts of our Lord and of His divine grace. These are evidenced by the convents founded by her according to the primitive Rule of our Lady of Mount Carmel, without any mitigation, but with as much religious observance and recollection, with such austerity, such unceasing prayer and as much manual labour as our weak human nature is able to bear. She herself was a living example of that manner of life, and she fully trusted that our Lord would grant to His servants spiritual and bodily strength to persevere to the end. So great were the charity and fervour of this Mother, such was her solicitude for the perfection of her daughters, that she did not content herself with the good example and the instructions she gave while alive, but wished that, even after her death, her words might remain and continue the work she had begun on earth. As one truly hungering after our Lord, and greatly experienced in all that concerns the religious life, she wrote the advice and the explanations contained in this book, so that the sadness caused to the nuns by her bodily absence might be counterbalanced by her spiritual presence; for indeed she seems living even in the dead letters. This, then, is one of the consolations with which her spiritual daughters may alleviate the sorrow caused by her death; another being the certainty that, where she now is, she will not abandon those whom she so ardently loved, because, so far from being less, charity is much greater in heaven than on earth.

It is no small consolation to see, albeit after her death, her spirit still alive in the doctrine of this book, which she composed through zeal for the spiritual improvement of her daughters, and which she earnestly requested me to get printed.

There being various manuscript copies, it was unavoidable that there should be many passages at variance with what she had written; this could only be obviated by printing the whole work, and therefore I willingly complied with her request.

In this book, then, she first recommends the practice of prayer and meditation which give a taste of that sweetness reserved by God for those who fear Him, rendering them prompt and ready for all the works of virtue. For, just as Satan, with the allurement of pleasure, leads men to vice, so the Holy Ghost opposes to the sensual a spiritual pleasure whereby He inclines them to the practice of virtue.

She further strongly recommends the mortification of our unruly appetites and our self-will, which is brought about by prayer which softens the heart, and by its sweetness compensates for the bitterness inseparable from mortification. These two virtues might be termed frankincense and myrrh, so often mentioned in the Canticle of Canticles; incense, having the property of rising into the air, represents prayer; and myrrh, which has a bitter taste, mortification.

Moreover, she recommends in this book interior recollection and the withdrawal from conversation with worldly people, were they even our own parents, according to the words of the prophet: 'Hearken, O daughter, and see, and incline thy ear; and forget thy people and thy father's house' (Psalm xliv. 11). She recommends manual labour with a view to lessen such conversations and to enable the nuns, who ought to be lovers of the poverty of Christ, to provide for their own needs without having recourse to their families for assistance. St. Paul himself, notwithstanding his care of all the churches, provided by the labour of his hands for his own requirements and those of his companions; how, then, could persons who have no such charge dispense themselves, with a good conscience, from this duty?

She likewise recommends the rigour and the austerity of the monastic life, and this rigour has ever been maintained. For the first obligation of religious persons, who have consecrated their body and soul to Christ their Spouse, is to follow the Lamb whithersoever He goeth, which means to imitate and follow Him, and we know that her whole life was a perpetual bearing of the cross, and that she was exceedingly zealous for the rigour and strictness of the Order, labouring hard that it might ever remain firm and never become weakened, for, if the least mitigation were allowed to creep in, relaxation would inevitably follow until the whole edifice came to grief; for our nature has a tendency towards ease, and drags us down. This austerity has a further advantage, inasmuch as those who might choose the religious life, not for the sake of God, but for earthly considerations, could never select a manner of life so entirely at variance with the inclinations of human nature. Just as the sea casts out dead bodies, so a strict Order frightens away those who, without being called by God, are only guided by human considerations. It follows that none will choose it but those ready to give up the world for the sake of Christ, and these, so far from chafing under the recollection and austerity of this kind of life, cherish it, and these are precisely the class of persons who maintain the Order in its integrity. This Mother also wished her nuns to be few in number, because small means are large enough for a few, and thus will be warded off the greatest danger that could befall a religious community, namely, that of paying more attention to the dowry than to the spirit and devotion of aspirants; otherwise some persons unfit for the religious life might be admitted. And as they must needs be strict in the choice of those whom they receive, they must be prompt in dismissing those who have not the required qualities. For this reason she thought it imprudent to receive nuns coming from a great distance, as it might not be convenient to send them back to their homes if the necessity arose.

These are the points, very reverend Mothers, that you will learn from this book, and which I have learnt from the life and the example of your Mother, together with many other particulars about the gifts and virtues with which our Lord had enriched her. One of these was her wonderful obedience to her spiritual fathers, which was such that sometimes, when she knew the will of God to be different from theirs, she obeyed them all the same, our Lord approving her manner of acting and testifying that He preferred obedience to confessors and superiors.[1]

She possessed another special gift of our Lord, namely this, that all the persons dealing with her changed their lives and advanced in virtue, as has been clearly seen in some religious deficient in gravity and learning, and also in many other persons. Not less remarkable was another gift she held from God, which enabled her to lead her visitors to the exercise of prayer and meditation, so that in a very short time and with great facility, they even became masters in that art, provided they had the necessary disposition.

Owing to the great desire I have that your Reverences should in all things imitate her and faithfully guard the treasure entrusted to you, I wished to remind you of these matters, trusting that our Lord, Who hath given you so rich a share of His spirit, will preserve it within you. Thus you will ever advance from virtue to virtue until you attain perfection, and will not be far from the glorious sight of your most sweet Bridegroom, our

[1] This applies to the will of God as manifested by visions, locutions etc., not, of course, to any positive command either of Holy Scripture or of the Church. An example is given in note 8, page 192.

Lord. For myself I desire no other reward than that the nuns into whose hands this book may fall should commend me to our Lord, asking Him that, since His Majesty has placed me in this high position, He may also give me the grace so to fill it that after this mortal life I may come to the enjoyment of His glory, which we believe this blessed Mother already possesses. I trust she will not forget those that loved her during life, nor those devoted to her since she has gone.

May Christ ever dwell in the souls of your Reverences with the abundance of His grace.

THEOTONIO, ARCHBISHOP OF EVORA.

CONTENTS

CHAPTER V

CHAPTER VI

CHAPTER VII

CHAPTER VIII

CHAPTER IX

CHAPTER X

CHAPTER XI

CHAPTER XII

CHAPTER XIII

CHAPTER XIV

CHAPTER XV

CHAPTER XVI

CHAPTER XVII

CHAPTER XVIII

CHAPTER XIX

CHAPTER XX

CHAPTER XXI

CHAPTER XXII

CHAPTER XXIII

CHAPTER XXIV

CHAPTER XXV

CHAPTER XXVI

CHAPTER XXVII

CHAPTER XXVIII

CHAPTER XXIX

CHAPTER XXX

CHAPTER XXXI

CHAPTER XXXII

CHAPTER XXXIII

CHAPTER XXXIV

CHAPTER XLI

CHAPTER XLII

INTRODUCTION

THE convent of St. Joseph at Avila having been inaugurated on August 24, 1562, and the storms occasioned by its foundation having somewhat subsided, St. Teresa received permission from the Provincial, Fray Angel de Salazar, to leave the monastery of the Incarnation and join her new community; she crossed the threshold of that 'Paradise,' as our Lord had vouchsafed to call it, about Mid-Lent 1563, never to leave the enclosure again—as she fervently hoped. She did not know then that God had destined her to more arduous work which would compel her to sally forth and establish convent after convent in distant parts of Spain. Her sojourn at St. Joseph's only lasted four and a half years, but, as she says, it was the happiest time of her life. The convent was small and poor, the observance as strict as human nature, strengthened by grace, can bear, but she enjoyed to the full the peace which, after the many struggles graphically described in the *Life*, had at length been granted her.

The visitor who has the privilege of penetrating

into the hallowed enclosure will have to reconstruct in his mind the convent as it was in St. Teresa's time. The handsome church was not yet begun, and what is now called the primitive chapel was in reality built at a later period, though undoubtedly on the original lines. For even now it is only about twelve paces long and eight paces wide, and the sanctuary, the sacristy, and the nuns' choir are of diminutive proportions. The main building of the convent, in the shape of a quadrangle, is likewise a later addition: in the Saint's time a few old and small houses served for a convent, and the kitchen, the refectory, and other dependencies being on a lower level than the surrounding land, were both dark and damp. There were then no lay sisters to do the house-work. The few choir nuns took it in turns to see to the washing, the scrubbing, the service in the kitchen and scullery, and Teresa, who had been nominated Prioress by the Bishop, and retained that office until her death (employing a Vicaress during her prolonged absences), took her share, and more than her share, in the common work. Never was the convent so scrupulously clean as when it was her turn to do the scrubbing. Never was the food so tasty as when she did the kitchen, though she might have been seen in an ecstasy, saucepan in hand. The Divine Office was performed with a devotion and a refinement which were at once a source of edification for the faithful and a revelation to the clerics who came to assist at it.

The convent was unendowed, and voluntary alms were anything but abundant; so the nuns spent long hours in spinning in order to earn their livelihood, and we know that Teresa herself was busy with the distaff, not only when alone in her cell but also when in the parlour with visitors. How, after all that, there remained any time for anything else is a wonder; but the fact is that during these four and a half years she did find the time to write two works which have brought light and peace into the hearts of thousands. She had been advised by Don Francisco Soto y Salazar, the Grand Inquisitor, to write a full history of her life, and to send it to Blessed Juan d'Avila, the man who, since the death of St. Peter of Alcantara, was better able than anybody in Spain to judge about spiritual experiences. She began it probably soon after having taken up her residence at St. Joseph's, and completed it in May or June, or, at the latest, in the course of the summer of 1565. The place where she wrote this marvellous work is still shown to the visitor. The cell inhabited by her has been left exactly as she left it herself when last she bade farewell to the convent. With the exception of a bed it contains no furniture: no table to put her books on, no chair to sit on. When writing she knelt or sat on the floor, the paper lying on a small projection of the wall in the window recess. Glass windows would have been too great a luxury for St. Joseph's convent; instead of these the nuns used canvas fixed in a frame and fastened in the open window. Had it not been for the fire burning within her, her fingers must have been numbed during the long evenings in cold Avila when she was writing, at a prodigious speed, at a window practically open.

The sisters, though perhaps free from inquisitiveness, could not have helped noticing how much their saintly Prioress was writing, and no doubt were told she was composing a work on prayer. Prayer being the very object for which they had joined her, and, at the same time, a subject on which careful and detailed instruction is required, no less than on the most recondite science, they were naturally anxious to read that work. There is so much in it that concerns any one desirous of doing more than merely repeat a set form of prayers. They lived a life of prayer, and they required a guiding hand. However, besides the incomparable treatise on the various phases of the contemplative life, it contains much that is intensely personal, and if Teresa was always anxious to lay bare her innermost soul before those who held the place of God in her respect, she was by no means willing to make known to the world, at least during her life-time, the wonderful graces showered on her. As to her failings and shortcomings, she was more than ready to proclaim them, even in exaggerated terms; but Divine favours—no! least of all to those over whom she exercised superiority: before these she only delighted in humbling herself.

However, the nuns would not be put off; they appealed to the confessor, Fray Domingo Bañez, who commanded the Prioress to write one more book, embodying the homely instructions she was wont to give her daughters. An order coming from God's representative always found ready compliance on her part. Thus, no sooner was the *Life* completed than she took up her pen once more.

Not much reflection was required about the title of the new work. 'The Way of Perfection' was a favourite expression of the Saint's. She found it in the *Imitation of Christ*:[1] 'Hence it comes to pass that I recognize the way of perfection'; and also in one of the Meditations of St. Peter of Alcantara:[2] 'But the servant of God that expecteth merit and comfort in the way of perfection', while she herself had repeatedly used it in the *Life*: 'Some of them began to walk in the way of perfection';[3] 'it requires greater courage in one not yet perfect to walk in the way of perfection'; 'I

[1] *Imitation*, bk. iii. ch. lv. 3.

[2] *Meditations of St. Peter of Alcantara*, translated by Giles Willoughby, p. 199 (Liverpool, 1843); and later by George Seymour Hollings.

[3] *Life*, ch. xxi. 9; xxxi. 19; xxxv. 14.

cannot understand what it is that makes men afraid of the way of perfection.' It is not the 'way of the perfect' of which the *Imitation* speaks in another place,[1] but the road that leads to perfection. Although she never grew tired of praising the perfection of the few nuns gathered around her,[2] she could not but foresee that others, less advanced, might come in the future, and she desired to address herself to these no less than to the former. This was all the more necessary as there appears to have been a slight misunderstanding about the title of the newly established Reform. St. Teresa called herself and her nuns 'Discalced', following in this the example of some other Orders which had been lately reformed and had made barefootedness the distinctive sign of the Reform, so much so that 'barefooted' and 'Reformed' came to be synonymous terms. But in Rome the new Reform of the Carmelite Order received a different title. The General, John Baptist Rubeo, called the Reformed members of his Order Contemplatives. Thus, in a patent of 1567 he speaks of 'houses and monasteries of contemplative Carmelites',[3] and again in 1570 he addresses 'the contemplative Carmelites of the Province of Castile'.[4] Both

[1] *Imitation*, bk. iii. ch. xxxii. 3.

[2] *Foundations*, ch. i. iv. sqq.

[3] Patent of August 16, 1567: '*casas y monasterios de Carmelitas contemplativos.*'

[4] Patent of August 8, 1570: '*ad Carmelitas contemplativos provinciæ Castellæ.*'

these documents, as well as some others, are of a later date than the first version of the *Way of Perfection*, but the expression may have been used before it was committed to writing. It will be noticed in various passages of the book, especially the second half of it, that some of the nuns seem to have been somewhat alarmed by that title, thinking perhaps that only those who possessed the supernatural gift of contemplation were called to the life led at St. Joseph's convent. St. Teresa wished to dispel these fears. She repeatedly explains that she is not treating of contemplation, but writes for those who are generously and faithfully doing their utmost in the service of the Lord, quite independently of the question whether or not they have received that gift; she wishes to put them on the road towards perfection, leaving it to Him Who alone can dispense heavenly favours to complete the work begun in their hearts. If in the present life they do not attain perfect contemplation, their faithfulness in small things will unquestionably lead them to the very highest degree of it in the next life. For those who are already in this world called to contemplation further instructions may be required, and these will be found in the book of her *Life*, should her confessor think it advisable that they should read it. For the others the present work will suffice, as it teaches that sanctity does not consist in doing extraordinary things, but in doing ordinary things extraordinarily well.

This it is that makes the *Way of Perfection* so useful for people of various conditions, and not only for those who serve God within the walls of an enclosed convent. Many who could not understand the Saint's teaching on mystical theology, and for whom the *Life* and the *Interior Castle* would be sealed books, will find in the *Way of Perfection* practical advice to last them a life-time.

St. Teresa knew this. She could not but notice the progress made by her nuns day by day in consequence of her oral instructions, of which this book is an epitome. She was therefore most anxious that her work should come into the hands not only of her contemporaries, but also of those that were to come in the future.

We do not know when the volume was completed. The only allusion to contemporary events refers to the ravages of the heretics in the south of France, of which heart-rending accounts must have reached the Saint. The destruction of Catholic churches, the profanation of the Blessed Sacrament, the pulling down of sacred images, the sacking of convents, and the murder of priests, made a terrible impression on her. One of her biographers also alludes to the destruction of convents in England, but that had taken place during her early life in the Order; yet perhaps some news may have reached her of the events in Scotland. Be this as it may, her own writings only refer to France. On the other hand, it must be taken for certain that the book was finished before the visit of the General, in April 1567, which led to the foundation of the convent at Medina del Campo and others, and was a land-mark in her life; she would certainly have mentioned it, had she then been engaged on the *Way of Perfection*. She says more than once that her confessor, Domingo Bañez, was to examine the book before it could be placed in the hands of the nuns. In fact, both he and Fray Garcia de Toledo read and approved it, though neither has left a written approbation, but there is reason to believe that some passages were deleted by Bañez. The original manuscript appears to have remained in the convent of St. Joseph at Avila until, in 1586, four years after the death of St. Teresa, it was lent to Fray Luis de Leon, who had been entrusted with the editing of her works; when he had done with it, it was presented to Philip II. for the royal monastery of the Escorial, where it has remained ever since, and where the present writer was privileged to see it. It is not in the library, but in a small room where some other precious manuscripts, as well as certain relics of saints, are preserved.

But it was not the intention of St. Teresa that

this book should be the exclusive property of the nuns of St. Joseph's. From August 1567, when she established the convent at Medina del Campo, until a few months before her death, she was engaged on the foundation of numerous convents after the pattern of the first; over a hundred pious women took the habit of Our Lady of Mount Carmel and dedicated themselves to a life of intercession and vicarious suffering. These, too, stood in need of the instructions contained in the *Way of Perfection* not less than of the regulations laid down in the Rule and Constitutions. Accordingly St. Teresa undertook to write the whole book over again, paying special attention to the corrections made by the reviser. In addition to these she introduced many changes, aiming at greater precision, rearranging whole chapters and developing some of her thoughts. Neither the date nor the place where this second edition was composed can now be ascertained. The manuscript, with the exception of a few leaves which have been lost or purloined, is preserved at the convent of Valladolid; it is bound in solid silver, and forms one of the chief treasures of that convent. This manuscript was repeatedly copied during the life-time of the Saint. One copy is at Toledo, another at the convent of El Pardo, at Madrid, and a third one at Salamanca: all containing variants in the handwriting of the Saint, but only the second and third bearing the signature of St. Teresa, who testifies to their being faithful copies. One more copy is to be found in the library of the Escorial, agreeing literally with the original of Valladolid. But this probably was not known to the Saint, and may have been made after her death. Other convents may also have procured copies of the book; but, if so, these must have been lost.

In a letter to her brother, Don Lorenzo de Cepeda, dated January 2, 1577,[1] St. Teresa says: 'The book which treats of the matter of which I have told you is the one where I explained the Pater Noster. There you will find considerations on the degree of prayer which you have reached, although the subject is not so fully developed as in the other book (the *Life*). I think it is in the explanation of these words: *Adveniat regnum tuum.* Read it again, at least the section on the *Pater Noster*; perhaps you will find something to satisfy you.' Thus Don Lorenzo must have had access to the work.

But copying a book with the pen was a long process, and there was always a danger of omissions and changes, which could only be obviated by having the whole work printed. To this end, she sent a copy, the one now at Toledo, to Don Teutonio de Braganza, Archbishop of Evora, requesting him to make the necessary arrangements.

[1] Letters, vol. ii. no. 161.

The letter is unfortunately not preserved, but in one of July 22, 1579[1] she says: 'Last week I wrote a long letter to your Lordship sending you my little book; I will therefore only write a few words to-day, as I forgot to ask your Lordship whether the *Life of our Holy Father Saint Albert* (which you will find in the same volume as my book) might be printed together with the latter. It would be a great consolation for us all, for that *Life* is only to be found in Latin.[2] It has been translated by a Father of the Order of St. Dominic, one of the most learned men we have in our country, and a great servant of God. He has done it for love of me, not knowing, however, that it was to be published. He has not received permission from his Provincial, neither did he ask for it, but this does not matter much, provided your Lordship is satisfied with the book and undertakes its publication.'

Don Teutonio was not quite satisfied with the manuscript of the *Way of Perfection* submitted to him. He returned it to the Saint, who in the meantime had gone from Valladolid to Salamanca, where she revised it once more with the assistance of Sister Hieronyma of the Holy Ghost; many

[1] Vol. iii. no. 291.

[2] St. Albert, Carmelite, born in Trapani in Sicily, about the middle of the thirteenth Century, died at Messina, August 7, 1306. His life, written by an anonymous author towards the end of the fourteenth Century (cf. *Analecta Bollandiana*, 1898, vol. xvii p. 317) was published at Venice in 1499 by Johannes Maria Polutianus de Novarola. The Spanish translation was made by Fray Diego de Yangüas.

passages were recast, and a whole chapter was omitted.[1] Don Teutonio granted the permission for printing the volume on October 7, 1580, but unforeseen circumstances must have caused a long delay, for his prefatory letter was only written in 1582, the book appearing the following year, after the death of St. Teresa. This first edition has become exceedingly rare, only three copies being known to exist. But it was so much appreciated that reprints appeared at Salamanca in 1585 and at Valencia in 1587.[2]

Meanwhile Fray Luis de Leon had been entrusted with the task of editing the complete works of the Saint. All the manuscripts then available were placed in his hands, among them the two autographs and the three copies containing corrections in the Saint's own handwriting. Taking the text of Valladolid for his basis, he incorporated with it many of the variants to be found in the other sources, so that his edition, which appeared in 1588, so far from being a reproduction of any one of the authentic texts, was rather a combination of all of them. It has been reproduced, times without number, until recent years; the two English translations, by Abraham Woodhead and his companion, in 1675, and by Canon

[1] See the new French edition, due to the indefatigable labours of the Carmelite nuns of Paris. (*Œuvres complètes de Sainte Térèse*, vol. v. Introduction. (Paris, 1901)

[2] *Ibid.* p 16.

Dalton in 1852, have followed it, though the latter allowed himself to be influenced by the French translation of Robert Arnauld d'Andilly, one (though, perhaps, the least dangerous) of the Jansenist leaders.

The merit of having returned to one of the originals, the manuscript of Valladolid, belongs to P. Marcel Bouix, whose French translation appeared in 1856. In 1883, on the occasion of the third centenary of the death of the Saint, Don Francisco Herrera Bayona, treasurer of the Metropolitan church of Valladolid, undertook the publication of a photographic reproduction of St. Teresa's autograph, as Don Vicente de la Fuente had already done for the *Life* and the *Book of the Foundations*. He was only allowed to photograph the manuscript of the Escorial, but every facility was accorded him to prepare a literal transcript of the one at Valladolid, which he printed in parallel columns with the transcript of the former version. Moreover, he confronted with these texts the three early copies of Toledo, Madrid, and Salamanca, as well as Don Teutonio's edition, adding to the volume a complete apparatus of variants. This edition has been utilized for the present translation, which was ready for the press four years ago, but the publication of which has been delayed owing to a prolonged absence of the present writer.

The question which text to follow in this

translation has been carefully discussed by those who were able to form an opinion. The first idea was to choose one of the two original versions, and to supplement it by the variants which would have been added as foot-notes, or at least printed in a different style; but, after various essays, it was found that such an arrangement would prove bewildering for the generality of readers, while the student, who alone can be interested in the gradual evolution of the text, finds the whole material in Don Francisco's edition. It was therefore decided, though not without reluctance, to follow the precedent (but not the text) of Luis de Leon, and to combine once more the various versions, so that this edition should contain everything written by St. Teresa. There are some chapters where the divergence between the versions of the Escorial and of Valladolid is so great that the translation resembles a mosaic composed of a large number of small bits, skilfully combined. But the work has been done most conscientiously, and while nothing has been added to the text of the Saint, nothing has been omitted, except, of course, what would have been mere repetition. No doubt the plan adopted in this translation will not meet with the approval of scholars, but as the translator desired to benefit the souls of the faithful rather than the intellect of the student, no other course could have been chosen. The present writer has repeatedly compared every word with the originals and can vouch for the accuracy of the translation.

A word must be added about another writing frequently attributed to St. Teresa, namely, the *Seven Meditations on the Pater Noster, for the Days of the Week.* This short work appeared for the first time at Antwerp in 1630 and has been frequently reprinted and translated into many languages, including English. But the book is not by St. Teresa. Not one of her biographers knew anything about it; it is never alluded to either in her correspondence or in the very numerous and minute depositions made by all sorts and conditions of persons during the process of canonization, while the Chronicler of the Order distinctly denies its authenticity, giving good reasons for his judgment. It is probably the work of some friar or nun, and deserves respect owing to the pious sentiments it contains. But no one acquainted with the style of St. Teresa could admit its authenticity.

BENEDICT ZIMMERMAN
Prior, O.C.D.

ST. LUKE'S PRIORY
WINCANTON.
October 15, 1910.

THE WAY OF PERFECTION

AUTHOR'S PROTESTATION

In whatever I may say in this book, I submit to what our Mother, the Holy Roman Church, teaches; if I write anything contrary to this, it will be unintentionally. Therefore, I beg of the theologians who are to read it, for the love of our Lord to examine it carefully and to correct any such faults as well as any other defects it may possess. If it has any good in it, may it be for the honour and glory of God and the service of His most holy Mother, our Patron and our Lady, whose habit I wear, although most unworthy of it.

(This Protestation, although not to be found in her autographs, was written by St. Teresa for the edition published after her death at Evora.)

BOOK ENTITLED

THE WAY OF PERFECTION

COMPOSED BY

TERESA OF JESUS

NUN OF THE ORDER OF OUR LADY OF MOUNT CARMEL. DEDICATED TO THE DISCALCED NUNS OF OUR LADY OF CARMEL OF THE PRIMITIVE RULE.

SUBJECT MATTER OF THE BOOK

JHS

This book contains advice and counsel given by Teresa of Jesus to her sisters and daughters, the religious, of the convents which, with the help of our Lord and the glorious Virgin Mother of God, our Lady, she has founded according to the Primitive Rule of our Lady of Carmel. It is specially dedicated to the sisters of the convent of St. Joseph, Avila, the first of her houses in which, while Prioress there, she wrote this treatise.[1]

[1] This title was written by the Saint herself on the first leaf of the Valladolid edition of the Way of Perfection.

INTRODUCTION

WHICH CONTAINS THE REASONS FOR WRITING THIS BOOK.

THE sisters of this convent of St. Joseph, having learnt that my confessor, Father Master Domingo Bañez, of the glorious Order of St. Dominic, had given me leave to write about prayer,[1] of which I appeared capable because of having spoken with so many spiritual and devout persons, have so importuned me that I have decided on complying with their wishes. Faulty and imperfect as my style may be, I know that the sisters' great love for me will give my words more influence with them than that of books far better written by those who know what they are writing about. Therefore I have determined to yield to the nuns' wishes and persuasions. I rely upon their prayers and on humility; perhaps by these means God may give me grace to say something useful concerning the life that ought to be led in this house and helpful to my sisters, and He may teach me, so that I may teach them.

If I fail, Father Master, who is to read these writings first, will either correct them or throw them into the fire: thus I shall have lost nothing

[1] *Rel.* vii. 9. *Way of Perf.* xlii.

by obeying the wishes of these servants of God, and they will discover what I really am when His Majesty does not assist me.

I intend suggesting remedies for certain minor temptations of the devil, which, because they are slight, are often disregarded; also to explain my object in founding this house, namely, to restore the perfect observance of our Rule that had been mitigated elsewhere.[2] I will also speak of other matters as our Lord may direct me, and as they occur to my mind. Not knowing of what things I shall treat, I cannot arrange them in proper order. I think, after all, that this is best, as it is quite incongruous for such a person as myself to speak about such subjects. May our Lord guide me in all I do, that it may be pleasing to His holy will, for this has always been my aim, faulty as my deeds may be.

I know that on my part there is no lack of love for my sisters, nor of a desire to do all I can to help their souls to make great progress in God's service. This affection, my age, and my personal experience in various convents, may assist me to write of such lesser matters better than theologians whose more important business and powerful minds make them overlook things, insignificant in themselves, yet which may do great harm to such weak creatures as we women are. The devil employs his most subtle wiles against strictly cloistered nuns, for he sees that he requires some new sort of weapon to injure them. Wicked as I am, I have been able to defend myself but ill against him, and I wish my

[2] *Life*, xxxii. 13, 14; xxxv. 13, 14; xxxvi. 27, 28.

sisters to take warning by me. I shall only speak of what I have learnt by my own experience, have witnessed in others, or that God has shown to me during prayer.

A short time ago I was told to write a history of my life, in which I have also treated of prayer: as perhaps my confessor may not permit you to read it, I shall repeat some of it here, besides adding other things which I believe are requisite. May God direct my work, as I have begged of Him, and may He order it all for His greater glory! Amen.

CHAPTER I

THE REASON WHY I FOUNDED THIS CONVENT IN SUCH AUSTERE OBSERVANCE

1. Why the Convent of St. Joseph at Avila was founded. 2. Reasons for the corporal austerities of this convent. 3. St. Teresa's grief at sin and the eternal loss of sinners. 4. She begs the nuns to intercede against these evils. 5. This, and not worldly matters, should be the object of our petitions.

1. THIS convent was founded for the reasons already given in the work above mentioned,[1] and also on account of certain favours that God showed me, in which He revealed that He would be served with great fervour in this house.[2] I did not at first intend that such rigorous bodily austerities should be practised in it, nor that it should possess no income; on the contrary, I wished it to have sufficient means to prevent the possibility of want; which shows how weak and wicked I am, although I meant rather to do what was right than to seek for self-indulgence.[3]

2. Just at this time I heard of the miseries France was suffering, of the havoc the Lutherans were making there, and how this wretched sect was increasing.[4] It grieved me bitterly, and as if I could

[1] *Life*, xxxii. 13. *Rel.* vii, 14.

[2] *Life*, xxxii. 14; xxxv. 13. *Castle*, M. VI. vi. 2; M. VII. iv. 21. *Foundations*, i. 6, 7.

[3] *Life*, xxxiii. 15; xxxv. 2-7.

[4] *Life*, xxxii. 9. *Rel.* ii. 14 *Way of Perf.* xxxv. 3. Luis de Leon relates that the mere mention of the ravages committed by the heretics on the monasteries of Germany and England so wounded St. Teresa's heart as to cause her constant pain. The first and chief reason for her founding the houses of Discalced Carmelites was to repair, to some extent, these wrongs done by the heretics. (Fuente, vol. VI. 130. Note 19.)

have done anything, or had been of any consequence, I cried to God and begged Him to cure this terrible evil. I felt that I would have laid down a thousand lives to save one of the many souls perishing there. Yet, as I am but a woman, feeble and faulty, it was impossible for me to serve God in the way I wished—indeed, all I cared for then, as I do now, was that, as the enemies of God are so many and His friends so few, these latter might at least be good ones. Therefore I determined to do what little was in my power, which was to follow the Evangelical counsels as perfectly as I could and to see that the few nuns here should do the same.[5] Trusting in the great mercy of God which never fails those who resolve to leave all things for His sake, I hoped that, as my sisters here are all that I ever wished them to be, their virtues would be strong enough to resist the influence of my defects and that I might be able to bring some comfort to our Lord. Thus, being all of us employed in interceding for the champions of the Church and the preachers and theologians who defend her, we might, to our utmost, aid this Lord of mine Who is attacked with such cruelty by those on whom He has conferred great benefits that it seems as though they would fasten Him to the Cross again, leaving Him no place to lay His head.

3. O my Redeemer! How it wearies my heart[6] to think of this! To what a state have Christians come! Must those who owe Thee most always

[5] *Life*, xxxv. 13; xxxvi. 26; xxxix. 14. *Found.* i. 1-4. *Castle*, M. V. iv. 5.

[6] Psalm cxviii. 53: 'Defectio tenuit me, pro peccatoribus derelinquentibus legem tuam.'

treat Thee worst?—those souls to whom Thou hast shown the greatest goodness, whom Thou hast chosen for Thy friends, amongst whom Thou dost dwell, to whom Thou dost give Thyself in Thy Sacraments? Are not Thy torments at the hands of the Jews enough for them? Indeed, my Lord, we forfeit nothing in retiring from the world, for if [Christians] show *Thee* such disloyalty, what could *we* hope for? Do we merit better treatment from them? Have we done more for them than Thou hast done, that they should be friends to us? How is this? What do we hope for—we, who by the mercy of God have escaped this plague-spot? For these men are already the slaves of the devil. They have earned a bitter scourging from the hands of the fiend and have justly bought eternal fire with the pleasures he has given them. That must be their fate, though it breaks my heart to see so many souls lose themselves. Would that the evil were not so great: fain would I not see more and more ruined every day.[7]

4. O my sisters in Christ! help me to pray to our Lord for this! This is why we live here together, why the Lord has brought you here; it must be your work, the object of your longings; your tears and prayers must beg for this and not for any worldly matters. I laugh, and yet I grieve, at the intentions recommended to our prayers,—even such matters as to ask His Majesty for success in business matters and lawsuits concerning money, and this from people who I wish would beg God

[7] *Life*, xiii. 14; xxxii. 9. *Castle*, M. V. ii. 13; M. VI. i. 5, 6. *Excl.* x. 9.

for grace to trample such things under foot. These people mean well; therefore, to tell the truth, I pray for them to God because of their piety in asking for it, although, for my part, I believe that He never listens to such prayers from me.

5. The world is in a fever[8]; men wish, as it were, to condemn Christ again, for they suborn a thousand false witnesses against Him: they want to level the Church with the ground—and shall we waste our time in petitioning for that which, were it granted, might cost some soul its entrance into heaven? No, sisters, this is no time to ask God for what is of little moment. Were there no need to humour the weakness of human nature, which seeks for help everywhere (and, indeed, it would be well if we could help it in any way), I should wish it to be known that these are not the matters for which God is so fervently entreated within the convent of St. Joseph.

[8] *Excl.* ix. 15. 'It may be said that the fever of love or desire is no less a fever than that of temperature. One heats the soul and the other the body. Avarice is one of our fevers; impurity is our fever, luxury is another; ambition and wrath are both our fevers.' *S. Ambros. Hom. in S. Luc.* lib. IV in cap. iv. *sub fine.*

CHAPTER II

THAT THE NECESSITIES OF THE BODY SHOULD BE DISREGARDED. OF THE ADVANTAGES OF POVERTY.

1. Nuns should leave the care of their health to Christ. 2. Perpetual poverty to be maintained in the Order. 3. Safeguards against loss of poverty of spirit. 4. Advantages of poverty. 5. Honours and riches are opposed to poverty. 6. Poverty always the badge of the Carmelite Order. 7. The convents, though poor, may possess hermitages. 8. Intercession to be made for benefactors.

1. Do not suppose, my sisters, that because you do not seek favour with the world you will be left to starve; I can reassure you about that. Never try to sustain yourselves by any human artifice, or you will perish of famine as you would deserve. Look to your Spouse; He must maintain you: if He is pleased with you, those who like you least will give you food even against their will, as you have learnt by experience.[1] If when you have done this, you should die of hunger, happy the nuns of St. Joseph! Thus our prayers will be pleasing to God and we shall have carried out what we professed. For the love of God, do not forget this: as you have given up your revenues, give up the care of your sustenance as well or all will be lost. People whom our Lord wishes to possess incomes are quite right in looking after such matters, for that is their vocation, but it is inconsistent in us. To calculate what we shall receive from others seems to me like reckoning up their riches, and all

[1] *Life*, xxxvi. 25. *Rel.* ii. 2. *Const.* 9. *Concep.* ii. 12; iii. 5.

your care will not change their minds nor make them wish to give you alms. Leave your case in the hands of Him Who bends all wills, Who is the Lord of riches and of rich men. We came here at His bidding: His words are sure and cannot fail; heaven and earth will fail first; let us not forsake Him, and never fear that He will forsake us. If at any time He did so, it would be for our greater good, as life forsook the saints when they were slain and beheaded for our Lord, that their glory might be increased by their martyrdom. It would be a good exchange to finish this life quickly so as to enjoy eternal satiety.

2. Be certain, sisters, that this matter will be most important for you when I am dead, therefore I leave it you in writing. While I live, by the grace of God I will remind you of it, knowing by experience how great are its benefits. When I have least I am most free from anxiety, and God knows that, as far as I can tell, it grieves me much more when I am well cared for than when I am in want.[2] I am not sure whether this has happened because I have always found that our Lord supplies our wants at once. We should be deceiving the world if we acted otherwise; if, having embraced poverty, we were not poor in spirit but only in externals. My conscience would prick me, as the expression is; it would seem like rich people asking for alms:

[2] St. Teresa dearly loved poverty. She was about to make a foundation at Toledo with twelve thousand ducats left her by a rich merchant, but for certain reasons she was not able to come to an agreement with the persons responsible for the payment of this sum, at which she was greatly pleased, saying: 'Now that the money-god has been pulled down, I feel more hopeful that the foundation will be made.' (Fuente, vol. VI. 284, Note 15.) From the relation of Mother Mary of St. Joseph.

God forbid that this should ever be done! Those who are so over-anxious about what will be given them will, some day or other, out of custom, ask for what they do not want and perhaps from people more needy than themselves. Although the latter will gain rather than lose by this yet *we* shall be the losers.

3. May God prevent this ever happening, my daughters! If it were necessary, I should prefer your possessing an income. Never let your minds dwell on the subject: I ask this as an alms from you. Let the very last in the community, if she sees such a thing being done, cry out to God against it and go to the Prioress, humbly telling her that she is doing wrong.[3] This is so important that otherwise, little by little, true poverty would be lost. I trust in God that it will never happen and that He will not abandon His handmaids: for this alone, if for no other reason, this book that you have bidden me write for you, wretched sinner as I am, may be of use by keeping you on the alert. I believe, my daughters, that it is for your sakes our Lord has taught me some of the benefits to be found in holy poverty, which those will discover who practise it, although perhaps not to the same extent as I have, for not only was I without poverty of spirit, although I had professed it, but I was prodigal in spirit.

4. Poverty includes in itself all the good things of this world and a great part of the advantages of all the virtues as well, I believe. This I dare not assert, not knowing the value of each virtue, so I

[3] *Castle*, M. I. ii. 21. *Visit.* 20, 21, 22, 34, 36.

will not discuss what I do not thoroughly understand. But, in my opinion, poverty comprises many virtues. It is a vast domain. I affirm that whoever despises all earthly goods holds dominion over them. What are kings and lords to me if I do not want their money, nor seek to please them if by so doing I should displease God in the very least? What care I for their honours, if I know that the honour of a poor man consists in true poverty? It seems to me that honours and riches nearly always go together: he who loves honour never hates riches, while he who hates riches seeks no honours.

5. You must understand this clearly; for I think that a thirst for honour always carries with it some regard for property and money; it is strange to see a poor man honoured by the world, for however much he may deserve it he generally remains unnoticed. True poverty, undertaken for the sake of God, bears with it a certain dignity in that he who professes it need seek to please no one but Him, and there is no doubt that the man who asks no help has many friends, as events have taught me. Much has been written on this matter that I could not understand, much less explain, but I confess that I was too engrossed by the subject to realize how foolish I was to discuss it. Now I am aware of it, I will be silent. But since I have said it, if it is well said, let it stand.

6. For love of our Lord, since our badge is holy poverty, so highly esteemed and strictly practised at the foundation of our Order by our holy Fathers, that, as I was told by one who knew, they kept no provisions from one day to the other, let us,

now that it is no longer observed so perfectly in exteriors, strive to practise it interiorly.[4] Life lasts but two hours: the reward is immense, but, even without that, by following the counsels of our Lord the very imitating His Majesty in any way would be an ample recompense.

This must be the motto embroidered on our banners, which we must try to follow in our house, our clothes, our words, and what is far more, in our hearts. With God's help, while this is done, no fear lest religious observance should decay here for, as St. Clare used to say, poverty is a strong wall.[5] With this, and with humility, she wished to surround her monasteries. True enough, if poverty is real it guards purity and all the other virtues better than do fine buildings. Keep to this, I beg of you by the love of God and by His Blood. If, with a good conscience, I could wish that the day you build a costly dwelling it may fall and kill you all — I say, if I could do so with good conscience—I *would* wish it and beg God to grant it. It looks very ill, my daughters, to build fine houses with needy men's alms![6] God forbid

[4] *Life*, xi. 3.

[5] 'St. Clare often taught the sisters that the Order would be pleasing to God while endowed with poverty, and that it would always prosper as long as it was fortified by the tower of strictest poverty.' (*Acta SS.*, Aug. 12.) While founding the convent of St. Joseph at Avila, St. Teresa tells us: 'St. Clare appeared to me in great beauty and bade me take courage and go on with what I had begun; she would help me. I began to have a great devotion to St. Clare; and she has so truly kept her word, that a monastery of nuns of her Order in our neighbourhood helped us to live; and, what is of more importance, by little and little she so perfectly fulfilled my desire, that the poverty which the blessed Saint observes in her own house is observed in this and we are living on alms.' (*Life*, xxxiii, 15.)

[6] 'This community had better take a small house suited to poor people,

it! ours should be poor and mean in every way. Let us to this extent at least resemble our King. He had no home except the stable of Bethlehem where He was born, and the Cross where He died. Within these houses few luxuries could be found!

7. Those who build large houses have their reasons for doing so and are led by religious motives, but any little corner does for thirteen poor women. If there should be any grounds (as there must be, on account of the enclosure and because they are a help to prayer and devotion,) by all means let there be hermitages in which to retire for prayer, for weak human nature requires some indulgence; but let the convents be neither large nor handsome.[7] God deliver us from such things! Remember, they must all fall down at the Day of Judgment, and who knows how soon that may be? It would not look well if the house of thirteen poor women made much noise when it tumbled, for the real poor make no commotion—they must be silent or none will pity them.

8. How happy you will feel if some one is saved from hell by means of the alms he gave you![8]

and enter it humbly and not burden themselves with debts.' (Letter to Father Gracian, Sept. 1, 1582. vol. VI. Let. 459.)

[7] On Hermitages, *Rule*, 2. *Const.* 34. *Visit.* 13. *Found.* xiv. 4. *Life*, xxxvi. 31. Sisters Isabel de San Domingo and Teresa de Jesus say that the principal hermitages built by St. Teresa at St. Joseph's, Avila, were: 1. Christ at the column, with St. Peter shedding tears of repentance; 2. the Annunciation; 3. St. Catherine of Alexandria; 4. St. Francis of Assisi; 5. St. Augustine; 6. St. Jerome, (in a subterranean grotto); 7. St. Dominic and St. Catherine of Siena; 8. Saint Hilarion; 9. St. Alexis. (*Œuvres*, vol. V. 42.)

[8] This happened in the case of Don Bernardino de Mendoza, brother of the Bishop of Avila, and founder of the convent of Valladolid. (*Found.* x. 2.)

This is quite possible, for you are bound to pray constantly for the souls of those who maintain you.[9] It is the will of God that, although all we have comes from Him, yet we should show gratitude to those through whom He gives it, and by no means must you neglect to do so. I cannot remember what I first began to speak about, for I have wandered from my subject. I think it must have been our Lord's wish as I never intended writing as I have done. May His Majesty always uphold us with His hand, so that we may never give up holy poverty! Amen.

CHAPTER III

THIS CHAPTER CONTINUES THE SUBJECT SPOKEN OF IN THE FIRST CHAPTER. THE WRITER EXHORTS THE SISTERS CONSTANTLY TO BEG GOD TO PROTECT THOSE WHO LABOUR FOR THE CHURCH, AND CONCLUDES WITH AN ARDENT APPEAL TO GOD.

1. Evils of the times. 2. Difficulties of religious and ecclesiastics who live in the world. 3. The two chief objects for prayer. 4. An appeal to God the Father on behalf of His Son. 5. Subjects for intercession with God.

1. LET us now return to the reason why our Lord has assembled us in this house, in which I am most anxious that we should please His Majesty. Seeing how great are the disasters of these times[1]

[9] *Const.* 24. Mother Inés de Jesus says: 'Our holy Mother was so grateful that she told me she had never, till that day, forgotten to pray for a man who, in some poor village, had given her a cup of water when she was very thirsty.' (Fuente, vol. VI. 271.)

[1] Extract from a letter from the Saint to Don Lorenzo de Cepeda, January 17, 1570: 'I think it would be a consolation to me to have you in Spain: I feel so little in anything connected with this world, that perhaps our Lord will grant me this, so that we may work together

(although some persons have imagined that force of arms could stop this great evil), and that no human power can quench the devouring flames of heresy which spread most rapidly, I think we should act as people do when, in time of war, the enemy has overrun the country and the king finds himself hard pressed. He retires into a strongly fortified town from whence he sometimes makes a sortie. The small company with him in the citadel, being picked men, are better than a large army of cowardly soldiers; thus they often come off victors, or at least, if not victors, they are not vanquished for there is no traitor in their ranks and famine alone can conquer them. No famine can force *us* to surrender—it may kill us—it cannot vanquish us! But why have I told you this? To teach you, my sisters, that we must ask God to grant that, of all the good Christians in this fort, none may desert to the enemy, that no traitor may be found here, and that the captains of this castle, or city—that is, the preachers and theologians—may be proficient in the way of our Lord. Since most of these are religious, you must pray that they may advance in perfection and may follow their vocation more perfectly. This is very necessary, for, as I said, it is the arm of the Church and not of the State which must defend us now. We, being women, can fight for our King in neither way: let us, then,

to promote His honour and glory and to help the salvation of souls. I am deeply grieved at seeing so many lost, and the Indians cost me many tears. May God enlighten them, for there are many miseries both in their country and in our own. I travel to many places and talk to many people, and I can only say that we are often worse than the beasts, for we do not understand the great dignity of our souls and we degrade them with the base things of this world. May God give us light!' vol. I. Let. 23.

strive so to live that our prayers may avail to help these servants of God who have laboured hard to arm themselves with learning and virtue with which to help their Sovereign. You may ask why I insist so much on this, and why I say we must help those who are better than ourselves. I will explain this, as I do not think you realize how much you owe to God for withdrawing you so entirely from all earthly cares, from occasions of sin, and from the society of the world.[2] This is a very special favour and one not shared in by the men of whom I have been speaking. Indeed, it would be less fitting for them now than ever, for they have to strengthen the weak and to encourage the timid. What a state soldiers would get into without their captain! These defenders of the Church must live amongst men and associate with them, they must frequent the Court, and even at times conform outwardly to its customs.

2. Do you think, my daughters, that it is easy to keep friends with the world, to live in it, to transact worldly business, and, as I said, to conform to its usages, and yet, in one's heart, to remain a stranger and enemy of this same world, like an exile? In short, not to be men but to be angels? Unless they are all this, they do not deserve the name of captains, and may our Lord prevent their ever leaving their cells, for they will do more harm than good. This is no time for defects to appear in the teachers, who, unless they be forearmed by knowing the need of spurning all things earthly beneath their feet, detached from all things transitory, and wholly devoted to what is eternal, are

[2] *Castle* M. VI. vi. 14.

bound to manifest their imperfections, strive as they may to hide them. For are they not dealing with the world? Do not imagine that it will pardon or fail to observe their shortcomings. Much that is good may pass unnoticed—or even perhaps be considered evil, but no fault or imperfection will ever escape criticism.[3]

3. I wonder who taught them all about perfection—not for their own practice, for they think it will suffice to content God if they keep the commandments fairly well, but that they may censure others, while sometimes they take virtue for self-indulgence? You see that, far from requiring but little help from God during the great struggle in which they are engaged, our defenders need it urgently. I wish you to lead such lives as to merit to obtain these two favours from God. Firstly, that among very learned theologians and religious there may be many with the qualifications I describe, and that our Lord may perfect those who are less fitted, for one who is perfect can do more than many who are imperfect. The other favour is that, when they are engaged in this war (which, as I said, is a fierce one), our Lord may uphold them with His hand and protect them from the many dangers of the world and may stop their ears, in these perilous seas, to the song of the Sirens. If we can prevail with God to grant any of these things, though we are enclosed in this house, we are fighting for Him,[4] and I shall think all my pains have been well spent in building this little nook where I also intended that the rule of

[3] *Found.* i. 5, 6. *Life*, xxxi. 19.
[4] *Life*, xxxvi. 28 and Note.

our Lady and Empress should be kept with all the perfection of its commencement.[5] Do not suppose it is useless to continue these petitions: some people consider it a hardship not to pray more for their own souls, yet what better prayer could there be? Perhaps you are troubled at thinking that it will not free you from the pains of Purgatory; but this prayer will cancel some of your debt, and if more is owing, never mind that. What does it matter if I stay in Purgatory until the Day of Judgment if my prayers save a single soul?—how much more if they save many and give glory to God? Care nothing for any earthly pain when there is a question of rendering some greater service to Him Who suffered so much for us. Constantly try to learn what is most perfect; I beg you always to consult those who are learned, and I will tell you why. I entreat you, for the love of God, to beseech His Majesty to hear us in this. Miserable wretch as I am, I beg Him to grant it, for it is for His glory and the good of His Church, which is my only care.[6]

4. It seems presumption in me to imagine that I have any power to obtain this—I place all my confidence, O my God! in these servants of Thine, who are with me and who, I know, neither desire nor seek to do aught but please Thee. They have left the little they possessed, only wishing they owned more to offer Thee. Thou art not ungrateful, O Thou my Creator, that I need fear Thou wilt refuse them what they ask, nor, O Lord of my soul, didst Thou repulse women whilst Thou

[5] *Way of Perf.* i. 4, 5; xx. 2. *Found.* i. 5. *Rel.* ii. 13.

[6] Escorial, iv. Treats of three very important matters touching the spiritual life.

wert in the world, but didst ever favour them and show them tender love and pitiful compassion![7] Thou didst put greater trust in them than in men, for amongst them was Thy most holy Mother whose merits we share, and whose habit we wear, unworthy as we are by reason of our sins. We can do nothing for Thee in public, nor do we dare to tell the truths over which we weep in secret lest Thou shouldst not hear our most right petition. Just and good as Thou art, O Lord! I will not believe that Thou wilt reject us. Thou art a just Judge, not like earthly judges who, being sons of Adam and stern men, have no faith in women's virtue. The day will come, my King, when all will be known. I speak not for myself, for all men know of my wickedness and I rejoice that it is made public, but, seeing in what manner of times we are living, it is not right to repulse the good and valiant though they are but women. When we beg of Thee honours, income, riches, any worldly things, do not listen to us, but how shouldst Thou not hear us when we ask for what concerns the honour of Thy Son? Why, O Eternal Father shouldst Thou refuse those who would forfeit a thousand honours and a thousand lives for Thee? Not for our sakes, O God! for we deserve it not, but for the sake of Thy Son and of His merits. O Eternal Father! should such stripes and insults and such bitter torments be forgotten? How can a heart so loving as Thine, my Creator, endure that what

[7] The following passage as far as 'though they are but women' is not in the MS. of Valladolid, and even in that of the Escorial it has been scratched out, but has been restored with the exception of two lines which remain illegible.

was instituted with such ardent love by Thy Son for the sake of pleasing Thee (for Thou didst bid Him love us) should be held of so little value as is the Blessed Sacrament in these days by heretics? For they drive It from Its dwelling-place when they destroy the churches. It is not as if He had left undone aught that could please Thee. No, He consummated everything! Was it not enough, O Eternal Father! for Him to have had no place in which to lay His head while He lived amidst incessant toils, that now they must deprive Him of the place to which He invites His friends, seeing that they are fainting and knowing that those who labour need to be supported by this meat? Has He not paid in overwhelming excess for the sin of Adam? Must this most meek and loving Lamb atone anew for every fresh sin we commit? Do not suffer it, my Sovereign King; let Thy Majesty be appeased; look not on our faults but on Thy most holy Son Who has redeemed us; reflect on His merits, on those of His glorious Mother and on those of the many Saints and Martyrs who have died for Thee! But alas, O my God! who am I who have dared to offer Thee this petition in the name of all? My daughters, what a wretched advocate you have to gain a hearing and to present your petition for you! What if my presumption should anger this supreme Judge, as would be only right and just? But remember, O my Sovereign and my Lord! that Thou art the God of mercy; do Thou prove it to this poor sinner and worm who is thus bold with Thee. Look, O God! upon my desires and on the tears with which I beg this of Thee, and, forgetting my evil actions for Thine own sake, take pity on the many perishing souls and have mercy on Thy Church. Do not permit these evils to increase in Christendom, O Lord, but illuminate its darkness!

5. For the love of our Lord, I beg of you, my sisters, to intercede for this poor, presumptuous creature, and fulfil your duty by asking Him to to give her humility. I do not charge you particularly to pray for kings and prelates of the Church, especially for our own Bishop,[8] as I see that you do so diligently, therefore I need not speak of it. But let who will come after me, be sure that if the Superior is holy the community will be the same, therefore ever crave this most important favour from God. If your prayers and desires, your disciplines and fasts are not performed for these intentions, know that you are not doing the work nor carrying out the design for which God placed you here, and I beg His Majesty, for the sake of His Godhead, never to let you forget this.

[8] Don Alvaro de Mendoza, a member of the family of the Counts of Ribadavia, for some time first chaplain of San Juan de los Reyes at Toledo, was nominated to the See of Avila in 1560, and became very intimate with St. Teresa, whose convent he took under his protection and jurisdiction. In 1577 he was promoted to the See of Palencia, and three years later he, together with the Archbishops of Toledo and Seville, was commissioned by the Pope to watch over the interests of the Discalced Carmelites. He died April 19, 1586, and was buried in the chapel of the convent of St. Joseph at Avila, where his tomb is still preserved. St. Teresa very frequently speaks of him, always in terms of the highest veneration. Many of her letters are addressed to him.

CHAPTER IV[1]

AN EXHORTATION TO OBEY THE RULE. THREE VERY IMPORTANT MATTERS IN THE SPIRITUAL LIFE. ONE MUST STRIVE AFTER SUBLIME PERFECTION IN ORDER TO ACCOMPLISH SO GREAT AN ENTERPRISE. HOW TO PRACTISE PRAYER.

1. The greatness of the work we have undertaken. 2. Prayer. 3. The three principal aids to prayer. 4. The evils of particular friendships. 5. Special danger of these in a small community. 6. Precautions against them. 7. Mutual charity. 8. Natural and supernatural love. 9. How to regard our confessors. 10. Discretion in our intercourse with them. 11. When a second confessor is needed. 12. Precautions against worldly confessors. 13. Evils caused by unsuitable confessors.

1. You see, daughters, upon how great an enterprise you have embarked for the sake of the Father Provincial, the Bishop of the diocese, and of your Order, in which all else is included, all being for the good of the Church for which we are bound to pray as a matter of obligation. As I said, what lives are not those bound to live who have had the courage to engage in this design, if they would not be confounded before God and man for their audacity? Clearly we must work hard; it is a great help to have high aspirations: by their means we may cause our actions to become great also, although there are different ways of doing so. If we endeavour to observe our Rule and Constitutions very faithfully, I hope that God will grant our petitions. I ask of you nothing new, my daughters, but only that we should keep what we have professed, which is our vocation and our duty, although there are very diverse ways of observing it.

[1] Valladolid edition, iv; Escorial, v.

2. The first chapter of our Rule bids us 'Pray without ceasing':[2] we must obey this with the greatest perfection possible for it is our most important duty; then we shall not neglect the fasts, penances, and silence enjoined by the Rule. As you know, these are necessary if the prayer is to be genuine; prayer and self-indulgence do not go together. Prayer is the subject of which you have asked me to speak: I beg of you, in return, to practise and to read, again and again, what I have already told you. Before speaking of spiritual matters, that is, of prayer, I will mention some things that must be done by those who intend to lead a life of prayer. These are so necessary that, with their help, a person who can hardly be called a contemplative may make great progress in serving God, but without them no one can be a thorough contemplative: any one who imagined that she was so would be much mistaken. May our Lord give me His grace for this task and teach me what to say that may be for His glory. Amen.[3]

3. Do not fancy, my friends and my sisters, that I am going to lay many charges on you: please God we may fulfil those that our holy Fathers enjoined and practised in our Rules and Constitutions, which include all the virtues, and by performing which our predecessors earned the name of Saints. It would be an error to seek another road or to try to learn some other way. I will explain three

[2] *Rule* 5: 'Meditating on the law of the Lord day and night, and watching in prayer.'

[3] Escorial edition. I.H.S. Ch. vi. Urges the nuns to practise three things. Speaks of the first, that is, the love of our neighbour and of the evil of particular friendships.

matters only, which are in our Constitutions: it is essential for us to understand how much they help us to preserve that peace, both interior and exterior, which our Lord so strongly enjoined. The first of these is love for one another: the second detachment from all created things: the other is true humility, which, though I mention it last, is chief of all and includes the rest.[4] The first matter, that is, fervent mutual charity, is most important, for there is no annoyance that cannot easily be borne by those who love one another: anything must be very out of the way to cause irritation. If this commandment were observed in this world as it ought to be I believe it would be a great help towards obeying the others, but whether we err by excess or by defect we only succeed in keeping it imperfectly.

4. You may think there can be no harm among us in excessive love for one another, but no one would believe what evil and imperfections spring from this source unless she had seen it for herself. The devil sets many snares here which are hardly detected by those who are content to serve God in a superficial way—indeed, they take such conduct for virtue—those, however, who are bent on perfection understand the evil clearly, for, little by little, it deprives the will of strength to devote itself entirely to the love of God. I think this injures women even more than men, and does serious damage to the community. It prevents a nun from loving all the others equally, makes her resent any injury done to her friend, causes her to wish she

[4] Valladolid edition, v. speaks of the first of these three subjects, namely, the love of our neighbour, and of the evils of particular friendships.

had something to give her favourite, to seek for opportunities to talk to her often, to tell her how much she loves her and other nonsense of the sort, rather than of how much she loves God. These close friendships rarely serve to forward the love of God; in fact, I believe the devil originates them so as to make factions among the religious.

5. When a friendship has the service of God for its object it is at once manifest that the will is not only uninfluenced by passion but is rather helped to subdue the passions. I am much in favour of such friendships in a large community, but in St. Joseph's, where there are and can be no more than thirteen nuns, all must love and help one another. For the love of God, keep free from partialities however holy they may be, for even among brethren they are like poison and I can see no advantage in them, but matters are far worse when they exist between relatives, for then they are a perfect pest, as Joseph's history shows. Believe me, sisters, though I may seem to you severe in excluding these attachments, yet this promotes high perfection and quiet peace, and weak souls are spared dangerous occasions. If we are inclined to care for one person more than another (which cannot be helped, for it is but human, and we often prefer the most faulty if they have more natural charm) let us control our likings firmly and not allow ourselves to be overmastered by our affections.

6. Let us love virtue and holiness and always try to prevent ourselves from being attracted by externals. O my sisters! let us not permit our will to become the slave of any save of Him Who

purchased it with His Blood, or, without knowing how, we shall find ourselves caught in a trap from which we cannot escape! Lord have mercy on us! the childish nonsense that comes from this is untold, and is so petty that no one could credit it who had not witnessed the thing. It is best not to speak of it here, lest women's foibles should be learnt by those who know nothing about them, so I will give no details, although they astonish even me at times. By the mercy of God I have never been entangled in such things myself, but perhaps this may be because I have fallen into far graver faults. However, as I said, I have often seen it, but as I told you, in a Superior it would be ruinous. In order to guard against these partialities, great care must be taken from the very first, and this more by watchfulness and kindness than by severity.[5] A most useful precaution is for the nuns, according to our present habit, never to be with one another nor talk together except at the appointed times, but that, as the Rule enjoins, the sisters should not be together, but each in her own cell.[6] Let there be no work-room in St. Joseph's, for although it is a praiseworthy custom, silence is better kept when one is alone. To accustom ourselves to solitude is a great help to prayer, and since prayer is the mortar which keeps our house together and we came here to practise it, we must learn to like what promotes it.[7]

7. To return to speak of our charity for one

[5] 'Any kind of attachment, even for a prioress, is utterly foreign to the spirit of Discalced nuns, and would prevent their soul's ever making progress. God wishes His brides to be detached, caring solely for Him.' (Letter to Ven. Anne of Jesus, May 30, 1582,) vol. IV. Let. 444.

[6] *Rule* 5. [7] *Rule* 14. *Const.* 5.

another. It seems superfluous to insist on this, for who would be so boorish as not to love those with whom they associate and live, cut off as they are from all conversation, intercourse, and recreation with any one outside the house, while believing that they bear a mutual love for God, as He loves all of them, since for His sake they have left everything? More especially as goodness always attracts love, and, by the blessing of God, I trust that the nuns of this convent will always be good. Therefore, I do not think there is much need for me to persuade you to love each other. But as regards the nature of this love and of the virtuous love that I wish you all to feel, and the means of knowing whether we possess this greatest of virtues—for it must be a very great virtue since our Lord so often enjoins it on us, as He did most stringently upon His apostles—of this I will speak to you for a short time as well as my inaptitude will allow. If you find the matter explained in any other books, you need not read mine, for perhaps I may not understand what I am talking about except when our Lord enlightens me.[8]

8. I intend treating of two kinds of love: one which is entirely spiritual, free from any sort of affection or natural tenderness which could tarnish its purity, and another which is spiritual but mingled with the frailty and weakness of human nature. The latter is good and seems lawful, being such as is felt between relatives and friends, and is that which I have mentioned. The first of these

[8] *Castle*, M. V. iii. 12. Escorial edition, vii. Speaks of two kinds of love and the importance of understanding what constitutes spiritual affection.

two ways of loving, and the one that I will discuss is unmixed with any kind of passion that would disturb its harmony. This love, exercised with moderation and discretion, is profitable in every way, particularly when borne towards holy people or confessors, for that which seems only natural is then changed into virtue.[9] At times, however, these two kinds of love seem so combined that it is difficult to distinguish them from one another, especially as regards a confessor. When persons who practise prayer discover that their confessor is a holy man who understands their spiritual state they feel a strong affection for him; the devil then opens a perfect battery of scruples on the soul, which, as he intends, greatly disturb it, especially if the priest is leading his penitent to higher perfection. Then the evil one torments his victim to such a pitch that she leaves her director, so that the temptation gives her no peace either in one way or the other.

9. In such a case it is best not to think about whether you like your confessor or not, or whether you wish to like him. If we feel friendship for those who benefit our bodies, why should we not feel as great a friendship for those who strive and labour to benefit our souls? On the contrary, I think a liking for my confessor is a great help to my progress if he is holy and spiritual, and if I see that he endeavours to profit my soul. Human nature is so weak that this feeling is often a help to our undertaking great things in God's service.

10. If, however, the confessor be a man of

[9] *Life* xxxvii. 6; xl. 24. *Rel.* ii. 8.

indifferent character, we must not let him know of our liking for him. Great prudence and caution are necessary on account of the difficulty of understanding his disposition: it is best, on this account, to conceal your feelings from him. You should believe that your friendship for him is harmless and think no more about it. You may follow this advice when you see that all your confessor says tends to profit your soul and when you discover no levity in him, but are conscious that he lives in the fear of God: any one can detect this at once unless she wilfully blinds herself. If this be so, do not allow any temptation to trouble you about your liking for him—despise it, think no more about it and the devil will grow tired and leave you alone. If, however, the confessor appears worldly-minded, be most guarded in every way; do not talk with him even when he converses on religious subjects but make your confession briefly and say no more. It would be best to tell the Prioress that he does not suit your soul and to ask for some one else; this is the wisest course to take if it is possible and can be done without injuring his reputation. I trust in God that it may be feasible for you.

11. In these and other difficulties by which the devil may seek to ensnare us, it would be best, when you are doubtful as to what course to pursue, to consult some theologian as the nuns are permitted to do,[10] to make your confession to him and to follow his advice in the case, lest some great mistake should be made in remedying the evil. How many people go astray in the world for want of

[10] *Castle*, M. VI. viii. 10, 11. *Found.* xix. 1.

seeking guidance, especially in what affects their neighbours' interests! Some redress must be sought, for when the devil starts such works, unless he is stopped at once the matter will become serious; therefore my advice about changing confessors is the best and I trust in God that you will be able to do so.

12. Be convinced of the importance of this: the thing is dangerous, a hell in itself, and injurious to every one. Do not wait until much harm has come of it, but stop the matter at once in every feasible way: this may be done with a clear conscience. I trust, however, that God will prevent those vowed to a life of prayer from becoming attached to any one who does not serve God fervently, as He certainly will unless they omit to practise prayer and to strive after perfection as we profess to do in this house. If the nuns see that the confessor does not understand their language nor cares to speak of God they cannot like him, for he differs from them. If he is of such a character he will have extremely few chances of doing any harm here, and unless he is very foolish he will neither trouble himself about the servants of God, nor disturb those who have few pleasures and little or no opportunity of following their own way.

13. Since I have begun speaking on this subject, I may say that this is the only harm or at any rate the greatest harm, that the devil can do within enclosed convents. It takes long to discover, so that great damage may have been wrought to perfection without any one knowing how, for if the confessor is worldly himself he will treat the

defect lightly in others. Deliver us, O Lord, for Thine own sake, from such misfortunes.

It is enough to unsettle all the nuns if their conscience tells them one thing and their confessor another. Where they are allowed no other director I do not know what to do nor how to quiet their minds, for he who ought to bring them peace and counsel is the very author of the evil. There must be a great deal of trouble, resulting in much harm, from these misplaced partialities, as, to my great sorrow, I have seen in certain convents, though not in my own,[11] therefore you need not be surprised at the pains I have taken to make you understand the danger.

CHAPTER V[1]

CONTINUES SPEAKING OF CONFESSORS: OF THE IMPORTANCE OF THEIR BEING LEARNED AND HOW WE SHOULD BEHAVE TOWARDS THEM.

1. Advantages of consulting more than one confessor. 2. One priest cannot know everything. 3. Difficulties of guiding souls. 4. No one may usurp the authority of the Prioress.

1. MAY God in His mercy prevent any one in this house from experiencing this trouble, or being reduced to such misery both of soul and body. I hope it may never happen that the Prioress and confessor are such fast friends that no one dare complain of the one to the other. Hence comes the temptation to omit confessing grave sins for

[11] In this as in other places, when St. Teresa alludes to 'her own house' or 'convent' she always refers to that of the Incarnation.

[1] Valladolid edition, vi; Escorial, viii.

fear lest the unfortunate culprit should get into trouble. God help us! What mischief the devil works in this way; how many a soul he may entrap, and how dear their miserable reserve and regard for honour costs people! Having no other director to consult, they imagine that they are preserving religious observance and the reputation of their monastery. Thus Satan schemes to ensnare souls whom he could entrap in no other way. If the poor nuns ask for another confessor they are told at once that this would destroy all religious discipline, and if he should be a priest of another Order, though as holy as St. Jerome, to speak to him is said to be an affront to the whole of their own Order. Thank God, my daughters, for the liberty you are allowed in this matter, for, though you cannot consult a large number of priests, there are some with whom you may confer besides your ordinary confessors and who can give you the requisite light.[2] For the love of our Lord, I beg the Superior to maintain this holy liberty, and to get permanent leave from the Bishop or Provincial,[3] for the nuns to have, besides their ordinary confessors, learned priests to whom they may all speak and open their souls,[4] especially if their own confessors, though holy, are not great scholars. God

[2] The holy Mother often charged her daughters, both by word of mouth and in her books, to endeavour to talk to learned and prudent theologians. She recommended the Dominicans for this purpose, on account of the sound doctrine taught by this holy Order. (Fuente, vol. VI. 280, Note 3. From the deposition of Father Giles Gonzalez de Avila).

[3] 'Or of the Provincial' was added afterwards above the line. With the exception of St. Joseph's, Avila, the conventss were under the jurisdiction of the Provincial of the Order.

[4] *Life*, xiii. 21, 28.

forbid that the religious should be directed entirely by one priest if he is ill-instructed, however saintly his spirit may appear, and perhaps may be in reality. Learning gives great light on all points; it is combined with holiness in some men. The greater favours our Lord shows you in prayer, the more need is there that you should be well informed about your devotions, prayer, and all your other duties.

2. You know that the foundation of all must be a good conscience; you ought to make every effort to free yourselves even from venial sin and to do what is most perfect. One would suppose any confessor knew this; however it is not the case. I had to consult one on matters of conscience who had gone through a whole course of theology, and he did me much harm by telling me certain matters were of no consequence.[5] Not that he intended to deceive me, nor had he any motive for doing so, but he knew no better: I have since met with two or three like him. Everything depends on our having light to keep the law of God perfectly; on this basis prayer rests solidly; without this strong foundation the whole building is out of the perpendicular. There is need, then, for the nuns to consult men who are both spiritual and learned.[6] If the confessor cannot lay claim to all this, let them occasionally see some one else: if they are forbidden to confess to any one but their regular confessor, let them seek counsel about their souls from such persons as I mentioned.[7] I dare go further and say that the sisters should sometimes go to

[5] *Life*, v. 6. [6] *Life*, xxv. 18. *Castle*, M. VI. viii. 10.
[7] Letter of Dec. 21, 1579, vol. III. Let. 304.

some other priest, even if their confessor possesses all these qualities, for he may be mistaken and it would not do for all to be misled by him. Nothing, however, must be done against obedience. Matters can always be arranged, and it is worth any trouble to help one soul—how much more to help a number?

3. All this is said to the Prioress whom I again entreat, for the love of God, to give the sisters this consolation since there are no comforts here except for the soul: God leads people by different ways and the same confessor may not understand them all. I assure you there will always be holy persons ready to guide and to console you if you live as you ought, however poor you may be. God, Who sustains your bodies and supplies them with food, will incite some one with the good will to enlighten your souls; and to bring a remedy for this evil which I fear more than any others. When tempted by the devil to levity or to mislead you on any point, the confessor will be more wary and circumspect in his conduct if he knows you will consult some other priest. If the evil one is stopped this entrance into the convent, I trust in God that he will never get in at all. Therefore, for the love of our Lord, I beg the Bishop for the time being to leave liberty on this point to the nuns, who will always be his most obedient children, and, when good and learned priests can be found, not to withdraw the permission. These will soon be known in a little town like this. Even though they may have other confessors, let the Bishop permit the sisters to confess to them and to

consult them on spiritual matters. I know this is expedient for many reasons and that any drawbacks it may possess are as nothing compared with the serious, hidden, and well-nigh irreparable harm that may otherwise be done. In convents good observance tends to decline quickly if not preserved with great care: evil customs, once begun, are most difficult to eradicate; they soon grow into habits, and the imperfections become a second nature to us.

4. I have both seen and heard of what I have been speaking and have consulted experienced, learned, and holy men who have considered what is best calculated to advance perfection in this house. Among the many dangers which beset us everywhere in this life, we shall find it safest for no Vicar[8] to be at liberty to go in or out of the convent or to give such leave to others, or to give any order: neither shall any confessor hold such power. They are to watch over the religious observance and piety of the house, and its interior and exterior well-being, in order to acquaint the Superior with any fault they may detect, but are not to be superiors themselves. As I said, there are grave reasons why this should be the most prudent regulation. Let the chaplain, if he is fit, be the usual confessor, but when it is clearly needful for a nun's soul she may go to confession to such priests as I have mentioned who are authorized by the Bishop. If his Lordship can trust the Prioress in this matter, let him leave it to her discretion. As the community is small, it will not take much time. This is our practice at the present day, not

[8] The Vicar, either the Bishop's nominee or the General's. *See* Letter to Father Gracian, Feb. 1581, vol. IV. Let. 369.

merely by my advice but by that of the prelate under whose obedience we live, as for many reasons we are not subject to the Order. The Bishop, Don Alvaro de Mendoza,[9] is of a noble family, a great servant of God, and highly favourable to all religious observance and holiness. He is a well-wisher of this house, both in spiritual and temporal matters, and esteems it very highly, desiring that the nuns should attain great perfection. Therefore I do not think that our Lord would permit him to be mistaken, as his only object is the glory of God. He assembled a number of men of learning, piety, and experience, who, together with myself, miserable as I am, after much prayer came to this decision. It is but reasonable that the future Superiors should, by the grace of God, observe this most important decree. It has been resolved on with careful deliberation by holy men, after fervently begging the Almighty to show them what was for the best, which this regulation most certainly is, as far as can at present be known. May God be pleased to promote its observance as may be most to His glory. Amen.

[9] *Life*, xxxiii. 19. *Found.* xxxi. 1.

CHAPTER VI[1]

RETURNS TO THE SUBJECT OF PERFECT LOVE

1. Supernatural love. 2. Love for others as felt by perfect souls. 3. Their detachment from seeking the love of others. 4. They realize its worthlessness. 5. Supernatural friendship.

1. I HAVE wandered far from my subject, but no one will blame me who realizes the importance of what I have said. Let us return, my sisters, to speak of the love we ought to feel for others which is lawful for us: that which I call entirely spiritual. I am not sure whether I understand what I am speaking about: at any rate, I think there is no need to say much about this love for I fear very few people possess it: if our Lord has granted it to any one among you she should thank and praise Him fervently, for she must have attained great perfection, and perhaps we shall profit by her example. I will say something about it, on the chance of its proving useful:[2] although the other sort of love is that we generally feel, for the sight of virtue, if we desire to win it, makes us love it. God grant us the grace to understand it and to strive to gain it! Please God I may even understand it myself, far more that I may succeed in explaining it, for I hardly know when love is spiritual and when it is partly sensual, or how to speak of it. I am like a person who hears a voice in the distance but cannot distinguish the words: for sometimes I do not understand what I write and yet our Lord is pleased to

[1] Valladolid edition, vii ; Escorial, ix.
[2] *Life*, vii. 33-37 ; xvi. 12 ; xxx. 6. *Castle*, M. II. i. 12.

grant that it should be correct. At times I may talk nonsense: it is most natural to me to do nothing well.

2. It seems to me that when God has clearly shown the soul what this world is, and that another world exists, and how different the two are—how that one is eternal while the other is but a dream—when the difference is seen between loving the Creator or the creature (which can only be found out by experience, not by holding a mere idea or opinion on the matter but by perceiving and proving what is gained by the one and lost by the other); when the soul understands what the Creator is and what the creature, with many other truths which our Lord manifests with certainty and conviction to those who seek to learn from Him in prayer, or to whom He chooses to reveal these verities—then that soul loves in a way very different from ours, who have not advanced thus far. It may seem needless to you, my sisters, to speak of this. You will say you know it already. God grant you do; that you know it practically; that it is graven in your hearts, so that you never forget it even for so short a time as a '*Memento*'. If you know it, you will see that I speak the truth in saying that souls which God has drawn so far feel such a love. These are generous, noble spirits who are not content with loving anything so wretched as a mortal body, whatever beauties and attractions it may possess: that is, with a love that dominates and enslaves them. Though the sight gives them pleasure, and they praise the Creator for it, yet as for dwelling on such qualities—no! I mean by souls

'dwelling' on them that they should love any one for such things, for this would seem to them loving a nothingness, a shadow: they would feel such shame as not to dare afterwards, without horrible confusion, to tell God that they loved Him.

3. You will declare that such persons do not know how to love or to repay the affection felt for them. At any rate, they care little for the latter; although they naturally feel a momentary pleasure in being loved, yet, returning to their senses, they see this is but folly unless the liking comes from one who can help them by counsel or by prayer.[3] All other affection wearies them, for they know it cannot profit, but may even injure th m. Yet they are grateful for it and requite it by commending their friend to God, thinking her attachment forms a debt laid on them by our Lord from Whom they believe it comes. Seeing nothing amiable in themselves, they think that others love them for the love of God, and leave His Majesty to reward them as they beg Him to do. Then they feel free from their debt and think no more about it. In my opinion, unless this fondness for us is felt by those who can lead us to perfection, it is often great blindness to wish to be loved.

4. Notice, that when we wish for any one's love it is always for the sake of self-interest or pleasure: those who are perfect, however, have so trodden under-foot all worldly goods, delights, and joys, that, even if they wished, as we might say, they could care for nothing outside God and speaking to others about Him; therefore what gain can

[3] Escorial, x. Of the great gain of being loved in such a way.

human love bring them? They cease to care for it, realizing this truth so clearly that they laugh at the thought of how anxious they used to be as to whether their affections were returned or no; for pure as our love may be, it is natural to wish for it to be repaid. Yet this repayment is but a thing of straw, an airy nothing, blown to and fro by the wind, for after we have been dearly loved, what remains to us? Therefore perfect souls care nothing whether they are cherished or no, except it be by those who can profit them, as I said; for human nature quickly tires of helping those we do not care for. Do you fancy such hearts can love or think of none except God alone? Indeed they love others far more, with a truer, more generous, and intense affection. In a word, this is true love. These souls are ever more ready to give than to receive,[4] even with their Creator. This, I say, merits the name of LOVE, for all other base affections have but usurped the title.

5. You may wonder, if such persons do not love what they see, what it is that they love. They do love what they see, and are drawn by what they hear, but what they see and hear is what is stable. If they care for any one, they do not arrest their eyes on the body but at once look into the soul to see if it contains aught they can love, or if not, whether it has germs or inclinations which show that, by digging deep enough they will find gold within the mine; loving this soul, no trouble wearies them, no service is too hard for them willingly to render it, for they wish their affection

[4] Acts, xx. 35: 'Beatius est magis dare quam accipere.'

for it to last, which they know is impossible unless their friend possesses virtue and the love of God.[5] I say it is impossible, though the other should render them immense services and even seek to die for them, and if she should do them every kindness in her power: though she should possess every natural attraction yet they could not force their wills to love her nor to remain attached to her. They know, and have learnt by experience, what these are worth, and cannot be cheated with false coin: seeing that their minds are not in unison they cannot continue to love her, for if their friend does not love God nor keep His law, they fear their attachment must end with this life and they will go to different regions. These souls in which our Lord has instilled true wisdom hold the affection which ends in this world no higher than its proper value—indeed, they hold it cheaper! To those who care for worldly things, such as pleasure, honour, and riches, it is of some worth if their friend be wealthy for the sake of the gaiety and amusement he provides.[6] Those who have spurned such things beneath their feet care little or nothing for such friendships. If they have any affection for such a one, it is a longing to bring her soul to love God so that they themselves can love her, for, as I said, they realize that no other sort of fondness can last but will cost them dear. Therefore they make every effort to benefit their friend and would lose a thousand lives to help her in the least. O priceless love, thus imitating the Captain of all love, Jesus, our only good!

[5] *Castle*, M. VI. xi. 10. *Life*, xxiv. 8. *Rel.* i. 16; ii. 8.
[6] *Life*, ii. 4; v. 9; xxi. 1. *Way of Perf.* xli. 4, 5.

CHAPTER VII[1]

CONTINUES TO TREAT OF SPIRITUAL LOVE, AND GIVES ADVICE HOW TO OBTAIN IT

1. Unselfishness of supernatural love. 2. Zeal for the loved one's eternal interests. 3. Benefits conferred by this love on its object. 4. How to gain this love for others. 5. The remembrance of our own defects should make us merciful to others. 6. How to practise perfect charity. 7. A good example is the truest sign of charity. 8. Obstacles to charity in communities.

1. It is strange to see how passionate is this tenderness! What tears, what penances and prayers it costs! How urgent is the care to recommend its object to the intercession of all who have power with God! what constant longing for the progress of its friend, and what disquiet if this be wanting! If the loved one seemed to be advancing and then falls back, the friend who is devoted to her knows no peace in life, and neither eats nor sleeps unhaunted by constant anxiety and dread lest the soul it loves so well should be lost and they two parted for ever. Such people care nothing for the death of the body—they will not attach themselves to what a breath can deprive us of beyond our powers of resistance. As I said, there is no thought of self in this affection; its only wish and care is to see its favourite enriched with divine graces. This is love indeed, not like a miserable earthly affection, even though the latter be not faulty—for from an unlawful attachment may God defend us! We need not tire ourselves with inveighing against what is a perfect hell, the least of whose ills is

[1] Valladolid edition, viii; Escorial, xi.

beyond exaggeration. We must never mention such a love, sisters, nor remember that it exists, nor must we ever hear it named either in jest or in earnest, nor suffer it to be discussed in our presence. It is utterly worthless, and the very mention of it may harm us. But I am speaking of the lawful affection we feel for one another, such as is felt between relations and friends. Our one anxiety is that they may not die; if their heads ache, our souls ache too; if they suffer, we lose all patience, and it is the same in other matters. It is not so with spiritual love, for, though through human weakness those who feel it grieve at their neighbour's trouble for the moment, yet reason resumes its sway; they reflect whether this cross is good for their friend's soul and whether it increases her virtue; they watch how she bears it; begging God to give her patience, that she may merit by her trials. If they see she is resigned, they are no longer disturbed, but feel happy and consoled.[2] Though they would rather suffer the pain themselves than let her bear it if their merit and benefit could all be transferred to her, yet they feel neither distress nor disturbance.

2. This affection seems exactly like that borne for us by the good Lover, Jesus: this is why it is so beneficial, for it embraces all the suffering for itself, that others without suffering may reap the reward. Even if such souls do not actually perform this, still they strive to lead their friends aright, more

[2] St. Teresa always looked cheerful, however much the trials of her friends may have grieved her. (Fuente, vol. VI. 310, Note. 9.) Deposition of Maria de San Francisco.

by actions than by words. I say, 'If they do not actually perform this;' that is, when the thing itself is impossible, for they strive incessantly to labour for, and to benefit, the one they love. Such an affection is a great blessing to its object, for either the friendship must come to an end or the lover will obtain grace from our Lord that the beloved may travel on the same road as herself, as did St. Monica for St. Augustine. Such a soul will never deal falsely with those it loves nor allow them to err while believing it can hinder them by reproof, which it will never neglect to give them because of its ardent desire to see them rich in virtue. What artifices does it not use in order to gain this end, although it cares for no earthly thing! It cannot resist doing this, nor can it flatter its friends, nor dissemble their faults.[3] Either they must amend or their mutual bond must come to an end, for this soul cannot otherwise endure it, nor ought it to do so, for there can be nothing but war between persons with such different aims. Though such a one may be indifferent to all others and take no heed whether they serve God or not, looking only to herself, yet she cannot act thus with her friends; no fault in them is hidden from her; she sees the smallest mote. I call this indeed a heavy cross to bear. Happy the souls thus loved, and blest the day on which they found such a friend!

3. O my God! of Thy mercy grant that many

[3] *See* Letter to Mary of St. Joseph, Jan. 1580, vol. III. Let. 309. 'Your Reverence must forgive me, because I am so anxious that any one I love dearly should never do amiss that I am unbearable. The same thing happened with Mother Brianda, to whom I wrote terrible letters, with but little result.'

may feel such love for me. I would far rather win this, O Lord! than the liking of all the kings and princes of the earth, and rightly so, for such affection labours with all its might to make us such that we may spurn the world under our feet and may hold beneath our sway all that it contains. If you ever meet persons of this kind, sisters, the Mother Prioress should make every effort to bring you together. Love them as much as you will: there are not many such souls, but our Lord always wishes their perfection to be known: people will tell you that there is no need of such help—God is enough. The company of God's friends is a good way of keeping near Him: it is of the greatest advantage, as I know from experience; for, after God Himself, I owe it to such persons that I am not in hell. I was most anxious that they should intercede for me with God, and used to beg them to do so. But let us return to our subject.

4. This is the kind of affection I wish we all possessed.[4] Although in the beginning our love may be defective, yet our Lord will correct it. Let us consider the way to obtain perfect love. Although at first we mingle some tenderness with it, no harm will be done as long as it does not amount to particular friendship. It is necessary at times to show some tenderness in our love[5] and even to feel it; we must sympathize with many of our sisters' trials and weaknesses, insignificant as they may be.[6] Sometimes a trifling matter gives as

[4] *Life*, vii. 32-37; xvi. 12; xxx. 6. *Castle*, M. II. i. 12.

[5] *Castle*, M. V. iii. 11.

[6] No one was in the company of this glorious Mother without receiving some consolation. All found solace from her in their crosses;

much pain to one person as a heavy cross would cause another. Sensitive natures feel very keenly slight troubles at which others would laugh. If you are stronger-minded, still, pity your neighbours and do not be astonished at them. Perhaps the devil has taken more trouble to wound their feelings thus than he has to grieve you by severe trials and crosses. It may be that our Lord spares us these sufferings to give us trials of other kinds, when perhaps what seems, and is indeed a heavy cross to us, will appear but a light one to our sisters.

5. We must not judge others by ourselves in such cases, nor compare ourselves to them at a time when, perhaps through no effort of our own, our Lord has given us greater fortitude; rather let us estimate ourselves by our weakest moments. There is need for this if we would know how to condole with our neighbours' griefs. Especially is this necessary for more courageous souls who, as they long for crosses, make little of their troubles. These should remember what they used to feel while they were still weak, and should reflect that if they have improved it is not their own doing. Otherwise, the devil may gradually cool our charity for others and lead us into mistaking an error for perfection. Constant care and vigilance are needed; Satan never sleeps, and is always especially wide awake when he watches more perfect souls; then his temptations are more subtle than ever, for he

she felt a deep compassion for the trials of the weak, whom she upheld by her words and prayers when she could do no more for them.' (Statement made by Father Pedro de la Purificacion: *Relaciones historicas de los siglos xvi. y xvii. publicadas por la Sociedad de Bibliofilos españoles*. vol. XXXII. p. 305. Madrid, 1896).

dare use no others; and unless we are very cautious the mischief is done before we know it.

6. In short we must always watch and pray,[7] for prayer is the surest way to discover the devil's snares and make him reveal himself. Be cordial with your sisters when they take their needful recreation,[8] and stay with them the whole of the appointed time, although it may not suit your taste.[9] I intended saying much of the other kind of love, but on second thoughts I do not think that it can flourish here, considering what life we lead; therefore I leave the subject alone, hoping that, with the help of God, there will be no danger of there being any less supernatural affection among those in this house, although the sisters may not always be quite perfect. It is right for the nuns to compassionate one another's needs, but beware lest this pity should be indiscreet, or contrary to obedience. Let no one know if the orders given by the Prioress seem harsh to you, unless you humbly say so to her yourself, otherwise you will do much harm. Make sure when it is right for you to sympathize with and to pity your sisters; you must always feel sorry for any conspicuous fault you see in one of them; charity is proved and tested in such a case by keeping patience and by

[7] St. Luke xxi. 36; 'Vigilate itaque omni tempore'

[8] *Const.* 27, 28. *Life*, xiii. 1. Sister Francisco de Jesus says: 'Our holy Mother was so fond of giving pleasure to the nuns that one night when she had retired to her cell at recreation time, on my asking her: "Isn't your Reverence coming to us?" (we had been told that she would be absent,) she answered laughingly: "Do you wish it, daughter? Well let us go together," and she came and was very merry.' (Fuente, vol. VI. 290, Note 5.)

[9] Escorial edition, xii. Of the great advantage of detaching ourselves from all interior and exterior things.

not being shocked.[10] Others bear thus with your faults, both those of which you are conscious and the many more of which you are ignorant. Pray constantly to God for your sister, and endeavour to practise perfectly the virtue contrary to her fault. Force yourself to do this, for you may thus teach her by deed, what by words or even by punishment, she could never attain to: whereas the sight of this virtue in another would make a great impression on her. This is good advice: do not forget it.

7. Oh! what an excellent and sincere love does that nun show who sacrifices her own interests to that of her sisters; who makes great progress in all the virtues and in the perfect observance of the Rule![11] There is more true friendship in this than in all the tender speeches that can be uttered, and which are not, and must not, be used in this house; such as: 'My life, my soul, my darling!' and other expressions people use to one another. Keep endearing words for your Spouse; you will often be alone with Him and will need them all, since His Majesty permits their use. However much you may repeat them to Him, they will not make you sentimental, and there is no need to address them to any one else. Such expressions are very womanish, and I do not wish you to be nor to appear so in any way, but rather valiant and manly. If you do your best, God will make you so strong that men will wonder at you. How easy this is to His Majesty Who created us out of nothing!

8. It is a great sign of love to relieve others of

[10] *Castle*, M. III. ii, 19; M. I. ii, 20, 21.
[11] *Castle*, M. VII. iv, 22.

their labour in the offices of the convent[12] and to take it on ourselves, also to rejoice and to thank God for our sisters' spiritual progress as if it were our own.[13] All these things (omitting the great good they bring with them), greatly conduce to peace and concord among the nuns, as by God's grace we have learned by experience. May His Majesty be pleased to increase this good feeling; it would be terrible were it otherwise and insufferable for so small a number to disagree with one another—God forbid it! But all the good that has been established here by the grace of God must be destroyed, or such a misfortune can never occur. If one of you should take offence at some hastily spoken words, let her at once atone for it and pray fervently on the subject, as also against any habitual fault, or grudge, or particular friendship, or desire of precedence, or regard for honour. My blood seems to freeze in my veins while I write this, at the thought that such a thing may be felt by any nun, for it is the special bane of convents. If it should really occur, give yourselves up for lost: know that you have driven your Spouse from the house and that, in a way, you have forced Him to seek some other home, since you have turned Him out of His own. Cry for aid to His Majesty, for, if your frequent confessions and communions do not prevent such ills, take heed lest there be some Judas among you. Let the Prioress be most

[12] *Life*, xxxi, 27. The Saint used to fold up the mantles of the nuns of the Incarnation.

[13] *Life*, xxxiv, 9 sqq. concerning Fr. Garcia de Toledo. *Castle*, M.V. iii, 11.

watchful on this point; let her prevent all chance of its occurring and stop it from the very first, for here lies all the mischief and its remedy. If gentleness will not suffice, let her inflict severe punishment. Should one of the nuns be found to be seditious, let her be sent to some other convent —God will provide her dowry. Drive away this pestilence: cut off the branches as best you can; or if this is not enough, pull up the roots. If this cannot be done, it would be better that such a person were imprisoned than that the whole community should be infected with such an incurable plague. What a terrible evil it is! God deliver us from a convent where this enters! I would rather it caught fire and burnt us all alive. But as I intend speaking more of this later on, on account of its great importance, I will only say I should prefer that the sisters loved one another tenderly with a demonstrative affection, if it were felt for all alike, although not with the perfect love I have described, than that they should disagree. May our Lord, being Who He is, never permit this! Amen.

CHAPTER VIII[1]

TREATS OF THE GREAT ADVANTAGE OF DETACHING OURSELVES FROM ALL CREATED THINGS, WHETHER INTERIOR OR EXTERIOR. OF THE MANY BENEFITS GAINED BY THOSE WHO HAVE LEFT THE WORLD BY SEVERING THEMSELVES FROM THEIR RELATIVES, AND HOW THEY WILL MEET WITH FAR TRUER FRIENDSHIP INSTEAD OF THAT WHICH THEY HAVE GIVEN UP.

1. Detachment. 2. Human affection for our relatives.

1. Now we will consider what is the detachment which we are bound to feel: if this be perfect it will include everything else. I say 'it will include everything else' because, if we cling to our Creator alone and care nothing for created things, His Majesty will infuse the virtues into us, so that, doing by degrees all that is in our power, we shall have little left with which to struggle, for our Lord will defend us against the devils and the whole world as well. Do you think that it is a small gain to give ourselves entirely to Him, keeping nothing for ourselves, since in His goodness all is contained as I told you? Be very grateful to Him, sisters, for bringing us here together where this is all that we care about.[2] I cannot tell why I am speaking about it to you, all of whom are capable of teaching me on the subject, for I own that, in this respect, I am not as perfect as I wish and as I know I ought to be; indeed, I am the most imperfect of you all.[3]

[1] Valladolid edition, ix; Escorial, xiii.
[2] *Castle*, M. VI. vi, 14. *Way of Perf.* ii, 8.
[3] *Life*, xviii, 6. *Found.* i, 4.

I have to say the same with regard to all the virtues and other matters which I treat of here, for it is easier to write of them than to practise them. Indeed, I may often fail even to write well of them, for sometimes one can only speak correctly of such things by experience, so that if I do succeed it must be by describing them as the opposite of my own qualities.[4] However, at your request, I will mention some matters which occur to me. It is clear that our lives are cut off from all outward things here: our Lord seems to wish to deprive us of all that would hold us captive to this world, so that He may, without impediment, draw us to Himself, O my Creator and my Sovereign! how have I deserved this great honour? Thou seemest to have sought for means whereby Thou couldst come nearer to us. By Thy mercy, permit us not to lose Thee. O my sisters! for the love of God consider what a signal grace our Lord has shown to those whom He has brought here. Let each of you realize it for herself, since of the twelve nuns His Majesty has chosen her for one. And how many, what a multitude, better than myself do I know of who would joyfully accept my place! Yet our Lord has bestowed this favour on me who so ill deserve it. Blessed be Thou, O my God! and may the angels and all creatures praise Thee, for I have as little merited this favour as I have the many others which Thou hast shown me. The vocation of a nun was an immense grace, yet I have been so wicked that Thou couldst not trust me, Lord. Among a number of people my guilt would not have been so noticeable

[4] *Const.* 16.

during my life-time and I should have hidden it as I did for so many years; but Thou, O Lord! hast brought me to where there are so few others that it seems impossible for my sins to remain unnoticed. That I might lead a better life, Thou hast removed me from all chance of evil. Therefore I confess, O Lord! that there is no excuse for my delinquencies and I have but greater need of Thy mercy to pardon me.

2. Remember, sisters, we are far more to blame than others if we are not so good, therefore, I earnestly beg her who feels beforehand that she has not fortitude of soul to observe what is practised here, to say so before her profession. There are other convents where, perhaps, our Lord may be served as well. Let her not disturb the small community which His Majesty has brought together here. There are many houses in which a nun is allowed to enjoy the society of her kindred: here, if relations are admitted, it is only for their own sake.[5] The sister who wishes, for her personal pleasure, to see her relatives and who does not weary of their society on their second visit, unless they are spiritual persons who help her soul, must recognize that she is imperfect, and not detached—she is not well, and will not obtain liberty of spirit nor perfect peace—she needs a physician. I affirm that unless she changes and is cured she is unfit for the house. As far as I know, the best remedy is that she should have no interviews with her relations until she feels emancipated from this bond, having obtained the grace from God by many

[5] *Const.* 14, 15.

prayers. When receiving her kindred has become a cross to a nun,[6] by all means let her see them sometimes for their own good, as she will certainly profit them and do herself no harm; but if she is very fond of them, if their troubles affect her deeply, and if she is delighted at their success in the world, let her be sure that she will injure herself and do them no good.

CHAPTER IX[1]

THOSE WHO HAVE GIVEN UP THE WORLD BENEFIT BY DOING SO AND GAIN TRUER FRIENDS: THIS, HOWEVER DOES NOT SUFFICE UNLESS WE FORSAKE OURSELVES ALSO.

1. Harm done by seeing much of our relations. 2. Detachment from them. 3. God will supply us with the friends we need. 4. Spiritual and corporal detachment.

1. OH, if we religious only understood the harm it does us to see much of our relations, how we should shun them! I cannot see what pleasure it can give us, for, setting aside the mischief done by it to our spiritual life, what comfort or solace can it obtain for us? We cannot share their amusements, nor would it be lawful for us; but we grieve over their unhappiness which often afflicts us more than it does them. I assure you that the soul and poverty of spirit pay dearly for any comfort that the body may gain. You are free from this evil here, for as everything is in common and no one may receive any private gift, all alms being given to the

[6] *Life*, ii, 6; vii, 10, 12; xxiv. 8. *Rel.* i, 6; ibid. x.
[1] Valladolid edition, x; Escorial, xiv.

community in general,[2] there is no obligation to repay your kindred for what they bestow, and, as you know, our Lord provides for us all together.

2. It astonishes me to see what harm the society of our kindred does us. It is incredible, save to those who have witnessed it for themselves; yet how this perfection seems forgotten by religious of the present day! at least by the greater number of them, although all the saints remembered it and wrote a great deal about it. I cannot tell what it is that we leave in this world, we who say we leave all for God, if we do not forego the chief thing of all—the society of our relatives. Things have come to such a pass that it is considered a defect in religious not to be fond of their kindred nor to see a great deal of them. They will tell you so, and allege their reasons for it. In this house, my daughters, we must pray a good deal for our relatives after having interceded for the Church, as I told you: this is only right; but having done this, we must blot them out of our memory as far as possible, because it is natural to us to fix our affection on them in preference to others. My relations were extremely fond of me, people say, and I loved them so much that I would not allow them to forget me. Yet I have learnt from experience, both in my own case and that of others, that (with the exception of parents, who only in very rare cases refuse succour to their children), when I have been in need my own kith and kin have helped me least of all, and it has been the servants of God who have come to my aid. It is right,

[2] *Const.* 10. On gifts. 31.

however, when our father and mother require comfort from us that we should not hold ourselves aloof from them: this is consistent with perfect detachment. The same applies to our brothers and sisters.

3. Believe me, sisters, if you serve God as you ought you will find no better kindred than those servants of His whom He will send you. I am convinced of the truth of this, and if you do what you know to be right (for to take any other course would be to fail in your duty to your true Friend and Spouse), you may be sure that in a very short time you will gain this liberty of spirit. Those who love you for His sake alone, who are more to be relied on than all your relatives, will never desert you, and you will find fathers and brothers where you never looked for them. For these latter help us because they wait for their reward from God, while the former, as they expect repayment from us, when they see our poverty and helplessness soon weary of assisting us. Though this does not always happen, yet it is the rule in this life; in short, it is the way of the world! If any one tells you it is a virtue to act in a contrary manner, do not believe him. It would take me a long time to tell you all the harm that results from such a course; as others who know better than I do have written on the subject, this will suffice. If, in spite of all my imperfections, I understand this so well, how far better more spiritual persons must realize it! As I said, much has been written elsewhere on this matter, many books treating of little else. There is no doubt that the saints do right in advising

us to fly from the world. Believe what I said to you—the thing that clings closest to us and is most difficult to shake off is the love of our kindred.

4. Those do right, therefore, who quit their country if it helps this detachment which I find consists not so much in bodily separation as in the spirit's resolutely embracing the good Jesus, our Lord, and forgetting all else since it possesses all things in Him. But it is a great help to keep apart from our relations until we are convinced of this truth. Later on, perhaps, it may be God's will that we should be in their society; we may then find our cross where we used to find our joy.

CHAPTER X[1]

THAT THIS ABNEGATION IS NOT ENOUGH UNLESS WE ALSO ARE DETACHED FROM OURSELVES. HOW THIS VIRTUE AND HUMILITY GO TOGETHER.

1. Detachment from self-will. 2. Humility and mortification. 3. Their effects. 4. Indifference to our health the first step to mortification. 5. Mortification and anxiety about health. 6. Relaxation of the Rule in convents.

1. SEPARATED from the world and our own kindred, in a state of absolute poverty, and enclosed in this convent under the conditions I have described, it would seem that we have done all and that there is nothing left to contend with. Ah, sisters, do not feel too secure, nor settle yourselves to sleep! You would be like a man who goes peacefully to rest after having bolted his doors securely against the

[1] Valladolid edition, xi; Escorial, xv. Treats of the humility accompanying the two virtues of detachment and the perfect love already described.

robbers already inside them. Have you not heard that the thief who lives in the house is the worst thief of all?[2]

Our natures are always the same, and unless we use the greatest care and each one of us makes it her most urgent business constantly to cross her self-will, many things will keep us from the holy liberty of spirit which we seek in order that our souls may rise to their Creator, unimpeded by any earthly, leaden weight.

2. A valuable aid towards this is the constant remembrance of the vanity of all things and of how quickly they pass away, that we may withdraw our affections from what is worthless and fix them on what is eternal. Though this means seems inefficient, yet I assure you it gives great strength to the soul. We must keep watch over ourselves carefully in the most insignificant matters: when we are attached to anything we must turn our thoughts from it and fix them on God. His Majesty will help us to do this, and it is a great grace from Him that, in this convent, the chief part of this is already done for us.[3] As this detachment from ourselves and crossing our own wills is a hard matter, the union being so close and self-love being very strong,[4] humility will now find its place.[5] This virtue and abnegation seem to me always to accompany one another; they are two sisters who

[2] St. Matt. x. 36: 'Inimici hominis domestici ejus.'

[3] St. Teresa practised strict poverty and disliked the nuns' becoming attached to any little article given them for their use. She therefore often made them change cells, breviaries, etc. (Fuente, vol. VI. 310, Note 16.) Deposition of Maria de San Francisco.

[4] Escorial edition, xvi. Of mortifying ourselves during sickness.

[5] *Life*, xxxi. 23, sqq.

cannot be separated. These are not the kindred I advise you to forsake: embrace and love them, and never be seen without them.

3. O sovereign virtues! rulers of all created things; queens of the world; our deliverers from all the snares and traps of the devil, dearly loved as you were by our Teacher, Jesus Christ, Who never for a moment lived without you! Those who possess you may sally forth and fight with all hell and the whole world and its temptations! Let them not be afraid, for 'theirs is the kingdom of heaven': they have no cause for dread for they care not if all be lost—nor do they count it loss—their sole fear is lest they should offend their God; they implore Him to preserve these virtues in their souls lest by their own fault they should lose them. It is true that these virtues have the property of hiding themselves from their owner's sight, so that he never believes he possesses them, whatever he may be told to the contrary. Yet he esteems them so highly that he is always striving to gain them and thus grows more perfect in them. The possessor of these virtues soon unwittingly reveals them to those who talk to him.

4. But what presumption for me to praise humility and mortification which have been so extolled by the King of Glory and exemplified by all His toils and sufferings! These are the virtues that you must labour to obtain in order to escape from the Land of Egypt. My daughters, when you possess them, you will find the manna:[7] then all things will taste sweet to you: however bitter

[6] St. Matt. iii, 3: 'Quoniam ipsorum est regnum cælorum.'
[7] Apoc. ii, 17. *Castle*, M. II, i, 13.

the world may find them, to you they will be delicious. Our first effort must be to cease loving our bodies;[8] some of us are naturally self-indulgent, therefore this is no easy work. Considering that we are nuns, it is surprising what a struggle these two things cost us, just as they do other people. Some of us seem to think we only entered the convent in order to keep ourselves alive and to nurse and pamper our bodies as well as we can, and this constitutes our principal pleasure. To tell the truth, there is very little opportunity of practising this here, but I do not want you even to wish for such a thing. Be convinced, sisters, that you came here to die for Christ, not to indulge yourselves for Him. The devil suggests that we need to take care of ourselves in order to observe the Rule. Such nuns are so exceedingly anxious to preserve their health so that they may be able to obey the Rule that they die without ever having observed it for a month, or perhaps, even for a single day. If good health is our object in life, I do not know why we came here. There is no fear lest we should fail in discretion on this point, for our confessors at once take fright lest we should kill ourselves with penances; and I wish our other faults of observance were as odious to us as is such want of prudence.

5. I know that those who practise the contrary will pay no attention to what I am writing, nor do I care if they say that I judge others by myself, which is true enough. I am sure that there are more who behave as I do, than there are nuns who

[8] *Castle*, M. I. ii, 14; M. III. ii, 9. *Concept.* ii, 20. *Const.* 21.

are offended at my words because they never themselves act in such a way. I believe that this is why our Lord permits us to have delicate constitutions; at least, He has shown me great mercy in doing so in my case, for as I was sure to pamper myself He wished me to have some excuse for it.[9] It is amusing to see how some worry themselves about this. At one time they have a mania for doing penances without either moderation or discretion:[10] this lasts for a day or so and then the devil puts it into their heads that penance makes them ill, so henceforth they never perform any more even when the Rule enjoins it, as they have found it injures them.[11] We do not obey even the least points of the Rule, such as silence, which could do us no harm. Directly we fancy our head aches, we stop away from choir which would not kill us either. One day we are absent because it aches, the next because it has ached, and three more lest it should ache again; but we love to invent penances for ourselves, so that we end by doing neither the one nor the other. Sometimes we feel stronger yet we think we are not obliged to mortify ourselves, but that by having obtained leave we are henceforth dispensed from everything.

6. You may ask why the Prioress gives these dispensations. If she could see into the state of your body perhaps she would refuse, but you tell her there is need of them and the doctor supports your cause, while a friend or relation stands by weeping, and though the poor Prioress sometimes sees that

[9] *Life*, xxiv, 2. *Rel.* xi, 2.
[10] *Castle*, M. I. ii, 19. *Way of Perf.* xxxix, 4.
[11] *Castle*, M. III. ii, 11. *Const.* 21.

too much is asked for, yet what is she to do? She feels a scruple lest she should be wanting in charity and would rather you erred than that she should: while it seems unjust to judge you harshly. Oh these complaints! God help us, among *nuns!* May He forgive me for saying so, but I believe it has already become the custom. I once saw a case of this kind: a nun said she had a headache, and complained of it a great deal. When it came to be inquired into, she felt no pain at all in her head, but suffered in some other part of her body. Such things may occur here at times, so I warn you against them now, for if the devil once begins to daunt us with the fear of losing our health we shall never do anything. May God give us light to accomplish all our duties! Amen.

CHAPTER XI[1]

CONTINUES TO TREAT OF MORTIFICATION AND EXPLAINS HOW TO GAIN IT DURING ILLNESS. HOW LITTLE THIS LIFE SHOULD BE VALUED BY ONE WHO TRULY LOVES GOD.

1. How a religious should behave during illness. 2. Sufferings endured by those living in the world. 3. How to master our bodies. 4. Strong resolution needed.

1. To be continually bewailing our slight ailments appears to me, sisters, to be a very great imperfection. Say nothing about them if you can help it. When the illness is severe it is self-evident—this is quite another sort of complaining, which at once makes itself known. Remember, you are few

[1] Valladolid edition, xii; Escorial, xvii.

in number, and if any of you has this habit she will weary all the rest if love and charity reign among you. If the indisposition is real, speak about it and take the necessary remedies[2]: if you have lost self-love, you will so dislike indulgence that there will be no fear of your wanting more than necessary, nor of your complaining without good cause. When there is a genuine reason you do right in mentioning it; this is far better than taking anything extra without leave and it would be very wrong of your sisters not to pity you. I am confident that, wherever prayer and charity prevail in however small a degree, the nuns will notice each other's wants, and the needful remedies and care will never be wanting.[3] As for the little indispositions women may suffer from—do not think of complaining of them: very often they are only fancies suggested by the devil, which come and go, and if you do not get rid of the habit of speaking about them (except to God) there will never be an end to them.[4]

2. I insist on this because I think it very important for us, and one of the things which greatly tend to relax discipline in monasteries. The body possesses this defect—the more you give it, the more it requires. It is wonderful how fond it is of comfort, and what pretexts it will offer to

[2] *Const.* 22. *Visit.* 10.

[3] The first thing that St. Teresa did on arriving at a convent was to visit the Blessed Sacrament. Then, if any of the nuns were ill, she went at once to see them, performing many deeds of kindness on their behalf. She charged the Prioresses to take great care of the invalids when it was requisite. (Fuente, vol. VI. 308. Note 2). Deposition of Catalina de los Angeles.

[4] *Concep.* ii, 17-20.

obtain it, however little needed; it deceives the unfortunate soul, and prevents its making progress. Remember how many poor people are ill and have no one to complain to—poverty and ease do not go together. Think too, what a number of married women there are, many of them, as I know, of good position in life, who, lest they should annoy their husbands, dare not speak of the serious maladies and poignant trials from which they suffer. Sinner as I am, no! we did not come here to be better treated than they are. How free you are from the great troubles of the world; learn, then, to suffer some little thing for the love of God without every one's knowing it. When a woman has made an unhappy marriage she does not say so, nor lament about it for fear her husband should know: she is very wretched but confides in no one: shall not we, then, keep secret between God and ourselves some of the ills He sends us for our sins? all the more because speaking of it does not lighten our load.

3. What I have said does not apply to serious illness attended with high fever, although, even then, I beg of you to be reasonable and patient;[5] but I allude to slight ailments with which we can go about without troubling other people concerning them. But what will happen if this is read by any one outside the convent? What will all the nuns say of me? How willingly I would bear this if I could help any one to improve! If a nun constantly complains, at last her sisters will not believe any one else who says she is really ill, even though

[5] *Rel.* iii, 2.

the doctor may confirm her words. However, as I am only speaking to my daughters they will forgive me for what I have written. Let us remember our holy Fathers, the ancient hermits, whose lives we profess to imitate: what sufferings they bore, what solitude, what cold and hunger, what scorching sunshine and heat, with no one to complain to but God. Do you think they were made of iron?[6] They were made of flesh and blood like ourselves. Believe me, daughters, when once we begin to subdue our wretched bodies, they do not trouble us so much. It is enough for you to see to what is needful. Do not desire anything extra, unless it is absolutely necessary.

4. Unless we resolve, once for all, to resign ourselves to death and ill-health, we shall never do anything. Endeavour to lose all fear of them and to leave everything in God's hands, come what may. What does it matter if we die? How many times have not our bodies mocked us! Let us mock them for once. Trust me, this resolution is more important than can be realized, for by keeping faithfully to it and practising it little by little until it becomes a habit, with the grace of God we shall vanquish the flesh, and you will experience the truth of what I say. Victory over such an enemy goes far to carry us through the battle of life. May God grant it to us, since He has the power, and we need His grace in all things: may He bring it to pass for His own sake! I am certain that only those who rejoice in

[6] *Imitation*, I. xviii, 2. St. Teresa knew the *Imitation of Christ* under the title of *Contemptus mundi*, translated by Luis de Granada and printed at Seville in 1536, and again at Lisbon 1544, and Alcalá 1548. There exists an earlier Spanish translation printed in 1490.

this conquest can estimate its value which is so great that I believe no one will regret any sufferings that have been endured in order to gain such peace and self-command.

CHAPTER XII[1]

THAT ONE WHO TRULY LOVES GOD MUST CARE LITTLE FOR LIFE OR HONOUR. THAT ONE WHO SEEKS AFTER PERFECTION MUST DESPISE HONOURS.

1. Having renounced all else, religious must renounce themselves. 2. The religious life a martyrdom. 3. Joy brought by mortification. 4. Contemplation incompatible with a desire for honour or riches. 5. Forsaking all things. 6. Humility. 7. Proud thoughts corrected by outward acts of humility. 8. Evil arising in convents from a regard for honour. 9. Wrong done by taking offence.

1. LET us now speak of other small matters which are very important, insignificant as they may appear. All this seems an enormous work, as indeed it is, being a warfare carried on against self; yet, when once we begin it, God so works in our souls, bestowing on them numerous graces, that all we can do in this life seems but a trifle. We nuns have done the greater part of our task; we have given up our liberty for the love of God and placed it in the power of another. We endure so much in our labours,[2] fasts,[3] silence,[4] enclosure,[5] attendance at choir,[6] that, however strongly we may wish for our ease, we can rarely enjoy it,[7] and perhaps, among the many convents I have visited, I may

[1] Valladolid edition, xiii; Escorial, xviii.
[2] *Rule*, 13. *Const.* 23. *Visit*, 11. [3] *Rule*, 10. *Const.* 11.
[4] *Rule*, 14. *Const.* 5. [5] *Const.* 13. *Found.* xxxi, 42. *Life*, vii, 5.
[6] *Rule*, 6. *Const.* 1-6. [7] *Life*, xiii, 30.

be the only nun who tries to obtain it! Why then do we draw back from interior mortification, which is the mainspring of all the rest, by which they become more meritorious and perfect and are finally performed with sweetness and peace?

2. This interior mortification, as I said, is acquired little by little through never following our own will or liking even in the most trifling matters, until we have subdued the body to the spirit. I repeat that this is entirely or at least mainly accomplished by renouncing all care for ourselves and our own pleasure. If we have really begun to serve our Lord, the least we can offer Him is our life, after having yielded our will to Him. What is there to fear in this? Whoever is a true religious or is genuinely devoted to prayer and aspires to enjoy divine consolations, should be convinced that she must not recoil from wishing either to die,[8] or to suffer martyrdom for His sake.[9] Do you not know, sisters, that the life of a good religious, and of one who wishes to be among the most intimate friends of God, is one long martyrdom? 'Long,' because, compared to decapitation, which lasts but an instant, it may be termed *long:* but a whole life-time is *short*, and sometimes very short indeed.

[8] 'Either to die or to suffer,' the genuine form of St. Teresa's motto, which occurs also in an undated letter to a Carmelite nun. 'To die or suffer—this should be our wish' *Letters*, vol. III. Let. 277. The usual wording, 'To suffer or to die,' is nowhere to be found in the Saint's writings. *Life*, xl, 27. 3, sqq.

[9] One of the nuns asked our holy Mother how to become a saint. She answered: 'Daughter, we are soon going to make a foundation; then you will learn the way.' They went, and the sister met with a great many trials: she told them to the Saint, who replied: 'Daughter, did you not ask me to teach you how to become a saint? This is the way'—meaning that sanctity lay in suffering for God. (Fuente, vol. VI. 318, Notes 20, 21. Deposition of Isabel de Jesus.)

How do we know that ours may not be so short as to end in an hour, or even in a moment, after we have determined to give ourselves entirely to God? It is quite possible, for we cannot depend on anything that passes away, much less on life, on which we must not reckon for a single day. Who, thinking each hour to be his last, would not spend it in labour?

3. Trust me, this is the safest view to take, therefore we must learn to cross our will in everything; although we may not succeed at once, yet little by little, by the help of prayer, as I said, without knowing how, we shall reach the summit. But how rigorous it sounds to say that we must never please ourselves, unless we are told of the consolation this self-denial brings with it, and of the security it obtains during this life! But, as you all practise it here, the principal part is already done; each one is urging her sisters on, and strives to excel the rest. Be most watchful over your secret feelings, especially such as concern precedence.[10] God deliver us, for the sake of His Passion, from saying, or from deliberately thinking, 'I am her senior in the Order': 'I am older than she': 'I have done more work': 'She is better treated than I am.'

4. When such thoughts arise in your minds, you must suppress them at once: if you dwell upon them or give them utterance they will prove contagious and will give rise to great evils in a religious house. Should your Prioress allow anything of this kind, however slight it may be, you must believe

[10] *Life*, xxi, 12; xxvii, 16. *Rel.* i, 28. *Castle*, M. V. iii, 10-12. *Concep.* ii, 15.

that God has permitted her to hold that office in punishment for your sins, and that it is the beginning of your ruin. Cry to Him for aid and let all your prayers be directed to obtain a remedy, for you are in danger. A religious, or a person who practises prayer with the genuine resolution of obtaining the graces and joys God grants to souls, is bound to this detachment from everything."[11]

5. You may think I insist too much on this, and that I treat it with excessive severity, as God bestows His consolations on souls wanting in this detachment. Doubtless this is the case, for in His infinite wisdom He knows they can be thus drawn to forsake all things for His sake. By 'forsaking all things'[12] I do not necessarily mean entering religion, for there may be obstacles preventing this, and in every state perfect souls may be detached and humble; however, this is more difficult whilst living in the world, for our surroundings influence us strongly. But rest assured of this—people may desire honours or possessions in monasteries as well as outside them (yet the sin is greater as the temptation is less),[13] but such souls, although they may have spent years in prayer, or rather in speculations (for perfect prayer eventually destroys these vices), will never make great progress nor enjoy the real fruit of prayer.

6. Ascertain, sisters, whether you care for these trifles, for you came here that you might spurn

[11] Escorial edition. xix. That care for honour and for the wisdom of this world must be avoided in order to arrive at true wisdom.

[12] St. Matt. xix, 27. St. Mark, x, 28. St. Luke, xviii, 28: 'Reliquimus omnia, et secuti sumus te.'

[13] *Concep.* ii, 30, 32, 33. *Way of Perf.* xxxvi, 2-7.

them. They give you no increase of honour, and you miss advantages which would have brought you more honour in the end; so discredit and loss are here combined. Let each one examine whether she is truly humble, and she will learn what progress she has made. I do not think the devil would dare to tempt a lowly heart with even the suggestions of a wish for precedence, for he is sagacious enough to fear the wound he would receive.

Such a temptation of the evil one can only strengthen and increase this virtue in a truly humble heart, which will reflect upon its former life, the little service it has rendered to our Lord compared with what it owed Him, and the wonders He performed in abasing Himself to give us an example of lowliness: it will recall its sins, and remember that it has deserved hell in return for them. These reflections so benefit the mind that Satan dares not return next day, for fear of getting a broken head.

7. Take this advice from me and do not forget it—that not only should you gain the victory within your own heart (where it would be very wrong not to benefit by the temptation), but even outwardly you ought to let your sisters be the gainers by its means if you would be avenged on the devil and escape from the repetition of such thoughts. As soon as they arise, tell the Prioress of them and ask her to give you some very mean employment, or else of your own accord do any sort of work of the kind. Meanwhile, study how to subdue your will in the things you are most averse to (our Lord will show you many ways of doing this), and perform some public penances such as are usual

in the house.[14] Thus the temptation will quickly vanish. God deliver us from people who try to serve Him yet who care for their honour or fear disgrace. What we gain by this only does us harm: as I said, honour is lost by those who seek it; above all by religious, especially in the matter of rank, for no poison in the world is so fatal to perfection.

8. You may say that this is a trifling fault and only human nature; that it is of no importance. Do not hold it lightly; it spreads in monasteries as quickly as foam gathers on the sea; nothing can be called trifling in so great a danger as these points of honour and sensitiveness about affronts. Would you like to know the chief reason—not to speak of other causes? Some slight annoyance, hardly worth mentioning, is offered you, and the devil instigates one of your sisters to consider it a grave insult: she even thinks it a charity to tell you of it and to ask you how you could bear such an injury: she says she begs God to grant you patience; she should offer it up to Him, for a saint could bear no more.[15]

9. In short, the evil one makes mischief through another's tongue: so that although you are resolved to suffer meekly you are tempted to vainglory on account of what you have not borne as well as you ought to have done. Human nature is so weak that though we overcome the temptation by telling ourselves there is no cause for annoyance, yet we think we have done something praiseworthy and feel we have been injured—how much more when others agree with us! This makes the trouble worse; we hold that we are in the right; our souls

[14] *Const.* 25.

[15] *See* Letter to Ven. Anne of Jesus. May 30, 1582. vol. IV. Let. 444.

lose an occasion of gaining merit and are left weaker than before, while a door is opened to Satan by which he can return another time to tempt us more severely. It may even happen that when you are willing to bear an injury, some one may come and ask you: 'Are you to be treated like a dog? surely every one ought to have some self-respect!' Oh! for the love of God, sisters, never show such indiscreet sympathy with one another respecting mere fancied injuries, which is like that shown to holy Job by his wife and friends.

CHAPTER XIII[1]

CONTINUES THE SUBJECT OF MORTIFICATION: THAT A NUN MUST AVOID THE TOUCHINESS AND WISDOM OF THE WORLD IN ORDER TO ATTAIN TRUE WISDOM.

1. We must imitate our Lord by suffering unjustly. 2. The evil of bad example. 3. One who is punctilious about honour is unsuited to the religious life. 4. A mortified spirit essential for a Carmelite. 5. Essentials of a Carmelite vocation.

1. I OFTEN tell you, sisters, and now I leave it to you here in writing, that not only those dwelling in this house but all who aspire after perfection must fly a thousand leagues away from saying, 'I was in the *right:* it was not *right* for me to suffer this, they had no *right* to do such a thing to me!'[2] Now God deliver us from such wrong *rights!* Do you think that there was any question of *rights* when our good Jesus suffered the injuries which were so *unrighteously* inflicted on Him? I do not know what any person is doing in a monastery

[1] Valladolid edition, xiv; Escorial, continuation of xix.

[2] *Const.* 30.

who will only bear a cross which people have a perfect *right* to lay upon her—let her go back to the world where people care nothing for such *rights*. Is it possible for you to suffer so much that you *ought* not to suffer any more! What *rights* have you in this? I do not know of them. When we receive honours or affection or kind treatment let us think what *right* have we to *them*, for certainly we have no *right* to them in this life; but when wrong is done to us we call it so, though it does us no wrong—I do not know why we should ever speak of it. Either we are brides of this great King or we are not. If we are, what faithful wife does not share her husband's disgrace, even against her will? In short, they share both honour and shame together. To seek to share in His kingdom and to enjoy His presence, and yet to shun all part in His ignominy and His toils is incompatible. God preserve us from such a wish! Let her who believes that her sisters hold her the last of all think herself the most fortunate, as indeed she is if she bears it as she ought, and she will not fail to be honoured for it, both in this world and in the next: you may trust my words.[3]

2. But what presumption for me to write 'You may trust my words' when He Who is true Wisdom tells us so, as does the Queen of Angels! Let us, my daughters, imitate, however feebly, the

[3] 'In order to profit and advance by means of persecutions and injuries we meet with, it is well to reflect that God has been offended by them before I have—when the blow strikes me, He has already been affronted by the sin. The soul that truly loves its Spouse ought to have already pledged itself to be entirely His, and if He supports the insult, why should we resent it? . . . Die or suffer—this should be our wish.' (See Ch. xii, Note 8).

most holy Virgin, whose habit we wear. Indeed, we feel ashamed to number ourselves among her nuns, because, however deeply we seem to humble ourselves, we are most unworthy to be called the daughters of such a mother, and the brides of such a Spouse, even if we copy her humility in any way—'in any way', I say. However, though we may all abase and humble ourselves, no one is so bound to do this as myself, who for my sins deserve to be insulted and despised by the devils themselves. Yet, although others may not have committed so many faults, it will be wonderful if they have done nothing that deserves hell. Therefore, I repeat, you must not consider the defects I have spoken of as insignificant, for, if you do not check them carefully, what seems a trifle to-day will become a venial sin to-morrow; this is a thing of such evil growth that if left alone it will spread and is most injurious in communities. We must be very watchful in such matters lest we injure those who are trying to help us and to give us a good example. If we only realized the immense harm that is done by introducing the bad habit of touchiness about honour, we should die a thousand times rather than be the means of doing so. That would be only the death of the body, but the loss of souls is a terrible one and seems never-ending, for when one generation dies, others succeed it, and perhaps they will all be influenced more by the one bad custom we began[4] than by the many virtues they see practised, for the devil takes care the evil habit is kept up, while the infirmity of human nature destroys our virtues.[5]

[4] *Found.* i, 3. *Castle*, M. VII. iv, 22. [5] *Const.* 5.

3. What genuine charity, and how true a service to God would it be, if the novice who sees that she cannot conform to the customs of this convent would acknowledge it and go away before being professed, thus leaving the nuns in peace. Other monasteries (if they will take my advice) will not keep her, nor allow her to take the vows without giving her several years' probation, to learn whether she will improve. I do not mean one who cannot bear penances and fasting, for though this be a fault, it does not cause so much harm, but I am speaking of those who wish to be esteemed and respected; who see others' faults but never know their own, and who possess other defects of the same kind, which all take their origin from a want of humility. If God does not favour such a character with a great deal of light and understanding, so that she amends in the course of years, may He prevent you from retaining her in your community; for, be assured that she will never be at rest herself nor leave others at peace. As you do not require dowries, God preserves you from many dangers, for I pity the monasteries which, for the sake of not returning the dowry or out of regard for her relations, keep a thief who robs them of this treasure.[6]

4. In this convent you have abandoned and lost the honour of this world, for the poor are not honoured; nor should you honour others at so dear a cost to yourselves. Our honour, sisters, is to serve God;[7] whoever should hinder this had better remain at home with her honour. It was to test

[6] Escorial edition, xx. The great importance of refusing to profess any one whose character is opposed to the virtues I have described.

[7] *Life*, xi, 4; xx, 34.

the disposition of novices that our Fathers ordered a year's probation for them[8] (which in our Order may be prolonged to four years),[9] and I wish that they were not professed for ten years, because a humble nun would care little for the delay, knowing that if she were good she would not be sent away, and if she were not, why should she wish to stay and damage Christ's community? By not being 'good' I do not mean an attachment to worldly vanities, for by the mercy of God, I believe that those in this house are far from anything of the sort, but I mean a want of mortification, self-esteem, or a care for human respect and self, of the kind mentioned. Let her who knows that she is not very mortified believe what I say, and not make her profession unless she wishes to live in a very hell in this life—and God grant she may not find herself in another hell in the next world—for there is much in such dispositions to make one fear such a fate for her, though perhaps neither she herself nor the nuns understand her case as I do. Trust my words, otherwise you will learn this truth in the future. The spirit of our Order bids us not only to be nuns but hermits, like our holy Fathers in times past; therefore we must be detached from all created things. This grace of detachment is to be found in any one to whom God has given our vocation, and

[8] *Visit.* 24, 25, 42. *Const.* 17, 41.

[9] 'Four years' probation.' There appears to be no record of such a custom, so that the thought presents itself that this was arranged between the Saint and the Bishop of Avila, who at that time was Superior of the convent of St. Joseph. It is certain that St. Teresa acted on this principle, because Maria de San José (Maria Davila), one of the first four Novices, was only professed on July 2, 1566, nearly four years after her entrance.

although at first she may not possess it in perfection, yet we know that she has it by her joy at seeing she is cut off from the world, and her delight in all the practices of the religious life.[10]

5. I repeat that any one who is worldly and who does not improve is not fit for our convents: she should go somewhere else if she wishes to be a nun—if not, she will see what will happen. Let her not complain that it is my fault because I founded this house, and that I do not warn her. This convent is a paradise (if paradise can exist on earth) for any one who finds her sole happiness in pleasing God,[11] and who cares nothing for her own comfort: such a person leads a very happy life here, but if she seeks for anything more, she will lose all the rest because nothing else is to be had. A discontented mind resembles a man suffering from violent nausea, whose stomach rejects all food however good it may be while loathing the meat which others relish. Any one with the character I have described may save her soul more easily elsewhere than here, and may by degrees attain the perfection which she would not gain in this Order, because here the mortifications must be accepted at once; for although time is allowed for attaining total interior detachment and mortification, these virtues must soon be practised outwardly because of the harm their absence may do to others. If seeing them performed by all the nuns and living among good companions should not improve the new-comer in a year, or in six months, I fear she will never make much progress

[10] *Found.* xxviii, 37.

[11] *Castle*, M.V. iv, 5. *Found.* i, 3. *Life*, xxxv, 13.

either in many years or in few. I do not say she must be as perfect in these qualities as the rest of the nuns, but she must make visible progress towards the recovery of her spiritual health, as she soon will do if the disease is not mortal.

CHAPTER XIV[1]

TREATS OF THE GREAT IMPORTANCE OF NOT PROFESSING ANY ONE OF A SPIRIT CONTRARY TO THE QUALIFICATIONS HERE DESCRIBED.

1. Qualifications requisite for a Carmelite nun. 2. On admitting novices to profession. 3. Responsibility of admitting novices.

1. I BELIEVE that God gives great grace to any one who is resolved to do right, therefore you must examine into what is the intention of a person entering the convent. She must not come here to find a home, as often happens nowadays, although if she has good sense our Lord may perfect even this intention. If she is wanting in sense, on no account receive her, for she will not know why she enters nor will her Superiors ever be able to teach her afterwards. As a rule, those who are defective in this way think they know, better than the wisest, what is good for them. I believe this ill is incurable, for it is seldom without some malice. Among a number of religious and in a large convent it may be borne with, but in our small community it would be intolerable. Good sense, when it once begins to see what is right,

[1] Valladolid edition, xv; Escorial, xxi.

clings firmly to it, convinced that this is the safest course, and although this may not lead to great spirituality, still such a person is useful when practical advice is required and in many other ways, and is not a burden to any one, but rather a help by her cheerfulness. However, I cannot see of what service in a community a person wanting in sense can be, though she may do much harm.[2] This defect, and the others I spoke of,[3] are not known at first, for many people speak well and understand ill, while others' speech is short and unpolished but they are at home with God. They are simple, holy souls who know little of this world's work and manners, but are apt for prayer.[4] Therefore inquiries must be made before receiving a novice, and a long probation given her before her

[2] Ribera says in his life of St. Teresa: 'She was singularly fond of intelligent people. Next to their having a vocation, what she cared for most in those she received as novices, even if only lay sisters, was a good understanding. People who knew her holiness and love of prayer were careful to praise the fervour and prayerfulness of the candidates they brought her, thinking this would make her accept them. But she only seemed to care to know whether they were sensible and apt. I myself was among their number, and, being greatly surprised, I asked her the reason. She answered: "Father, our Lord will give her devotion when she enters, and we will teach her prayer. As for those who have practised prayer outside, we very often have to teach them to forget all they have learnt—but as for intelligence, we cannot give it to them. Besides, a devout, good nun, if she has no brains, is only of use to herself. But I can put a sensible nun at the head of the house and trust her with any of the offices."' (*Ribera*, IV, xxiv).

[3] Ch. xiii, 3. *Const.* 13, 17, 41.

[4] When St. Teresa set out for Soria she chose Catalina de Cristo, of the convent of Medina del Campo, as Prioress of the new foundation. 'But she reads only with difficulty, and does not even know how to write,' remarked some one. 'She is a saint,' said the foundress, 'and that is enough to make a good Prioress of her.' On June 27, 1581, she had occasion to write to Fr. Gracian: 'The Prioress fills her place admirably.' Letters, vol. IV. Let. 387.

profession. If the world once understands that you are free to send away new-comers (as there is often good reason for doing in a convent where austerities are practised), no one will feel offended by your doing so.

2. I say this because these times are so disastrous and our weakness is so great that the rules of past generations do not suffice to make us disregard all pretences about dignity; that is, that we must not, because of a consideration for the feelings of a novice's relations or for fear of giving some slight offence, allow the former good customs of the convent to be forgotten. God grant that those who receive unsuitable candidates may not suffer for it in the next world! there is always some slight pretext for thinking we may admit them, though in a case of such importance no excuse is valid.

3. I believe that when the Prioress is uninfluenced by affection or prejudice, and only seeks the welfare of the house, God will not permit her to fall into error. When, however, she is swayed by regard for other people's feelings or the demands of etiquette, she will be sure to make some mistake. Each one of us must consider the matter for herself and pray about it and must encourage the Prioress when she feels misgivings. The affair is of the utmost consequence, therefore I beg God to enlighten the nuns about it. You do well in taking no dowries: it sometimes happens that, for the sake of not repaying money which they have not in hand, religious keep in their house a thief who

robs them of their treasure, to their great misfortune. Never receive dowries in this convent, for what seems a gain will prove to be a great loss.[5]

CHAPTER XV[1]

THE GREAT ADVANTAGE OF NOT EXCUSING OURSELVES EVEN WHEN UNJUSTLY BLAMED.

1. Submitting to unjust blame. 2. A penance that all may practise. 3. A prayer to share our Lord's obloquy. 4. Benefits of bearing with false accusations. 5. Liberty of spirit thus gained.

1. I AM overwhelmed with confusion at speaking on this subject, and I do not know how to fufil my task. The fault is yours, sisters, for you bade me undertake the work—you must read it as best you can since I do my best to write it and you must not criticize its shortcomings. Such a book requires leisure: as you know, I have so little that I have been unable to go on with it for a week, and I forget both what I have already written and how I intended to continue. I can do nothing but blame myself for my failings, and beg you not to imitate me by excusing yourselves as I am doing here. Not to exculpate ourselves when unjustly accused is a sublime virtue,[2] and very edifying and meritorious; but, although I have often taught it you, and by the mercy of God you practise it, yet His

[5] When making a fresh foundation, St. Teresa always admitted two or three good and poor young girls without dowry, and she said they were a great comfort to her. (Fuente, vol. VI. 317, Note 12.) Deposition of Isabel de Jesus.

[1] Valladolid edition, xvi; Escorial, xxii.

[2] *Const.* 30, 47.

Majesty has never given me the grace to do so myself—may He grant that I do before I die! Yet there always seems to me some good reason for thinking it would be better to make some excuse for myself. This is often lawful, indeed, sometimes it would be wrong to omit it, yet I have not sufficient discretion—or rather, humility—to know when it should be done. For indeed it requires great humility to see oneself blamed without cause, and to be silent; we thus imitate our Lord, Who freed us from our sins. Be most careful to act in this way, sisters; it does us great good, while I can see no use in our exculpating ourselves, unless, as I said, when we might cause offence or scandal by not telling the truth. Any one who is more prudent than I am will easily understand this. I think it is a great gain to accustom oneself to practise this virtue, and to endeavour to obtain from God the true humility that must be the result. Whoever is really humble ought to wish sincerely to be despised,[3] persecuted, and condemned for serious offences without any just cause.[4] If you seek to follow our Lord, in what better way can you do so? No bodily strength is needed here, nor the help of any one save God.

2. I wish these great virtues, my sisters, to be both our study and our penance. You know that

[3] *Found.* xxvii, 19, 20. *Life*, xix, 12; xxxi, 13-17, 25. *Rel.* ii, 4. *Castle*, M.VI. i, 7-11.

[4] Saint John of the Cross gives these three rules for mortifying the desire of honour: 1. Do those things which bring thee into contempt, and desire that others also may do them. 2. Speak disparagingly of thyself, and contrive that others may do so too. 3. Think humbly and contemptuously of thyself, and desire that others may do so also. (*Ascent of Mount Carmel*, I. xiii, 8.)

I restrain you from other severe and excessive austerities, which if performed imprudently might injure your health. Here, however, there is nothing to fear; for however great the interior virtues may be, they do not weaken the body so that it cannot keep the Rule of the religious life. These strengthen the soul, and, as I have often told you, by constantly conquering yourselves in little things you may train yourselves to gain the victory in great matters. But—how well I have written this, and how badly I practise it!—indeed, I have never been tried thus in any important affair, for I never heard any ill spoken of me that did not fall far short of the truth, if not in that particular matter, yet often enough in similar things: only too often in other ways have I offended our Lord God, and I thought people showed me a great kindness in not speaking of these.[5] I always prefer that they should find fault with what I have not done, for the truth is very painful to hear; but for a false accusation, however grave, I care nothing, and in minor matters I follow my natural bent without thinking of what is most perfect. For this reason, I wish you to understand from the first, and I desire each one of you to consider, how much is gained by this habit of not excusing yourselves.[6] I think it can

[5] *Castle*, M. VI. i, 12. *Way of Perf.* xvii, 4.

[6] St. Teresa was wonderfully patient under persecution. Sometimes I used to speak to her of the calumnies uttered against her. She would answer with perfect simplicity and sweetness: 'Whoever has said any harm against me has done me a great favour.' One day she said to me: 'I assure you, Father, that whenever I hear that people have spoken ill of me, I always pray to God for them. I beg Him to preserve their heart, their lips, and hands from all offence; I do not look upon them as ill-intentioned, but I see in them the ministers of Jesus Christ, instruments used by the Holy Ghost to do me good and to further my

never do any harm, while its chief advantage is that we thus, to a certain degree, imitate our Lord. I say, 'to a certain degree', for we are never wholly innocent when blamed but are always guilty of many sins, for 'the just man falleth seven times a day',[7] and 'if we say we have no sin, the truth is not in us';[8] therefore, though we may not be guilty of this particular fault, yet we are never altogether free from offence as was the good Jesus.

3. O my Lord, when I remember in how many ways Thou didst suffer, Who yet in no way didst deserve it, I know not what to say for myself, nor of what I am thinking when I shrink from suffering or defend myself from blame! Thou knowest, O my only Good! that if there is aught that is right in me it comes from Thy hands. Why shouldst Thou not give me much instead of little? If it is because I do not deserve it, neither have I deserved the graces Thou hast already bestowed on me. Can it be that I should wish men to think well of

salvation. Believe me, Father,' she added: 'the best and most efficient means of winning heaven is patience during trials; this makes man master and ruler of himself as our Lord told His Apostles.' I remember that sometimes, when I spoke to her about scandals that had been spread about her, she used to laugh and say: 'I should have done far worse things if our Lord had not upheld me. What we must fear and what I feel the most, is the harm the soul does to itself by such slander: I should be willing to suffer not only all kinds of insults, but any tortures, to prevent an offence against God, and to deliver that soul from sin. As for the person who is slandered, the only harm she suffers is to have an opportunity of gaining merit.' (Deposition of Father Pedro de la Purificacion, Discalced Carmelite: *Las Relaciones historicas de los siglos xvi. y xvii. publicadas por la Sociedad de Bibliofilos españoles*, vol. XXXII. 309. Madrid, 1896).

[7] Prov. xxiv, 16: 'Septies enim cadet justus, et resurget.'

[8] 1 John. i, 8: 'Si dixerimus quoniam peccatum non habemus, veritas in nobis non est.'

a thing so vile as I am, when they said such evil things of Thee, Who art above every other good? Do not permit this: forbid it, O my God! nor let me wish that anything displeasing to Thine eyes should be found in me, Thy handmaiden. See, O my Lord! I am blind and I care but little for the light. Enlighten me and make me sincerely desire that all men should hate me, since I have so often abandoned Thee Who lovest me so faithfully. Why do we act thus, O my God? What joy do we think to find by pleasing creatures? What does it matter of what guilt they accuse us if we are guiltless before Thee, O Lord?

4. Ah, my sisters, how far we are from grasping this truth! We shall never reach the summit of perfection unless we come to understand what is the great reality, and what is of no account.[9] Were there no other gain but the shame felt by your accuser at seeing that you permit yourselves to be unjustly condemned, it would be very great, for to witness such an action sometimes benefits a soul more than listening to ten sermons. We must all strive to preach by our deeds since the Apostle and our own incapacity forbid our doing so by word of mouth.[10] Do not imagine that either the good or the ill you do will be concealed, however strict your enclosure may be. And can you fancy that if you do not defend yourselves, no one else will take your part? See how our Lord answered for the Magdalen in the house of the Pharisee,[11] and when

[9] Escorial edition, xxiii. Continues the same subject.

[10] I Cor. xiv, 34: 'Mulieres in ecclesiis taceant.'

[11] St. Matt. xxvi, 10: 'Quid molesti estis huic mulieri?'

her sister blamed her.[12] He will not treat you with such rigour as He kept for Himself. He did not permit even the thief to speak in His defence until He hung upon the cross.[13] When there is need, His Majesty will find you an advocate: if not, it will be because you do not require one.

5. I know that this is true, for it has been fully proved to me by experience. Yet I do not wish you to reckon on it: I would rather have you rejoice at being accused. Time will show you how your soul will benefit by this: you will gradually gain liberty of spirit and will not care whether you are well or ill spoken of; you will feel as if the matter concerned some one else, or as if two people were holding a private conversation in which you do not want to take part. It is the same here: we have grown so accustomed to returning no answer that it does not seem as if any one had spoken to us. People who are unmortified and very sensitive may think this impossible. Though difficult at first, I know that this liberty of spirit, abnegation, and detachment may, by the grace of God, gradually be obtained.

[12] *Life*, xxvii, 7; *Excl.* v, 2, 3. *Castle*, M.VII. i, 14; M.VI. xi, 12. *Rel.* vii, 26.

[13] St. Luke xxiii, 40: 'Neque tu times Deum, quod in eadem damnatione es?'

CHAPTER XVI[1]

THE GAME OF CHESS.

1. The game of chess. 2. Meditation and contemplation. 3. Difficulties of rising to contemplation. 4. The virtues usually required for it. 5. Sufferings borne for us by Christ. 6. Why God sometimes raises imperfect souls to contemplation. 7. Abandonment to God's care. 8. That all should aim at sanctity.

1. Do not imagine that a great part of my work is done. No, I have only been 'placing the board' for the game. You asked me to teach you the foundation of prayer, my daughters, although God did not establish me on this foundation, for I am almost destitute of these virtues; yet I know no other. But, be sure that any one who does not understand how to set the pieces in the game of chess will never be able to play well, nor, if he does not know how to give check, will he ever succeed in effecting checkmate. You may blame me for speaking of a game, for such things are neither played nor permitted in our convent.[2] This will show you what a mother God has given you, skilled even in such vanities as this! Still, they say that sometimes the game is lawful, and how well it would be for us to play it, and if we practised it often, how quickly we should checkmate this divine King so that He neither could, nor would, move out of our check! The Queen is His strongest opponent in the game, and all the other pieces help her. No queen can defeat Him so soon as can

[1] Fuente, xvi. This chapter is omitted in the Valladolid edition as far as paragraph 3. Continuation of ch. xxiii. in Escorial.

[2] *Const.* 27.

humility.[3] It drew Him from heaven into the Virgin's womb,[4] and with it we can draw Him by a single hair[5] into our souls. And doubtless, the greater our humility, the more entirely shall we possess Him, and the weaker it is, the more reluctantly will He dwell within us. For I do not and I cannot understand how humility can exist without love, or love without humility,[6] nor can either of these virtues be held in their perfection without great detachment from all created things.

2.[7] Perhaps you ask me, my daughters, why I speak to you of these virtues: they are taught in plenty of books and you only wish me to write about contemplation. If you had asked me about meditation, I could have instructed you, and I advise every one to practise it[8] even though they do not possess the virtues, for this is the first step to obtain them all; it is most essential for all Christians to begin this practice. No one, however desperate his case may be, ought to neglect it if God incites him to make use of it. I have written this elsewhere, as have other people who understand the subject, which, as God knows, I certainly do not. Contemplation, however, is quite another thing, daughters. We fall into a mistake on this point, so that if any one thinks about his sins every day for a certain time (as he is bound to do if he

[3] *Castle*, M. IV. ii, 8. *Life*, xxii, 16.

[4] 'Non horruisti Virginis uterum.' *Te Deum*. *Castle*, M. I. ii, 9; M. II. i, 13; M. III. i, 15; ii, 3, 8; M. IV. ii, 8.

[5] Cant. iv, 9: 'Vulnerasti cor meum . . . in uno crine colli tui.'

[6] *Life*, x, 2; xix, 2.

[7] Escorial, xxiv. Shows how necessary the foregoing explanations were as an introduction to the treatise on prayer.

[8] *Life*, iv, 11; xi, 20. *Found.* v, 2, 3. *Castle*, M. II. i, 19, 20; M. VI. vii, 12.

is a Christian in anything but name), we at once call him a great contemplative, and expect him to possess the sublime virtues proper to such a state: he even thinks so himself; but he is quite wrong. He has not yet learnt how to 'place the board,' but thinks he can effect checkmate simply by knowing the names of the pieces—in this he is deceived; this King will not let Himself be taken except by one who is entirely given up to Him.[9]

3. Therefore, daughters, if you wish me to tell you the way to attain to contemplation you must allow me to speak at length on certain matters, although to you they may seem unimportant. I think that they are important, and unless you intend learning and practising them, continue your mental prayer all your life; for I assure you, and all others who aspire to this state, that you will never otherwise attain to genuine contemplation. I may be deceived about this, but I judge from my own experience; and I have been striving to become a contemplative for the last twenty years.

4. I will now describe mental prayer, as perhaps some of you do not understand what it is. God grant that we practise it as we ought, but I am afraid this can only be done by a great effort unless we possess the virtues, although they are not here necessary in so high a degree as for contemplation. The King of glory will not come into our souls, so as

[9] Valladolid edition, xviii. Escorial, xxv. On the difference between contemplatives and those who content themselves with mental prayer. That it is possible for God to raise a worldly soul to perfect contemplation occasionally, and the reason why He does so. This chapter must be carefully noted as well as the following. [By an error of calculation this chapter is counted xviii. instead of xvii. in the Valladolid manuscript.]

to be united to them, unless we strive to obtain the highest virtues. I will explain this, for if you once found me out in an untruth you would believe me no longer—as would be only right if I told one purposely; but God preserve me from any falsehood! my error would come either from ignorance or want of understanding. I wish you to know that He sometimes shows great favour to people whose souls are in an evil state, that by this means He may snatch them out of the devil's grasp. I do not mean persons who are in mortal sin, but those who are very faulty: our Lord may permit them to behold some very high vision in order to turn their hearts to Him.[10] I cannot, however, believe that He would actually raise them to contemplation, for this is a divine union in which our Lord takes His delight in the soul while the soul rejoices in Him, and there is no way in which heavenly purity can take pleasure in what is impure, nor can He Who is 'the Joy of the Angels' find His happiness in one who is not His own. We know that those in mortal sin are the slaves of Satan and must find their joy in him, since they have gratified him; the pleasures he gives are, as we know, nothing but ceaseless torment even in this life. Still without taking those who are not His, yet His Majesty will do what He has often done—snatch them out of the hand of the enemy and make them His own.

5. O my God, how often do we force Thee to struggle with the devil on our account! Was it not enough that Thou didst suffer him to bear

[10] *Life*, xxii, 22, 23. *Castle*, M. IV. 1, 3. *Concep.* v, 3. *Way of Perf.* xli, 2.

Thee in his arms to the pinnacle of the Temple,"[11] to teach us how to vanquish him? What a sight, daughters, to see this Sun encompassed with darkness, and what terror that wretch must have felt although he did not know the reason why, for God did not permit him to understand it! Blessed be such immense pity and mercy! How ashamed we Christians ought to feel, as I said above, at constraining our Lord to combat daily this unclean beast! There was need for Thine arms to be so strong, O Lord, but how was it that they were not weakened by the many tortures Thou didst endure upon the cross? Oh, how soon all hurts borne with love are healed! I believe that if Thy life had lasted longer, the love Thou hast for us would have healed Thy wounds without need of any other medicine. O my God! who will apply such a lotion to all the trials which give me pain and trouble? How eagerly I should desire them, if they were to be cured by such a health-giving ointment! It seems extravagant for me to speak thus, as my actions are in such contrast to it, yet divine love does greater things than this. But lest I should seem fond of what is sensational (as indeed I am), and that I may not set you a bad example, I will not tell you about them."[12]

6. But, to return to what I was saying—God knows that He can attract certain souls to Himself by means of divine favours: He sees they are on

[11] St. Matt. iv, 5: 'Tunc diabolus statuit eum super pinnaculum templi.'

[12] Escorial edition, xxvi. God can sometimes raise a worldly soul to perfect contemplation, and the reasons for His doing so. This chapter is very noteworthy.

the way to be lost, but He does not wish it to happen through any fault of His, therefore, though they are in a bad case and are lacking in goodness He gives them consolations, delights, and tenderness of devotion which begin to excite their desires; He even sometimes raises them to contemplation, although but rarely and for a very short time. This is to prove whether such a grace will induce them to prepare themselves to enjoy His favours more often.[13] But if they do not respond to Thee, and are unwilling to pardon their enemies, then pardon us, O Lord! for it is a terrible misfortune for a soul which thou hast thus drawn to Thee to become attached afterwards to any earthly thing. I feel sure there are many souls which our Lord God puts to this proof, but few who correspond rightly to the favour, for when He acts thus, unless we offer any hindrance, I am convinced that He never ceases bestowing His graces until He has brought us to a very high state of prayer. If we do not yield ourselves to Him as entirely as He gives Himself to us,[14] He does what suffices by leaving us to mental prayer and visiting us now and then, as servants working in His vineyard. But the other souls are His beloved children whom He will not allow to quit His side, nor will He leave them, since they do not wish to forsake Him. He seats them at His table and ministers to them so far[15] that (as they say) He takes the meat from His own mouth to feed them with.[16]

[13] *Castle*, M. IV. iii, 9, 10; M. V. i, 2, 3; ii, 4, 5; iii, 2, 6, 12.
[14] *Castle*, M. V. i, 3. *Life*, xi, 2-4; xxii, 18, 19.
[15] St. Luke xii, 37: 'Et transiens ministrabit illis.'
[16] Psalm liv, 15: 'Qui simul mecum dulces capiebas cibos.' *Rel.* iv, 6.

7. O happy custody, my daughters! O joyful renunciation of things so trifling and so base, which leads us to such a blessed state! What does it matter if all the world blames you[17] and deafens you with abuse while you are resting meanwhile in the arms of God? He is powerful to deliver you from all. *Once* only did He command that the world should be created, and it was created[18] —with Him to will is to do.[19] Except for the greater gain of those who love Him, He will not permit them to be spoken against:[20] His love for them is not so weak. Then why, my sisters, should we not show Him all the love we can? See what a rich exchange—to give our love for His; to give it to Him Who can give us all things, while we can do nothing without His aid. But what is it that we do for Thee, O Lord our Creator? We do nothing but make a paltry resolution. If then His Majesty wills that we should purchase all things by this mere nothing, let us not be so mad as to refuse it.

8. O Lord! all our ills come from not fixing our eyes on Thee: if we looked at nothing else but where we are going we should soon arrive, but we fall a thousand times and stumble and go astray because we do not keep our gaze bent on Him Who is the 'Way.' It looks so new to us that one would suppose nobody had walked in it before. Indeed, this is a grievous pity: one would think we were not Christians at all, nor had ever read the Passion in our lives. Lord have mercy on us—we are touched on a point of honour! If people tell us

[17] *Life*, xl, 30. [18] Psalm xxxii, 19: 'Ipse dixit et facta sunt.'
[19] Philip. ii, 13: 'Qui operatur in vobis et velle at perficere.'
[20] *Way of Perf.* xvii, 4. *Castle*, M. VI. xi, 12.

not to notice it, we at once call them unchristian—I laugh, or I *grieve* sometimes, at what I hear of such foibles in the world, as I do at my own foibles in religion. To be undervalued in the least is unbearable to us: we at once cry out: 'We are not angels, nor saints!' That is true enough. God deliver us, my daughters, when we fall into any imperfection, from saying: 'We are not angels! We are not saints!' Although we are not, still, it is the greatest help to believe that, with the aid of God, we can be if we strive our hardest. There is no fear of His failing to do His part if we do ours. Since we came here for nothing else, let us put our hands to the plough,[21] as they say. Let there be nothing which we know would further our Lord's service that we dare not undertake with the assistance of His grace. I wish such audacity to exist in this house—it always increases humility. Ever nourish this holy daring, for God aids the valiant and is no respecter of persons.[22] Both to you and to me He will give the help needed. I have wandered from my subject, to which I will return; that is, instruction on mental prayer and contemplation. It may appear presumptuous on my part, but you will excuse everything. Perhaps you may understand my rough style better than other more polished writings. May our Lord grant me His assistance. Amen!

[21] St. Luke, ix, 62: 'Nemo mittens manum suam ad aratrum, et respiciens retro, aptus est regno Dei.'

[22] St. Matt. xxii, 16: 'Non enim respicis personam hominum.'

CHAPTER XVII[1]

THAT SOME SOULS ARE NOT SUITED TO CONTEMPLATION, AND OTHERS ARE LONG IN ATTAINING IT. EVERY ONE WHO IS TRULY HUMBLE SHOULD BE CONTENT TO GO BY THE WAY OUR LORD CONDUCTS HER.

1. Humility is necessary for prayerful souls. 2. All who practise prayer cannot become contemplatives. 3. Vocal prayer less dangerous than contemplation. 4. In the active way we serve like Martha. 5. Both the active and contemplative life serve our Lord. 6. The cross the surest way.

1. I SEEM now to have come to the subject of prayer, but there still remains something important for me to say: it concerns humility, which is most requisite in this convent because it is the principal aid to prayer. As I said,[2] it is very necessary for you to know how to practise humility on every occasion: this is one of the chief points, and most essential for persons given to prayer. How can any one who is truly humble think herself as good as others who are contemplatives? God may, by His goodness and mercy and by the merits of Christ, make her deserve to receive such graces as they do, but, if she takes my advice, she will always rank herself in the lowest place, as our Lord taught us both by His word and example.[3] Let her respond to His call if God leads her by the way of contemplation:[4] otherwise, if she thinks herself happy in being allowed to wait upon the servants of God, humility will serve in its stead.[5] Let her praise His Majesty for having placed her in their company

[1] Valladolid edition, xix; Escorial, xxvii. [2] Ch. xvi, 1.
[3] St. Luke x, 42: 'Recumbe in novissimo loco.' *Life*, xxii, 18.
[4] *Castle*, M. IV. ii, 8. [5] *Castle*, M. III. ii, 16.

although she deserves to be the slave of the devils in hell. I have good cause for saying this, for, as I told you, it is important to understand that His Majesty does not lead all souls in the same way, and perhaps she who thinks herself the least of all may be the highest in His eyes.

2. Thus it does not follow, because all the nuns in this convent practise prayer, that they must all be contemplatives. Such an idea would greatly discourage those who do not understand the truth that contemplation is a gift of God which is not necessary for salvation nor for earning our eternal reward, nor does any one here require us to possess it. She who is without it, yet who follows the counsels I have given, will attain great perfection. It may be that she will gain far more merit, as she has to work harder[6] on her own account; our Lord is treating her like a valiant woman and keeping until hereafter all the happiness she has missed in this life. Let her not be disheartened nor give up prayer or the other practices of which her sisters make use—sometimes our Lord comes very late, and pays as much all at once as He has given to others during many years.[7] For more than fourteen years I could not meditate without a book.[8] There are many people of this kind, and others cannot meditate even with the help of reading, but are obliged to recite vocal prayers which to a certain extent arrest their attention. Some have so volatile an imagination that they cannot fix their thoughts, which are always wandering, upon one thing; if they try to think of God

[6] *Castle*, M. V. iii, 4, 5. [7] St. Matt. xx, 12. [8] *Life*, ix, 6.

they are troubled with a thousand foolish fancies, scruples and doubts.

3. I know a very old nun of most exemplary life, (would to God my life were like hers!) very holy, very austere, and a perfect religious, who has spent many hours, and even a number of years, in vocal prayers, but cannot make use of mental prayer: the utmost she can do is to pause a little, from time to time, during her Ave Marias and Paternosters, which is a very holy custom. Many people resemble her: if they are humble, let them not think they are more imperfect or believe they will be any the worse for it in the end, for they will be quite as well off as those who enjoy many consolations. In one way such souls are safer, for we cannot tell whether spiritual delights come from God or from the devil: if they are not divine they are very dangerous, for Satan tries to excite pride by their means: however, if they are sent by God there is nothing to fear for they bring humility with them,[9] as I fully explained in another book.

4. Other souls, receiving no spiritual consolations, are humble, for they doubt whether it is not through their own fault and are most anxious to improve. When they see any one else weeping, unless they do the same they think they must be much more backward than she is in God's service, although perhaps they are more advanced, for tears,[10] though a good sign, do not always indicate perfection. Humility, mortification, detachment,

[9] *Life*, xv, 16; xix, 2; xx, 38. *Rel.* ii, 15; vii, 7; viii, 7, 9. *Castle*, M.VI. iii, 25; v, 5; ix, 9.

[10] *Castle*, M. VI. vi, 6-9.

and other virtues are the safest: there is no cause for fear, nor need you doubt that you may become as perfect as the greatest contemplatives. St. Martha was holy,[11] though we are never told she was a contemplative; would you not be content with resembling this blessed woman who deserved to receive Christ our Lord so often into her home, where she fed and served Him, and where He ate at her table, and even, perhaps, off her own plate? If she had always been enraptured like the Magdalen there would have been no one to offer food to this divine Guest. Imagine, then, that this community is the house of St. Martha where there must be different kinds of people. Let not the nun who is called to the active life murmur at others who are absorbed in contemplation, for she knows our Lord will defend them;[12] as a rule, they themselves are silent, for the 'better part'[13] makes them oblivious of themselves and of all else. Remember that some one must cook the food, and think yourself favoured by being allowed to serve with Martha. Reflect that true humility consists in being willing and ready to do what our Lord asks of us: it always makes us consider ourselves unworthy to be reckoned among His servants.

5. If contemplation, mental and vocal prayer, nursing the sick, the work of the house, and the most menial labour, all serve this Guest Who comes to eat and drink and converse with us, why should

[11] *Excl.* v. 2, 3. *Castle*, M. VII. i, 14. *Life*, xxii, 13.
[12] *Excl.* v. 2, 3. *Castle*, M. VI. xi, 12. *Way of Perf.* xv, 4.
[13] St. Luke x, 42: 'Maria optimam partem elegit, quae non auferetur ab ea.'

we choose to minister to Him in one way rather than in another?[14] Not that I mean that we have any choice as to the labours we shall perform, but you should practise them all, for the decision does not rest with you but with our Lord. But if, after many years' trial, He makes it clear what place each one is to fill, it would be a strange humility for you to choose for yourself. Leave that to the Master of the house: He is wise and powerful and knows what is best for you and for Himself.[15]

6. You may be sure, if we do all we can and prepare ourselves for contemplation with all the perfection I have described, that if He does not grant it to us (though I believe, if our humility and detachment are sincere, He is sure to bestow this gift), He is keeping back these consolations in reserve only to give them to us all at once in heaven. As I said elsewhere, He wishes to treat us as valiant women,[16] giving us the cross His Majesty ever bore Himself. What truer frendship can He show than to choose for us what He chose for Himself? Besides, perhaps we should not have gained so rich a reward by contemplation. His judgments are His own—we have no right to interfere with them. It is well the decision does not rest with us, for, thinking it a more peaceful way, we should all immediately become contemplatives! What a gain is ours if, for fear of losing by it, we do not seek to gain by what we think is best, since

[14] Escorial, xxviii. How much is gained by preparing ourselves for contemplation, and the bad result of making our own choice.

[15] *Life*, xii, 5-8, 12; xxii, 13, 15-19.

[16] Ch. vii, 7. *Life*, xi, 16-20. On the Cross, xv, 17; xxvii, 4. *Castle*, M.II. i, 15, 17.

God never permits the truly mortified soul to lose aught save for its greater gain!

CHAPTER XVIII[1]

CONTINUATION OF THE SAME SUBJECT. SHOWS THAT CONTEMPLATIVES HAVE TO BEAR FAR HEAVIER CROSSES THAN PEOPLE WHO LEAD THE ACTIVE LIFE. THIS CHAPTER OFFERS GREAT CONSOLATION TO THE LATTER.

1. Trials of the contemplative life. 2. Its reward. 3. Preparation for contemplation. 4. Contemplatives bear the standard of humility. 5. The virtues preferable to supernatural favours. 6. Obedience. 7. Danger of supernatural favours.

1. DAUGHTERS, I assure those of you whom God does not lead by the way of contemplation that both by observation and experience I know that those following it do not bear a lighter cross than you: but indeed you would be aghast at the different kinds of trials God sends them. I know a great deal of both vocations, and am well aware that the sufferings God inflicts on contemplatives are of so unbearable a kind that, unless He sustained such souls by the manna of divine consolations, they would find their pains insupportable. God guides those He loves by the way of afflictions; the dearer they are to Him, the more severe are their trials. It is incredible that He should hate contemplatives whom He Himself praises and calls His friends, and absurd to imagine that He would admit self-indulgent and easy-going people into His friendship; I feel certain that God gives by far the heaviest crosses to His favourites. The road He chooses for

[1] Valladolid edition, xx; Escorial, continuation of xxviii.

them is so uneven and rugged as to make them fancy that they have lost their way and that they must turn back again and start afresh. Then His Majesty is obliged to give them some refreshment[2] —*water* would not be enough, it must be *wine*:[3] inebriated[4] with this draught from God they become unconscious of their pain and enabled to sustain it. Thus one rarely finds true contemplatives who are not valiant and resolved to suffer. If they are weak, the first thing our Lord does is to infuse courage into them so that they may fear no trials.[5] I believe that those who lead the active life, when they see that contemplatives occasionally receive consolation, imagine that their life consists of nothing else; yet perhaps you might not be able to bear such trials as theirs for a single day.[6] Our Lord knows for what everybody is suited, and gives each one what is best for her soul, for His own glory, and for the good of her neighbour. As none of you have chosen your own work, you need have no fear that it will be labour lost.

2. Pay attention to what I am saying, for we all have to serve God, and that not for one or two years, or for ten years either, that we should desert our duties like cowards. It is well to show our Lord that we are not defaulters; we must be like soldiers

[2] Cant. ii, 4: 'Introduxit me in cellam vinariam'. *Concep.* vi, 1 seqq. *Life*, xviii, 17.

[3] *Castle*, M, V. i, 10; ii, 11. *Concep.* iv, 4-8; v, 5; vii, 2-5.

[4] Psalm xxii, 5: 'Calix meus inebrians, quam præclarus est.'

[5] Escorial, xxix. Continuation of the same subject. The trials in store for contemplatives are much heavier than those borne by persons engaged in the active life. This is consoling for the latter.

[6] *Castle*. M. V. ii, 8; M. VI. i, 3, sqq. M. VII. iv, 7.

who receive their pay whether they fight or no, and so must always stand at their post, ready to set to work whenever their captain gives his orders. How much better pay shall we receive from our King than they get from theirs, for sometimes the poor fellows die in battle and God knows what wages they get afterwards! The captain reviews his regiment as it stands on service and knows the capabilities of each soldier, although not so well as our heavenly Captain knows ours. He assigns to them the duties for which they are fit, but if the men were absent they would receive neither pay nor orders.

3. Therefore, sisters, practise mental prayer, and if you cannot manage that, then vocal prayer, reading, and the colloquies with God which I will teach you later on. Never give up your hours of prayer: you do not know when the Bridegroom will summon you, and you might share the fate of the foolish virgins.[7] Our Lord may give you some heavier cross under the guise of divine consolations. If He does not, be convinced that you are not meant for contemplation but for the active life. This will give you an opportunity of gaining merit through humility. Let such a one believe that she is unworthy even of the place she holds. Let her cheerfully do what she is told, and as I said,[8] if only her humility is genuine, blessed is such a servant in the active life, for she will complain of none but herself, and I would far rather resemble her than some contemplatives with whom I am acquainted.

[7] St. Matt. xxv, 2: 'Quinque autem ex eis erant fatuæ, et quinque prudentes.'

[8] Ch. xvii, 2.

4. Let her leave others to wage their own wars, which are no easy ones. Though standard-bearers, like officers, do not actually fight, yet they expose themselves to great danger and must suffer, in a way, more than the rest of the men because they carry the colours which they must not relinquish, even though they themselves are being cut to pieces. In the same way, contemplatives must uphold the standard of humility, and must bear all the blows aimed at them without making any reprisal, for their duty is to suffer as Christ did, bearing aloft the cross and never letting it fall, whatever the danger may be, unless they would prove cowards in suffering. It is for this they are advanced to their high and honourable office. Do you suppose the position given them by the King is an easy one? For the sake of some slight distinction they undertake to incur far more danger than the rest, and if they turn cowards the battle will go against their side. Let contemplatives, then, look to their conduct, for if the standard-bearer quits his colours the day will be lost: in the same way, I believe that souls less advanced in religion are much injured by seeing those they hold as captains and friends of God act in a way ill suiting their position. The common soldiers march as they can: if sometimes they withdraw from the thick of the fray, no one notices them and they lose neither their honour nor their lives, but all eyes are on the standard-bearer who cannot move without being seen. His duty is a noble one and a great honour, and the King shows him special favour by his choice; but he has undertaken a heavy responsibility.

5. My daughters, as we do not understand our own needs nor what to ask for, let us leave all to our Lord[9] Who knows us better than we know ourselves. A lowly heart is content with what is given it, yet there are people who ask for favours from God as a matter of simple justice.[10] What humility! Therefore He Who knows all things rightly abstains from granting these gifts to such persons, seeing them unfit to drink of His chalice.[11] The best sign that any one has made progress is that she thinks herself the last of all and proves it by her behaviour, and that she aims at the well-being and good of others in all she does. This is the true test[12]—not sweetness in prayer, ecstasies, visions, and other divine favours of the same kind. The value of these latter we cannot estimate rightly until the next life, but the former are current coin, a constant revenue and a perpetual inheritance, not mere part-payments which, when acquitted, cease—I speak of great humility and mortification, and implicit obedience[13] which will not disobey one tittle of the orders given by the

[9] 'Love, Who dost love me more than I can love myself, or can conceive: why do I wish for more than Thou dost will to give me? . . . Perhaps what my soul fancies would be its gain might be its ruin. If I ask Thee to free me from a cross by which Thou seekest to mortify me, what do I ask of Thee, O my God? If I entreat Thee to send me such a trial, perhaps it may be beyond my patience which is too weak to bear the heavy burden; or were I to endure it, but were wanting in humility, I might fancy I had performed some great deed, while Thou, O my God, didst do it all!' (*Minor Works, Excl.* xvi, 1-3).

[10] *Castle*, M. III. i, 11; M. IV. ii, 8; M. VI. ix, 13-19. *Life*, xii, 2, 5; xxxix, 21-23.

[11] St. Matt. xx, 22: 'Potestis bibere calicem?'

[12] *Castle*, M. V. iii, 7, 8.

[13] *Life*, Prologue, p. 2; iv, 2. *Castle*, Preface.

Prioress, but submits to them as to the commands of God, of Whom she is the representative.[14]

6. Obedience is of the greatest importance; she who is lacking in it is not a nun at all: I will say no more about this, as I am speaking to nuns who are good religious, I believe, or at least desire to be so. But as obedience is most essential I mention it lest you might forget this. I cannot understand what any one is doing in a monastery if, after she has made a vow of obedience, she does not fulfil it as perfectly as possible.[15] I can assure her that while she fails in this she will never reach contemplation, or even lead the active life well: of this I am certain. Those who have not undertaken this obligation, but who wish to become contemplatives must, if they would walk in safety, resolutely submit their will to an experienced confessor. It is a well known fact that they will thus make more progress in a year than they would otherwise have done in a very long time. Much has been written on this subject;

[14] When St. Teresa was journeying to make a foundation she always put her companions under obedience to some religious who was with them, or, if there were none, to the priest who accompanied them, and though on account of her office and dignity she had so much claim to exact obedience, yet she was the first to obey. So dearly did she love this virtue that when she conferred on one of her nuns the post of Prioress to a new foundation, she, who had herself held that position for so many years, immediately rendered obedience and subjected herself, not as foundress, but as one of the last members of the house, and asked permission for everything she did. She behaved in the same manner when staying at convents of nuns of other Orders, submitting at once to the Superior as if she had been one of her community. (*Yepes*, bk. II, xxxvi.)

[15] St. Teresa was prompt in her obedience. One day during prayer-time in choir, she happened to make a slight noise. The Prioress said: 'Whoever made that disturbance must go away.' And the Saint withdrew in silence. (Deposition of Sister Francisca de Jesus. Fuente, vol. VI. 290, Note 9).

however, as it does not concern you I will not enlarge upon it.

7. These, then, are the virtues that I wish you, my daughters, to possess and to strive to obtain, and of which you should feel a holy envy. You must not be distressed if you do not experience these other devotional feelings which are unreliable. Although in the case of other people they may come from God, yet in yours He might permit them to be an illusion of the devil, who would mislead you as he has misled others. Such illusions are very dangerous for women. Why run into danger in serving our Lord when there are so many safe ways of doing so? Who wants you to incur such risk? There is need for much insistence on this point for we are weak by nature, though God will strengthen those He calls to be contemplatives. I am glad to have given this advice to other persons: it will also animate those called to the contemplative life to practise humility. If you say you do not require it, daughters, perhaps some novice may enter later on who will be glad of it. May our Lord give us light to follow His will in all things, and then we shall have nothing to fear!

CHAPTER XIX[1]

HOW SOULS SHOULD PRAY IF THEY CANNOT MAKE USE OF THE UNDERSTANDING IN PRAYER.

1. Of books on meditation. 2. Method in prayer. 3. Difficulties of mental prayer. 4. The 'living water' of the Samaritan. 5. Comparison of the water and the live-fire. 6. An ardent love for God subjects all things under our feet. 7. The heavenly water cools our desires. 8. And purifies our souls. 9. Meditation and contemplation. 10. This water slakes our thirst for God. 11. Moderation to be kept in this thirst. 12. The consequences of over-indulging it and their remedies. 13. Subterfuges of Satan. 14. The living water is intended for every one.

1. It is a long time since I wrote the last pages and I have had no opportunity of resuming the book, so that unless I read over the latter part I cannot remember what I said. However, to save time, I must go straight on, without either order or connection. For methodical minds and for souls who practise prayer and who are able to keep their attention fixed,[2] there are so many suitable books[3] written by good authors that it would be a mistake to come to me for advice on the subject. There are volumes containing meditations[4] for every day of the week on the mysteries of our Lord's life and sacred Passion, on the last judgment, hell, our own nothingness, the mercies God has

[1] Valladolid edition, xxi; Escorial, xxx.

[2] 'The habit of recollection is not to be gained by force of arms, but with calmness, which will enable you to practise it for a longer space of time . . . . There is no remedy for having given up a habit of recollection except to recommence it, otherwise the soul will continue to lose it more and more every day, and God grant it may realize its danger.' (*Castle*, M. II. i, 18).

[3] *Life*. iv, 10, 14.

[4] *Found*. v, 2, 3.

granted us, and our many debts to Him.[5] These books contain excellent teaching and a good method for the beginning and conclusion of mental prayer.

2. One who is accustomed to this kind of prayer requires no further instruction: our Lord will thus bring her to the port of light; such a good beginning is sure to end well. Those who can walk in this way enjoy peace and security, for when the thoughts are kept under control the journey becomes easy. But with God's permission I wish to offer some help to those who cannot practise such prayer. Even if I fail, at least you will have learnt that many others suffer in the same way as yourselves, so that you need not be distressed about it. When you begin to practise prayer I will give you some advice about this matter.

3. Some minds are as disorderly as unbroken horses—no one can quiet them: they rush about, hither and thither, and are never at rest. And although the rider, if adroit, may not always be in danger of his life, yet he is at times. Even if he does not run the risk of being killed, he risks looking foolish and has to keep perpetually on his guard. I pity souls to whom this is natural or to whom God allows it to happen. Perhaps no vital injury may be done, yet there is a risk of making mistakes, and the soul is in a continual state of agitation and trouble. Either this is natural to certain persons or God permits it. I pity them deeply. They are like a man parched with thirst, who sees water in the far distance, and, while trying to get to it, is

[5] Such are the *Meditations* of St. Peter of Alcantara.

hindered by other people, both at starting, when he has got half-way, and again just before the end of his journey. They resemble those souls who, after a great effort and immense trouble, have defeated their first enemies yet are beaten by the second adversaries, and would rather die of thirst than drink of water which costs them so dear. They lack strength, their courage fails them: though sometimes they overcome their second set of opponents yet they succumb before the third.

4. Perhaps they were not two steps off the living fountain of water of which our Lord spoke to the Samaritan woman,[6] promising that whoever drank of it should never thirst again.[7] How true is this which was told us by Truth Himself! For the soul thirsts no more for the things of this world, although its craving for the next life exceeds any natural thirst that can be imagined. Yet how the heart pines for this thirst, realizing its priceless value! This drought brings its own remedy with it: it allays all desire of created things and satisfies the soul. When it has been satiated by God, one of the greatest graces He can bestow on the spirit is to leave it with this thirst, which, after drinking, increases the longing to partake again and again of this water.[8]

5. As far as I can remember, water has three properties—there must be many more, but these suit my purpose. One property is that it chills

[6] St. John iv, 13: 'Qui autem biberet ex aqua quam ego dabo ei, non sitiet in æternum.'

[7] *Castle*, M. VI. xi, 5. *Excl.* ix. *Life*, xxx, 24.

[8] Escorial ed., xxxi. A comparison symbolizing perfect contemplation.

other things. However warm any one may be, he is cooled by plunging into a river, and water extinguishes the fiercest fire except wild-fire, which it only kindles the more. How strange it is that water should only increase this fire, which is fierce, raging, and subject to none of the elements, so that its opposite, instead of putting it out, only adds fuel to its flames. I could explain a great deal by this if only I understood philosophy. If I knew the properties of things I should be able to make my meaning clear: as it is, though I am amused and interested by them I do not know how to express myself—perhaps I do not even understand the matter. When God gives you this water, sisters, this comparison will please you and you will understand, as those do who drink of it, how a genuine love of God that is powerful and freed from earthly dross rises above mortal things and is sovereign over all the elements of this world. Though water may flow from the earth, there is no fear of its quenching the fire of divine love, over which it has no empire. Although they are the antidotes of one another, its flames are beyond the influence of water and are all-powerful. Do not be surprised then, sisters, at the stress I have laid in this book on your gaining liberty of spirit.

6. Is it a small thing that an insignificant little nun of St. Joseph's should obtain the mastery over the globe and all the elements? What wonder that the saints, with the help of God, did what they pleased with them? Fire and water obeyed St. Martin,[9] the birds and fish were subject to Saint

[9] Sulpicius Severus, in his Dialogues, tells us that St. Martin, having set fire to a heathen temple, prevented the flames from spreading

Francis,[10] and many other saints possessed this power over created things which they had evidently gained by striving to despise the world and by subjecting themselves with their whole hearts to the Lord of creation.[11] They did their utmost, therefore they may almost seem to have claimed this power as a right, for, as the Psalmist says: 'Thou hast subjected all things under his feet.'[12] Do you think this applies to every one? I see some men 'under the feet' of the things of this world. I knew a gentleman who was literally kicked to death in a struggle with his horses—you see how miserably he was 'subject' to them! Things occur every day that witness to the truth of what I say. Indeed, the Psalmist could not speak untruth, being guided by the Holy Ghost. However, I may be mistaken in his meaning, or misquote the text as saying that perfect souls are rulers of the whole earth. The water I spoke of has an earthly source, and has no influence over the fire of the love of God, whose flames rise high above it and spring from nothing so base. There are fires of a tepid love for God,

elsewhere by standing in their way. (Ch. vii). By his prayers he made a cool and refreshing space for himself in the midst of a burning room. He freed a whole district from an annual hailstorm which used to devastate it. A tempest in the Tuscan Sea was calmed by an invocation of the 'God of St. Martin' uttered by a heathen merchant. (Ch. xiv). (From the Nicene and Post-Nicene Fathers, Oxford, 1894).

[10] St. Francis stopped the swallows twittering during his sermon. At another time he preached to the birds who gathered round and listened, and flew away at his bidding, singing sweetly in praise of God. At Rimini he spoke to a multitude of fish which ranged themselves in front of him in the river to listen. This miracle so touched some of the heretics of the city as to convert them. (*The Little Flowers of St. Francis of Assisi*, xvii, xl).

[11] Job, v, 23: 'Et bestiæ terræ pacificæ erunt tibi.'

[12] Psalm viii, 8: 'Omnia subjecisti sub pedibus ejus.'

which any passing event may extinguish, but although a tempest rose against it, fervent charity would not be destroyed, but would vanquish its enemy: if water should rain from heaven,[13] instead of putting out this fire, it would revive the flames. These two elements are not opposed to one another, but spring from the same origin. There is no fear of their harming one another—they only increase each other's effects. The water of genuine tears, shed during real prayer, is a gift from the King of heaven: it feeds the flames and keeps them alight, while the fire helps to cool the water.

7. Ah, how delightful and wonderful a thing is this fire! When it is combined with the rain from heaven from whence flow the tears I spoke of, it chills and even freezes all worldly affections. These waters are given us; not obtained by any effort of our own: thus they leave no warmth that might attract us in anything of this world, unless it is something tending to feed this fire, which by its nature is insatiate and would, if possible, envelop the whole world in its flames.

8. A second property of water is the cleansing of what is foul. What would become of mankind with no water to wash in? This living, celestial water is limpid, undisturbed, and unmixed with any earthly matter, for it has come straight from heaven. The soul which has once drunk of it is cleansed and left pure and free from all sins.[14] As I said elsewhere,[15] we are powerless to obtain this

[13] *Castle*, M. VI. vi, 8, 9. *Life*, xviii, 12, sqq.
[14] *Castle*, M. VI. iv, 3. *Rel.* ix, 4.
[15] *Life*, xix.

water for ourselves, because perfect contemplation and divine union are high and supernatural graces given by God to the soul that it may be washed and left stainless and purified from the mire contracted by its sins. The water of sensible devotion,[16] obtained by the use of the intellect, has run its course over the earth and is not imbibed directly from the source itself; therefore whatever benefit it confers, it always contains a certain amount of mud, and is never so pure and limpid as the other. I do not call prayer made by thinking over a subject 'living water,' for I believe that, in spite of all our efforts, owing partly to physical causes and partly to human nature, it always retains something from which we should like it to be free.

9. I will explain myself more clearly. While meditating on the world and the contempt it deserves on account of its short duration, almost without knowing it we find ourselves thinking about the worldly matters we used to care for. Although we try to check these thoughts, they distract us all the more by the remembrance of what happened and speculations about what will come of it, what will be the consequences, what we did, and what we shall do. By pondering over the means of freeing ourselves from faults, we sometimes run into fresh danger. Not that we ought to omit such meditation, but we must be cautious and watchful. In contemplation our Lord Himself takes care of us, for He will not entrust us with our own interests. Our souls are so dear to Him that He prevents their running into danger

[16] *Castle*, M. IV. i. 4-7; ii, 4.

while He is bestowing this grace on them. He at once calls them to His side, and in a single instant shows them more truths and gives them a clearer knowledge of the nothingness of all things than we could gain for ourselves in many years. For our sight is not clear— our eyes are blinded by the dust on our path; but here, we know not how, our Lord brings us at once to the end of the journey.

10. The third property of water is to satisfy and quench thirst. Thirst seems to me to be a desire of something which we need so greatly that we should die were we altogether deprived of it. Water is a strange thing! we die for want of it, yet too much of it kills us —see how many men it has drowned! O Lord! is any one plunged so deeply into this living water as to die of it? Could such a thing happen? Yes. This love and desire of God may increase until nature can bear it no longer and men have perished from this cause. I know some one, to whose aid God came promptly with such abundance of this living water that she was almost drawn out of herself in raptures.[17] Her thirst and growing desire were such that she realized it was quite possible to die of such longing were it not remedied. I say 'drawn out of herself' as it were, because her soul found rest in ecstasy. Such a soul appears overcome by its loathing for this world, but it revives in God: His Majesty thus enables it to enjoy this grace which, if left to itself, it could not have borne without loss of life.

[17] The Saint herself. *Castle*, M. VI. xi, 8. *Rel.* iv, i. *Concep.* vii, 2. *Life*, xx. *Minor Works*, Poems 2, 3, 4 and Notes.

Blessed be He Who in the Gospel invites us to drink of this water.[18]

Most certainly, our Lord and our supreme Good possesses no imperfection, and all He does is for our welfare; therefore, however abundant this water may be, it is never in excess for there is nothing superfluous in His gifts. If He gives a deep draught He makes the soul capable of drinking it, just as a glass-maker moulds his vessels the right size to contain the fluid he means to pour into them. It is always wrong of us to wish for this water: it is solely through the grace of God that we reap any benefit from such a desire. We are indiscreet and think that, as this pain is sweet and enjoyable, we cannot have too much of it. We covet it beyond all measure, and do all we can to augment our longings, so that sometimes people die of such emotions. What a blessed death! Yet perhaps, by living, one might have helped others to die with the desire of such a death. I believe the devil has a hand in this: he knows what harm such people do him by living, and incites them to perform imprudent penances so as to destroy their health, which would be no small gain to him.

11. I strongly advise any one who feels this excessive thirst to be very cautious, for this temptation is sure to occur. Although possibly it may not kill her, yet her health may be impaired; besides, however unwillingly, she will show her feelings by exterior signs which ought by all means to be avoided. Sometimes all our efforts to hide

[18] St. John vii, 37: 'Si quis sitit veniat ad me, et bibat.' Escorial edition, xxxii. Tells us how we can sometimes moderate supernatural impulses.

our sentiments are fruitless. Let us be careful not to yield to any strong impulse towards fomenting this longing, but gently put it aside by turning our thoughts to some other subject.[19] Occasionally nature may have as much to do with these feelings as divine love: some characters are eager about everything, both good and bad. I do not consider such persons very mortified, yet mortification is always good.

12. It seems foolish to hinder so good a thing, yet it is really wise conduct. I do not mean that these longings should be stifled, but moderated, which may be done by encouraging some other desire that would be quite as meritorious. I will explain my meaning by an example—a man has a vehement longing to be with God and to be delivered from 'this prison',[20] as St. Paul styled it. No small mortification will be needed to restrain this most delicious pain; indeed, it cannot always be done. But he may be so overcome by it as almost to lose his reason; I saw this happen to some one a short time ago. Although naturally impulsive, she was so used to breaking her own will that, from what I witnessed on other occasions, I thought she had completely overcome it, yet once I saw her almost driven mad by this pain and by her violent efforts to overcome her feelings. In such an extreme case, in my opinion humility should make us fear, for we ought not to believe that our charity is fervent enough to bring us to such a state: I think there would be no harm in our changing the bent of our wishes, although

[19] *Castle*, M. VI. vi, 6.

[20] Rom. vii, 24: 'Quis me liberabit de corpore mortis hujus?'

sometimes this is impossible. We may consider that by living longer[21] we might serve God more, and might be able to enlighten some soul that would otherwise be lost; and that if we did more for God we should deserve to enjoy Him more. Besides, we ought to feel alarmed at thinking how little we have done for our Creator. These are fitting consolations for this great distress. Thus we shall assuage our pain and gain great merit, since for the sake of serving the God we long for so keenly we are willing to suffer and to bear our cross. It is like comforting some one who is in great sorrow by bidding him to be patient and to resign himself into the hands of God, that the divine will may de done in him: this resignation of ourselves is always the safest course to take.

13. But what if the devil were in any way concerned in these vehement desires? This is probable, as in a case mentioned by Cassian, I believe, of a very ascetic hermit whom the evil one persuaded to throw himself down a well in order to see God sooner.[22] I do not think the hermit's life can have been either humble or holy, or our Lord, Who is faithful, would never have allowed him to be so

[21] *Excl.* xiv, 4.

[22] The hermit Heron was so austere that he refused to join the brethren even at their usual feast at Easter. Deceived by his presumption, he obeyed the order of Satan, disguised as an angel of light, who assured the recluse that if he threw himself down a deep well in the neighourhood he would prove his sancitity by remaining unhurt. Heron was pulled out by the brethren and died three days afterwards from the injuries he had received, still persisting in his delusion. The Abbot Paphnutius considered that he had committed suicide and was with great difficulty persuaded to allow him the usual memorial and oblation granted to those at rest. (Cassian's *Conferences*; Conference of the Abbot Moses, v.) The edition used by St. Teresa is not known.

utterly blinded. Most certainly, if the impulse had been divine, it would have done the man no harm. Celestial inspirations infallibly bring with them prudence, light, and moderation, but this deadly enemy of ours seeks to injure us in every way—since he is wary, let us be the same. Moderation is often useful in similar cases, such as shortening our time for prayer, however much we may be enjoying it, if it tells on our health or begins to make our head ache, for discretion is always necessary.

14. Why do you think, my daughters, that before the battle has begun, I have told you of the end of the conflict and shown you its rewards by describing the benefits of drinking of this fountain of living water? I did it to prevent your being dismayed at the hardships and difficulties of the way, that you may be courageous and not grow weary, lest, when you have reached the spring and only have to stoop to drink of it, you may draw back and forfeit all this grace, imagining that you lack the strength to gain it and that it is not meant for you. Remember, our Lord invited 'any man': He is truth itself; His word cannot be doubted. If *all* had not been included He would not have addressed everybody, nor would He have said: 'I will give you to drink.' He might have said: 'Let all men come, for they will lose nothing by it, and I will give to drink to those I think fit for it.' But as He said unconditionally: 'If *any* man thirst let him come to me,' I feel sure that, unless they stop half-way, none will fail to drink of this living water. May our Lord, Who has promised to grant it us, give us grace to seek it as we ought, for His own sake.

CHAPTER XX[1]

SHOWS HOW, IN ONE WAY OR ANOTHER, PRAYER ALWAYS BRINGS US CONSOLATION. THE SISTERS ARE ADVISED TO SPEAK TO ONE ANOTHER CONSTANTLY ON THIS SUBJECT.

1. Consolations of prayer. 2. Advantages of mental prayer. 3. The society of seculars. 4. How to hold intercourse with them.

1. THE last chapter seems to contradict what I said, when in order to console those who were not contemplatives I told them that God had made many ways of reaching Him, just as He has made 'many mansions'.[2] I repeat that His Majesty, being God, knows our weakness and has provided for us. He did not say: 'Let some men come to Me by drinking this water, but let others come by some other means.' His mercy is so great that He hinders no one from drinking of the fountain of life. May He be for ever praised! What good reasons there were for His forbidding it to me! Yet, as He did not order me to refrain from it when first I approached it, but plunged me into its very depths, decidedly He will stop no one else. Indeed, He calls us loudly and publicly to do so. He is so good that He will not force us to drink it, but He gives it in many ways to those who try to follow Him, so that none may go away disconsolate or die of thirst. For from this overflowing river spring many rivulets, some large, others small, while there are little pools for children—enough for them as

[1] Valladolid edition, xxii; Escorial, xxxiii.

[2] St. John, xiv, 2: 'In domo Patris mei mansiones multæ sunt.' *Castle*, Introd. p. xxviii. M. I. i, 2.

they would be frightened at much water—by 'children' I mean beginners, unformed in virtue. You see, sisters, there is no fear you will die of drought on the way of prayer. The waters of comfort are never so utterly wanting that thirst becomes unbearable. Then take my advice; do not loiter on the road, but struggle manfully until you perish in the attempt, for you only came here for battle. Resolve firmly to die rather than miss the end of your journey. If at times our Lord lets you feel parched and arid during this life—in eternity He will give you abundance of water with no fear of its ever failing through any fault of yours. God grant that we may never fail Him! Amen.

2.[3] Let us now consider how to start on this journey. This is most important, or we might wander off the right track from the very first: indeed I believe everything depends upon it. I do not mean that no one who is not firmly resolved to persevere in prayer ought to begin to practise it, for our Lord will gradually lead her on to perfection. Prayer has such virtue that she need never fear to lose by it: if she takes but one step she will be richly rewarded, for it brings us many graces, great and small. It is like an indulgenced chaplet[4]—one bead earns a certain indulgence and several beads gain many more, yet if we never used the chaplet but kept it shut up in a box, it would

[3] Escorial edition, xxxiv. Advice to the sisters to encourage people to practise prayer.

[4] *Cuenta de perdones*—beads strung together, blessed by the Pope, who attached to them certain indulgences on condition of reciting the prescribed prayers. Don Vincente de Fuente says he saw two which were kept in St. Christopher's church, Salamanca.

be better for us to be without it. Thus, though many people do not persevere in prayer, any little progress they have made in it will give them light for other things, and the further they have advanced, the more light they will have. In short, they will certainly not harm themselves by beginning to practise it: good never brings forth evil. If you perceive a disposition or wish for prayer in people you see, try to remove any fear they may feel of beginning. I ask you, for the love of God, always to make your conversation helpful to your visitors. Your prayers are for the good of souls,[5] for whom you are bound to intercede continually with God, and it seems wrong not to try to help them in every other possible way. If you would be a good kinswoman, this is genuine affection: if you would wish to be a true friend, this is the only feasible way. Let the truth grow as it ought in your hearts by meditation and you will know what sort of love we should bear for our neighbours.

3. This is no time for child's-play; and worldly friendship, even when innocent, seems nothing else. Neither with your relations nor with any one else must you indulge in such foolish talk as: 'Do you love me? Do you not like me?' unless it serves some real end by benefiting a soul. To persuade your kindred, or a brother, or any other person to listen to and to admit the truth, some such words and signs of affection, which are always grateful to the senses, may be needed. Perhaps he will be better pleased by one kind word, as he would call it, than by a great deal you might say about

[5] Ch. iii, 3-5; iv, 1, 2.

God afterwards: however, it will make him more inclined to talk about religion. I do not forbid your using such endearments for a good end; otherwise they are useless and may do harm without your knowing it.

4. Every one knows you are nuns and that prayer is your business. Never say to yourselves: 'I do not wish to be thought good.' People will receive either profit or harm from what they see in you. It is very blameworthy of you, who are bound to speak solely on religious subjects,[6] to refrain from doing so, unless sometimes greater good may be done in this way. Your intercourse and character must be devout. Let those acquire it who wish to talk to you, but beware of learning worldly ways —they would be a hell to you. Never mind if you are considered ill-bred—still less if you are taken for a hypocrite—this would be an advantage. No one would wish to see you unless they spoke your language, for if one cannot understand Arabic one does not want to talk to a person who knows no other tongue: thus the world would neither weary you nor hurt you, for to spend all your time in learning a new dialect would be no small hurt. Not having had my experience, you cannot understand as I do how this injures the soul, which forgets one thing while learning another. It is a perpetual source of worry; this must by all means be avoided, for peace and quiet of mind are essential

[6] In most of the Carmelite convents in Spain the following lines are painted in the lobby:

Hermana, uno de dos:
O callar ó hablar con Dios;
Que en la casa de Teresa
Esta ciencia se profesa.

for the prayer of which I am about to speak. If your acquaintances ask to learn your language,[7] although it is not for you to teach it to them, yet you can tell them what great graces are gained by it. Never tire of doing this kindly, lovingly, prayerfully, in order to help your friends, so that, realizing its value, they may seek some master to teach it them. Our Lord would be doing you no small favour if He enabled you to persuade some one to practise prayer. When once one begins to speak of this way of prayer, how many matters there are to discuss, even by one as faulty as I am. Alas! I ought to write with both hands in order not to omit one subject for another. May it please our Lord to teach it you, sisters, better than I have hitherto done. Amen.

CHAPTER XXI[1]

THE IMPORTANCE OF MAKING A FIRM RESOLUTION, FROM THE VERY FIRST, TO PERSEVERE IN PRAYER AND TO HEED NO OBSTACLES RAISED AGAINST IT BY THE DEVIL.

1. Fortitude needed for mental prayer. 2. Subjects suited to it. 3. The Pater Noster used as mental prayer. 4. The world's objections to mental prayer. 5. God provides teachers to help us. 6. Perseverance necessary in the practice.

1. Do not be surprised, daughters, at the number of matters that have to be considered before starting on the heavenly road that leads to Paradise. This journey gains such vast treasures that no wonder the cost should seem dear. Some day we shall discover that all we have paid was nothing

[7] *Const.* 14.
[1] Valladolid edition, xxiii; Escorial, xxxv.

compared with the prize it has purchased for us. Let us return to speak of those who wish to travel by this path to the very end, and to the fount itself, where they will drink of the water of life. Although there are books written on the subject, yet I do not think it will be waste of time to speak of it here. How must one begin? I maintain that this is the chief point; in fact, that everything depends on people having a great and a most resolute determination never to halt until they reach their journey's end,[2] happen what may, whatever the consequences are, cost what it will, let who will blame them, whether they reach the goal or die on the road, or lose heart to bear the trials they encounter, or the earth itself goes to pieces beneath their feet.[3] Men will warn us again and again of the risks we run: 'Such a person was lost through this; another fell into error through it; some one else who practised prayer went wrong; it injures virtue, and is unfit for women whom it may lead into illusions; it is best for them to keep to their spinning; they have no need of all these subtleties—the Pater Noster and the Ave Maria are enough for them.' So they are, sisters; most certainly they are enough! You are always right in founding your prayer on the prayer that came from our Lord's own lips. Well may men say so. If we were not so weak and tepid we should need no fresh system of meditation nor any other books or prayers than these.

2. As I said, I am speaking to those who cannot

[2] 'Sic enim incepta pergitur via secure.' (*Imitation*, bk. III. xxvii, 5.
[3] *Life*, xv, 5, 7, 8. *Castle*, M. II. i, 16, 19.

meditate on other mysteries, which seem to them too systematic: besides, there are people so fastidious that nothing pleases them. For these reasons, I think it is well to lay down some rules for the beginning, the middle, and the end of prayer, without discussing anything very sublime, for, as I said, such matters are already treated of elsewhere. You cannot altogether be deprived of books—for no one can take these sacred books away from you[4]—and if you study them and humble yourself, you will need nothing more. The words of the Gospel, which came from our Lord's most sacred mouth, have always been dear to me and arouse a more fervent devotion in me than the most carefully written and learned books, especially those that were not composed by an approved author, for in such a case I never cared to glance at them.

3. I will keep close to the side of this Master of all wisdom, Who perhaps may teach me to write what will meet your needs. I do not say that I will explain these divine petitions—I dare not presume to do so. Much has been written on the subject, and even if it had not, it would be absurd for *me* to undertake the task. I will only put before you

[4] In 1559 the Grand Inquisitor, Don Hernando de Valdes, published an Index in which, besides many heretical books, he also proscribed excellent Catholic works of devotion on the plea that they were unfit for 'the wives of carpenters.' St. Teresa herself suffered very severely by this unprecedented regulation, as she tells in her *Life*, ch. xxvi. 6: 'When we were deprived of many books written in Spanish [literally, 'When they took away many books'—de romance—'in the vulgar tongue, lest they be read'] . . . I felt it deeply—for some of these books were a great comfort to me, and I could not read them in Latin—our Lord said to me: "Be not troubled: I will give thee a living book . . ." His Majesty has been to me a veritable Book, in which I saw all truth.' (Morel-Fatio, *Les Lectures de Sainte Thérèse*, Paris, 1908).

some consideration on the words of the Pater Noster, for sometimes too many books destroy our devotion just when we need it most. There is no doubt that a master has a kind feeling for his pupils, that he wishes them to understand his teaching, and does his best to make them comprehend it.[5]

4. Take no notice of the warnings people give you or the dangers they suggest. It is absurd to suppose that one could travel along a road full of bandits to reach a costly treasure without running any risks. Men of the world think happiness consists in journeying peacefully through life, yet for the sake of gaining a farthing they will sacrifice their sleep night after night, and leave other people no peace of mind or body. If, when you are trying to earn or 'bear away' this treasure for yourselves, for, as our Lord says, 'The violent bear it away[6]—and are travelling by the royal and safe road by which our Lord, all the elect, and the saints passed— if, even then, men warn you of so many dangers, so many horrors—what must be the risks incurred by those who seek these riches with no path to guide them? O my daughters! there can be no comparison between the hazard of those travellers and our own. Yet such souls never realize this until they fall headlong into peril, with no one to help them out of it. Thus they lose this water altogether; they drink of it neither much nor little, and do not even taste it from a pool or

[5] Escorial edition, xxxvi. Continues the same subject: that the objections raised by people against mental prayer are false, and we must not trust everybody's word.

[6] St. Matt. xi, 12: 'Violenti rapiunt illud.'

streamlet. How can they travel among so many dangers without a drop of it to support them? At the best, they must die of thirst, for whether we will or no, daughters, we must all journey to this fountain, although we may take different routes. Take my advice, and let no one mislead you by pointing out any other way than prayer. I am not discussing here whether mental and vocal prayer are necessary for *everybody*, but I say that *you* require them both. This is the work of religious: if any one tells you it is dangerous, look upon *him* as your greatest danger and shun his company. Keep my words in mind, for you may need them. A want of humility, of the virtues, may endanger you, but prayer—*prayer!* Never would God permit this! The devil must have originated these fears and so brought about, by crafty tricks, the fall of certain souls that practised prayer. See how blind men are! the world never reckons the thousands who have fallen into heresy and other flagrant crimes through never practising prayer and not even knowing what it means—which is a very real danger: yet if, among the multitudes of souls, Satan, to suit his own purposes, has won a paltry few who were given to prayer, people at once take fright at this holy custom. Let those Christians beware who sanction their neglect of prayer by this pretext, for they are avoiding good in order to save themselves from evil. I never heard of a more malicious fiction—it seems fiendish.

5. O my God, defend Thyself! See how men misunderstand Thy words: permit no weakness in Thy servants. There is one great mercy: you will

always find some one to help you. The real servant of God, to whom He gives light to see the true way, when beset by these fears only tries to hasten on. He sees clearly that the devil is going to attack him, and, avoiding the blow aimed at him, he splits open his enemy's skull. Satan's rage at this exceeds by far any pleasure he receives from those who gratify him. In troublous times, when the enemy has sown his cockle and seems leading all mankind in his wake, half blinded as they are by misguided zeal, God raises up some one to open their eyes, who bids them look at the mists the devil has raised to hide the way from them. How great God is! Sometimes the one man[7]—there may perhaps be two—who speaks the truth, overcomes all the rest. By degrees he points out to them the right course, and courage is given him by his Maker. If people say prayer is dangerous[8] he endeavours to teach them its benefits by his deeds, if not by his words. If objections are raised against frequent Communion, he has recourse more often than before to the most Blessed Sacrament. Thus if only one or two souls, throwing aside all misgivings, follow the better way, our Lord gradually regains what had before been lost.

6. Therefore, sisters, banish these misgivings: take no notice of public opinion. This is no time to believe everything you hear. Be guided only by those who conform their lives to that of Christ; try to keep a good conscience; practise humility; despise all earthly things; firmly believe the teaching of our holy Mother the Church—then you may

[7] *Excl*, x, 9. [8] *Found.* ch. iii, 3.

feel sure you are on the right road. Cast aside these causeless fears. If any one tries to frighten you, humbly explain the matter to him: tell him that our Rule bids us pray constantly[9]—which is the fact—and that you are bound to obey it. If people say that this only applies to vocal prayer, ask whether your mind and heart ought not to take part with your lips. If they answer 'Yes'—as they must, for they can do nothing else—you see that they admit that you are obliged to practise mental prayer and contemplation too, if God should give it you.[10]

[9] *Rule* 5.

[10] As far as I can understand, the gate by which to enter this castle is prayer and meditation. I do not allude more to mental than to vocal prayer; for if it is prayer at all, the mind must take part in it. If a person neither considers to Whom he is addressing himself, what he asks, nor what he is who ventures to speak to God, although his lips may utter many words, I do not call it prayer. Sometimes, indeed, one may pray devoutly without making all these considerations because one has practised them at other times. The custom of speaking to God Almighty as freely as with a slave—caring nothing whether one's words are suitable or not, but simply saying the first thing that comes to the mind from being learnt by heart by frequent repetition, cannot be called prayer: God grant that no Christian may address Him in this manner! (*Castle*, M. I. i, 9.)

CHAPTER XXII.[1]

SHOWS WHAT MENTAL PRAYER IS.

1. Vocal prayer implies mental prayer. 2 Reverence needful for prayer. 3. God is the King, we are His petitioners. 4. A prayer for guidance. 5. Christ is the Bridegroom of our souls. 6. By mental prayer we learn to know and love Him.

1. You must know, daughters, that there is no need to keep our lips closed in order to pray mentally. If while I utter a prayer I carefully consider its meaning and pay more attention to what I am saying to God than to the words themselves, this is both mental and vocal prayer. Should people affirm that you are praying to God if, while you recite the Pater Noster or the Ave Maria, you are thinking of earthly things—then I have no more to say. But if you wish to behave with due respect to such a mighty Monarch, you should reflect on Who He is you are addressing and what you yourself are, that you may show fitting reverence. For how can you accost Him, and petition His Majesty the King, or know what ceremonies to use, unless you realize His rank and your own position? This it is that regulates the respect to be paid, and you must learn it unless you wish to be turned away as a boor, with your requests ungranted. More than that, unless you are well versed in the matter, you should take care to find out the proper titles to use. I happened once, before I was accustomed to deal with grandees, to be brought in contact concerning business matters with a person of rank,

[1] Valladolid edition, xxiv. ; Escorial, xxxvii.

whom I was told to address as 'your Ladyship'. But my wits are dull and I am unused to such customs, so when I met her I forgot all about it and made a mistake. I thought it best to explain the case laughingly, and to ask her to allow me to call her 'your Honour', which she did.[2]

2. How canst Thou, Ruler of all creation as Thou art,[3] bear this want of reverence from men? Thou hast been King, my God, from all eternity, for Thine is no borrowed empire but Thine own, and it will never end. Blessed mayest Thou be! I always feel a peculiar joy at reciting in the Creed: 'Of Whose kingdom there shall be no end.'[4] I will praise and bless Thee for ever, Lord, for Thy kingdom shall last for ever. Permit not that men should think it right for them to praise Thee or speak to Thee with their lips alone. What are you saying, Christians, when you affirm that there is no need for mental prayer? Do you understand your own words? Really I think you cannot do so, and you wish us all to fall into the same mistake. You do not know what mental prayer is, how vocal prayers must be said, nor what contemplation is, or you would not distrust and condemn in one place what you approve of in another.

3. Whenever I remember it, I will always speak of mental and vocal prayer together, my daughters, lest I should alarm you. I know how such matters

[2] 'Your Honour' was the term used to others in ordinary life, even between brothers and sisters. The lady was probably Luisa de la Cerda, in whose palace St. Teresa spent the first part of the year 1562.

[3] Psalm cxliv. 13: 'Regnum tuum regnum omnium sæculorum; et dominatio tua in omni generatione et generationem.'

[4] 'Cujus regni non erit finis.' *Credo.*

end, having suffered a great deal of trouble from them, and I do not wish any one to disturb you, nor to confuse your mind on the subject, for timidity about prayer injures the soul. It is most important for you to know the right way to set about it. If one told a traveller that he had mistaken his way, he would wander to and fro and would tire himself out and lose his time by trying to find the path and would only arrive at his journey's end all the later. Who could blame any one for recollecting Whom she is about to address and what she herself is, before she begins to recite the 'Hours' or the Rosary? Yet I assure you, that if you considered these two points as you ought, before saying your vocal prayers you would spend a considerable time first in mental prayer. We must not speak to a prince with the same freedom that we should use towards a labourer or some poor creature like ourselves, whom we may accost in any way we choose. Yet this King is so humble that, however unmannerly my speech may be, He does not refuse to hear me on that account, nor do His guards repulse me. For the angels who attend Him know that their Monarch prefers the rusticity of a lowly shepherd, who would be more polite if only he knew how, to the courtly speeches of a learned but proud man. To atone for what God suffers from bearing with the loathsome presence of such a creature as myself, we ought to try to understand His purity and His sublimity. True, we know already Who it is that we approach when we draw near Him, as we recognize the magnates of this world. When we have been told who their father was and what their revenues and titles are, there is no more to know, as we honour them, not for their good character, but for their money. O wretched world! Thank God, daughters, that you have left so vile a thing, where men are esteemed not for their real selves but for the money which their tenants and the labourers they employ bring to them, for if the rich lose their incomes they at once lose their prestige with it. It is a mockery: you should laugh at it among yourselves during recreation, for it does us good to make merry over the blindness men show in this life.

4. O Thou our Monarch! King of glory, Lord of lords, Sovereign of all princes, Chief among the Saints! O Power, dominating over all else! Wisdom above all knowledge, having neither beginning nor end! limitless in all Thy works, which are infinite and incomprehensible and a fathomless abyss of wonders! O Beauty containing all other beauty! Thou art strength itself; Thou art the truth, O Lord, and the genuine riches: do Thou reign for ever! Most merciful God! would that I possessed the combined eloquence of all the human race, with wisdom to understand—as far as the understanding can attain in this life, which is but utter ignorance—that I might succeed in telling at least a few of the many things that might be pondered over, in order to obtain some feeble idea of the perfections of this our Lord and only Good.[5]

5. Before prayer, endeavour to realize Whose Presence you are approaching and to Whom you

[5] Escorial edition, xxxviii. Continues to explain mental prayer.

are about to speak, keeping in mind Whom you are addressing. If our lives were a thousand times as long as they are we should never fully understand how we ought to behave towards God, before Whom the very Angels tremble, Who *can* do all He *wills*, and with Whom to wish is to accomplish. Ought we not, my daughters, to rejoice in these perfections of our Spouse, and to learn to know Him and what our lives should be? In the world, when a girl is going to be married, she knows beforehand who her husband is to be and what are his means and position—and shall not we, who are already betrothed, think about our Bridegroom before He takes us home on the wedding-day? If these thoughts are not forbidden to an earthly bride, why should I be prevented from discovering Who this Man is, Who is His Father, to what country He will take me, what are the riches He promises to endow me with, and what rank He holds? May I not know how best to please Him, what are His tastes, and how to bring my mind to harmonize with His? For if a woman is to lead a happy married life, people advise her to make these things her first consideration, no matter how low her husband's station may be. And art Thou, O my Spouse! to be treated with less respect than is shown to men? If the world honours Thee not, let it at least leave Thy brides to do so in peace, since they spend their lives with Thee. Sometimes a husband is so jealous that he will permit his wife to speak to no one but himself. In order to please him and to live happily with him, this is but a small sacrifice for her to make: she should not wish to talk to others since she has all she can desire in him.

6. To understand these truths, my daughters, is to practise mental prayer. If you like to meditate on them and to pray vocally also, that is all well and good, but never address your words to God while you are thinking of something else—whoever does so, knows nothing of mental prayer. I think I have explained the matter clearly: God give us the grace to know how to practise it! Do not let yourselves be alarmed by any misgivings. Praise God who is almighty, and let no one hinder your making mental prayer. If any one of you cannot recite her prayers with such attention, let her know that she does not fulfil her obligation. If she wishes to pray with perfection, she must try with all her heart to be recollected, unless she would fail in her duties as the bride of this great King. Beg Him, daughters, to enable me to practise what I have taught you, for I fall very short of doing so. May His Majesty aid me, for His own sake! Amen.

CHAPTER XXIII[1]

HOW IMPORTANT IT IS THAT ONE WHO HAS ENTERED ON THE WAY OF PRAYER SHOULD NOT TURN BACK.

1. *Why we should persevere in prayer.* 2. *Because we must be generous.* 3. *Perseverance in prayer defeats the devil and gives us courage.* 4. *Reward gained by mental prayer.*

1. How I have wandered from the subject! It is essential, I think, to begin the practice of prayer with a firm resolution of persevering in it. The reasons for this are so many that it would take too long to enumerate them—besides, they are explained in a number of books. I will content myself, then, with mentioning two or three. Firstly, when we pay this attention (slight in itself) of our thoughts—an attention which is not fruitless, but which brings us a rich reward—when we render this homage to God, Who has bestowed so much on us and Who continues to shower benefits upon us, it would be wrong not to give it Him entirely; not as one who gives a thing, meaning to take it back again. This cannot be called 'giving': in fact, any one who has received a present always feels more or less annoyed at its being reclaimed by the donor, especially when he had come to look upon it as his own property. If this occurs between friends, and the giver is indebted for many gratuitous favours to the recipient, the latter may justly consider that meanness and want of affection are shown if nothing has been left him as a gage of love. Where can a wife be found who, after

[1] Valladolid edition, xxv; Escorial, xxxix.

receiving a number of valuable jewels from her husband, will not give him in return even a ring, not so much for its value (for all that she possesses is his), but as a pledge that she will be faithful to him unto death? Does God merit less than this, that we should mock Him by first giving Him this trifle and then taking it away? Since we have resolved to devote to Him this short space of time (which we should otherwise bestow on our friends, who would not thank us for it) let us yield it Him with thoughts that are free and withdrawn from all else. Let us fully resolve never to take it back, whatever crosses it may bring us, and in spite of all aridities.[2]

2. We must no longer reckon this time as our own: we should feel that God will have the right to call us to account for it unless we render it entirely to Him. When I say 'entirely' I do not mean that we should be taking it back if we missed it for a day or two on account of lawful duties[3] or illness, but that you should keep your resolution unchanged. God is not exacting: He does not scrutinize details, and if you seek to please Him you are offering Him a gift. The other way of acting suits spirits so miserly that they have not the heart to give, but will only lend. Still, even then, they do something: this Lord of ours takes any payment and accommodates Himself to our humours. He is liberal, not exacting about His dues: however heavy our debts may be, He easily remits them in order to win us. He watches us so closely that you need never fear He will leave you

[2] *Castle*, M. II. i, 15. [3] *Castle*, M. II. i, 18.

unrewarded if you but raise your eyes to heaven with the thought of Him.

3. A second reason why our resolution should be firm is that this lessens the devil's power of tempting us. He is very frightened of determined souls, knowing by experience how they injure him, and that by trying to do them mischief he only profits them and others and damages himself. Still, we must not grow careless or trust to this, for we have to deal with traitors who, though too cowardly to attack the wary, yet inflict great harm on the negligent. If they find that a soul is fickle, irresolute, and wanting in perseverance in the right path, they will never leave it alone day or night and will suggest to it endless fears and difficulties. Experience has convinced me of this, and I have been able to explain it to you: most people do not realize its gravity. A third and very weighty reason is that a resolute soul fights more courageously, knowing that, come what may, it must never retreat. It is like a soldier in the midst of the fray, who knows that if he is vanquished he must expect no quarter, but that, if he does not fall during the battle, he will be killed afterwards. I am sure that he must fight the more doggedly and intend to sell his life the more dearly for this, as the term goes. Besides, he would care less for his wounds, realizing the price of victory and that his life depended upon gaining it.

4. We ought to feel no doubt that, unless we allow ourselves to be defeated, we are sure to succeed. This is certain, for however insignificant our conquest may be we shall come off with great

gains. Never fear that our Lord will allow us to die of thirst after inviting us to drink of this fountain. I have said it before and I shall often repeat it, for people who have not learnt our Lord's goodness by experience, but only know of it by faith, are often discouraged. It is a great grace to have proved for oneself what friendship and caresses He bestows on those who walk by the way of prayer, and how, as it were, He defrays all the costs. It does not surprise me that those who have never practised it should want the security of receiving some interest. You know that we receive a hundredfold even in this life,[4] and that our Lord said: 'Ask and ye shall receive.'[5] His Majesty has promised this in several places in the Gospels: if you do not believe Him, sisters, it would be of little use for me to wear myself out with telling you about it. However, I can assure any one who still feels doubtful, that she has little to lose by beginning the practice, and that prayer has the advantage of gaining for us more than we ask or can even desire. This is incontestable: I know it from experience. If you find it is false, never believe a single word I have ever said to you. Those who, by the mercy of God, have learnt it for themselves can bear witness to what I affirm. It is well to have said this for the sake of those who will come after me.

[4] St. Matt. xix, 29: 'Omnis qui reliquerit domum . . . propter nomen meum, centuplum accipiet, et vitam æternam possidebit.'

[5] St. Luke xi, 9. St. Matt. vii, 7: 'Et ego dico vobis: Petite et dabitur vobis; quærite et invenietis; pulsate et aperietur vobis.' (*Castle*, M. IV. i, 11. *Life*, xix, 8.)

CHAPTER XXIV[1]

HOW VOCAL PRAYER MAY BE MADE WITH PERFECTION. ITS CLOSE CONNEXION WITH MENTAL PRAYER.

1. How vocal prayers should be said. 2. Recollection and vocal prayer. 3. Involuntary distractions during prayer. 4. Our part in obtaining recollection.

1. Now let me address myself to those souls I mentioned who can neither recollect themselves, nor concentrate their minds on mental prayer, nor can they meditate. We must not mention either of these words before them, for they will not hear of such things. In fact, many people are terrified at the mere name of mental prayer or meditation, yet perhaps some such persons may enter this convent, for as I said, all are not led by the same way. What I will advise you about, or I may say *teach* you (for as Prioress, I am your mother, and have the right to teach), is how to pray vocally, because you ought to understand the words you utter. Since long prayers may tire one who cannot fix her mind on God, I will not speak of them, but only of those which, as Christians, we are bound to repeat—namely the *Pater Noster* and the *Ave Maria.*[2]

2. Clearly, we ought to attend to how we say our prayers; then no one can say we speak without understanding our own words. Perhaps we think it is enough for us to pray as a matter of habit and that it suffices if we simply pronounce the words. Whether it *suffices* or no, is not for me to say: I

[1] Valladolid edition, xxvi; Escorial, continuation of xxxix.

[2] Escorial edition, xl.

leave the decision to theologians: God will give them light to guide those who consult them, and as to those who do not belong to our state of life, it is no business of mine. But, my daughters, I do not wish us to content ourselves with this. When I recite, in the *Credo*, 'I believe . . .' it seems to me that I ought to know and to understand what it is that 'I believe.' If I say, 'Our Father,' love requires that I should know *Who* is 'our Father', and *Who* the Master that teaches us this prayer, for there is an immense difference between one master and another. If you tell me that it is enough to know this once for all and to think no more about it, you might as well say that it is enough to recite the prayer itself once in a life-time. It is shameful to forget even our human teachers, especially if they were very holy and were our spiritual guides: we could not do so if we were faithful pupils. We should preserve a strong affection and respect for them, and should often speak of them. God forbid, then, that whenever we say this prayer we should not think of such a Master, so loving and desirous of our good. Still, human nature is so frail that we may often forget Him.

3. You know that His Majesty taught us that the first point is that prayer should be made in solitude.[3] He practised this Himself; not because it was requisite for Him, but for the sake of our instruction. I have already explained that we cannot speak both to God and to the world at the same time. Yet what else are we doing if, while we pray, we listen to other people's conversation

[3] St. Matt. vi, 6 : 'Tu autem, cum oraveris, intra in cubiculum tuum, et clauso ostio, ora Patrem tuum in abscondito.'

or let our thoughts dwell unchecked on whatever subject occurs to them? I am not alluding to times when people are out of health (especially if they suffer from melancholia), or when their brains are tired, for then no effort will control the attention. On other occasions God permits a tempest of difficulties to assault His servants for their greater good: then, though the soul may grieve at its distractions and try to stop them, this is found to be impossible. Such a person cannot attend to what she is saying, strive as she may, nor can she fix her thoughts on any other subject: indeed she seems bereft of reason and her wits wander—still the pain this state causes her proves her to be blameless in the matter. She should not trouble herself about it; this would only increase the evil; let her not tire herself by trying to reduce her mind to reason, of which in such a state it is incapable. Let her pray as best she can, or leave off praying and rest her brain as if she were ill, occupying herself with some other good work. This advice applies to persons who watch carefully over themselves and who grasp the truth that they cannot speak both to God and to the world at the same time.

4. On our part, we can endeavour to be alone—God grant this may suffice to make us realize in Whose presence we are and how He answers our petitions. Do you suppose He is silent, though we cannot hear Him? He speaks to our hearts when our hearts speak to Him. It would be good for us to believe that He teaches this prayer to each one of us in particular. This Master is never so

far off that His scholars need raise their voices to make Him hear: He keeps very close to them. I want to show you that, to say the *Pater Noster* well, you must not leave the side of the Tutor Who teaches it you. Perhaps you will say that this is meditation, and that you cannot pray except vocally nor do you wish to do so. Some people are impatient and self-indulgent, and find it difficult to collect their thoughts when they begin to pray, being unused to the habit; therefore to avoid some little trouble, they say they do not know how, nor can they do more than pray vocally. You are right in calling that which I am speaking of 'mental prayer,' but I assure you that vocal prayers, properly recited, cannot be separated from it if we are to realize with Whom we are speaking. We are bound to pray with attention, and may God grant that, with the aid of all these means, we may succeed in saying the *Pater Noster* well without wandering thoughts. I sometimes suffer from them, and I find that the best remedy is to keep my mind fixed on Him to Whom my words are addressed. You must be patient, and try to accustom yourselves to this most necessary practice, which for nuns—and, in my opinion, for all good Christians—is indispensable.

CHAPTER XXV[1]

THAT GREAT PROFIT IS REAPED BY THE SOUL FROM PRAYING VOCALLY WITH PERFECTION, AND THAT GOD THEN SOMETIMES RAISES IT TO A SUPERNATURAL STATE.

1. Difference between vocal and mental prayer and contemplation. 2. Mental and vocal prayer. 3. Contemplation is a gift from God.

1. To prove to you that vocal prayer, made perfectly, brings with it no small profit, I may tell you that it is quite possible, while you are reciting the *Pater Noster* or some other prayer (if you say it well), that God may raise you to perfect contemplation.[2] His Majesty thus shows that He is listening to His handmaid and speaks to her in return, suspending the understanding and stopping the thoughts—one might say, taking the words out of her mouth—so that speech becomes impossible, or at least requires a strong effort. The soul understands that the divine Master is teaching it without the sound of words. He suspends the faculties,[3] which by their action would hinder rather than favour contemplation. They are happy without knowing why: the soul is inflamed with love without comprehending how it loves: it feels that it enjoys the Beloved, yet how it does so it cannot tell. It realizes that this delight can never be gained through any desire of the mind itself: the will embraces its joy without apprehending how, yet it dimly perceives that every good work

[1] Valladolid edition, xxvii; Escorial, xli.
[2] *Concep.* iv, 1, sqq.
[3] *Life*, xviii, 1-3, 14-19. *Rel.* i. 1; viii, 7. *Castle*, M. V. i, 3, sqq.

mankind could perform in this world would not merit such a reward, for it is the gift of the Lord of heaven and earth Who gives it in the manner befitting His Godhead.

2. This, daughters, is perfect *contemplation*. Now you can see how it differs from mental prayer, which as I explained to you consists in thinking over and realizing what and with Whom we speak, and who we are that presume to address this great Sovereign. To consider these and other matters, such as how little we serve Him, and how greatly we should do so, is *mental prayer*. Do not fancy that it is some 'shibboleth', nor take fright at the word. To recite the 'Our Father', or the 'Hail, Mary', or any other petition is *vocal prayer*—you see what discord this would make without the accompaniment of mental prayer: even the words would go wrong sometimes.

3. With the assistance of God's grace we can help ourselves to a certain extent in these two matters; not so in contemplation:[4] this is beyond our natural powers, and He does all, for it is His work. In the history of my life, which was written by their command for my confessors, I have spoken at length about contemplation and explained it to the full extent of my knowledge, so I will only touch upon it here. If those of you whom God has so blessed as to lead into this state of prayer (and, as I have said, several of you are among the number) can obtain this book, you will find certain points and advice contained in it which will afford you great comfort, for our Lord

[4] *Castle*, M. V. ii, 1-5.

was pleased to enable me to make the matter clear —at least, so it appears to me and to others who have read it, and who always keep the book by them because of their high opinion of it. How ashamed I feel at telling you that they have a high opinion of me! God knows how confused I am at writing on some of these sublime subjects: may He be praised for His patience in bearing with me! Those of you who have reached a supernatural state of prayer should procure the volume after my death; the others have no need of it: only let them try to practise what I have taught them here and to advance by all the means in their power. Let them make every effort to obtain this grace from God, begging Him fervently to grant it them: let them help one another and then leave the rest in His Hands. The gift is His: He will not refuse it if you do not linger on the road but force yourselves to persevere to the end and to keep up the struggle, as I told you.

CHAPTER XXVI[1]

SHOWS HOW TO COLLECT THE THOUGHTS,[2] SUGGESTING MEANS OF DOING SO. THIS CHAPTER IS USEFUL FOR THOSE BEGINNING TO PRACTISE PRAYER.

1. The soul should keep close to Christ during prayer. 2. The advantages of doing so. 3. We must gaze on the Bridegroom of our souls. 4. He accommodates Himself to our needs. 5. How we may address Him. 6. We ought to share in His sufferings. 7. As did our Lady and the Magdalen. 8. How to become intimate with Jesus. 9. Aids towards obtaining this habit.

1. LET us return to speak of mental prayer, in order that we may pray intelligently, and may perform it in such a manner that, without our understanding how, God may give us all the rest. You know that, first of all, you must make your examination of conscience, say the *Confiteor* and make the sign of the cross—then, my daughters, as you are alone, seek for some companion—and where could you find a better one than the Master Who taught you the prayer you are about to say? Picture this same Lord close beside you. See how lovingly, how humbly He is teaching you—believe me, you should never be without so good a Friend. If you accustom yourselves to keep Him near you, and He sees that you love to have Him and make every effort to please Him, you will not be able to send Him away. He will never fail you, but will help you in all your troubles and you will

[1] Valladolid edition, xxviii.; Escorial, xlii.

[2] The word used is *pensamiento* sometimes used by the Saint for the imagination and sometimes for wandering thoughts. Hugh of St. Victor and Francis of St. Thomas define it as a 'wandering of the mind, aimless and useless, in which the thoughts roam hither and thither.' Perhaps 'idle fancies' would sometimes be the right interpretation.

find Him everywhere. Do you think it is a small thing to have such a friend at your side?

2. O my sisters! let those among you who cannot pursue a train of thought nor restrain the freaks of your imagination, practise it—practise it! I am sure that you can do this, for during many years I bore the trial of being unable to fix my attention on any subject. This is indeed a heavy cross, yet I know that our Lord does not so abandon us as to refuse us His company if we humbly ask Him for it. If we cannot attain to this in one year, let us wait for it many years: do not let us grudge spending our time so well. Who is there to hurry us? We have the power to accustom ourselves to this practice, and to cultivate it, and to keep close beside our dear Master.

3. I am not now asking you to meditate on Him, nor to produce great thoughts, nor to feel deep devotion: I only ask you to look at Him. Who can prevent your turning the eyes of your soul (but for an instant, if you can do no more) on our Lord? You are able to look on many ugly and vulgar things: then can you not gaze upon the fairest sight imaginable? If He does not appear beautiful to you, I give you leave never to think of Him, although, daughters, He never takes His eyes off you! He has borne with many offences and much unworthiness in you, yet these have not sufficed to make Him turn away: is it much to ask that you should sometimes lift your gaze from earth to fix it on Him? See: He is only waiting for us to look on Him, as the bride says.[3]

[3] Cant. vii, 10: 'Ego dilecto meo, et ad me conversio ejus.'

You will find that He suits Himself to whatever mood you are in. He longs so keenly for our glance that He will neglect no means to win it.

4. They say that a wife must do this if she wishes to live happily with her husband. If he is sad, she too must appear unhappy: if he is merry, (although she may be feeling far from cheerful), she must appear light-hearted also: see from what bondage you are freed, sisters! This is what our Lord really does with us. He subjects Himself to us and wishes us to take the command, and He will do our will. If you feel happy, think of Him at His Resurrection, for the very thought of how He rose from the tomb will delight you. How He shone with splendour! How beautiful and majestic, how victorious, how joyful He was! What spoils He brought away from the battle, where He won a glorious kingdom that He wishes to make all your own! Is it much for you to look but once on Him who gives you such riches? If you have trials to bear, if you are sorrowful, watch Him on His way to the garden. What grief must have arisen in His soul to cause Him, Who was patience itself, to manifest it and to complain of it! See Him bound to the column, full of suffering, His flesh all torn to pieces because of His tender love for you—persecuted by some, spat upon by others, denied and deserted by His friends, with none to plead for Him. He is stiff with the cold, and in such utter loneliness that you may well console one another. Or look on Him again—laden with the cross, and not allowed to stay to take breath. He will gaze at you with those beautiful,

compassionate eyes, brimming with tears, and will forget His own grief to solace yours, only because you went to comfort Him and turned towards Him.[4]

5. 'O Prince of all the earth, Thou Who art indeed my Spouse!' you may say, if your heart has been so melted at seeing Him in this state that not only do you look at Him, but you feel delight in speaking to Him, (not in any fixed form of prayer, but out of your compassion, which greatly touches Him:) 'art Thou reduced to such sore straits, my Lord, my only Good, that Thou art willing to consort with such a miserable comrade as myself? Yet Thy looks tell me that Thou findest some comfort even in me. How can it be that Thou art forsaken by the angels, and that Thy Father consoles Thee not? If it be Thy will to suffer thus for me, what do I suffer for Thee in return; Of what have I to complain? Shame at seeing Thee in such plight shall make me endure all the trials that may come to me: I will count them gain that I may imitate Thee in something. Let us go together, Lord: "whither Thou goest, I will go," and I will follow where Thou hast passed.'[5]

6. Never mind if the Jews trample you underfoot, if only you can save Him any pain. Take no notice of what is said to you; shut your ears to all murmurings; stumble and fall with your Spouse, but do not draw back from the cross[6] nor abandon it. Often recall His weariness and how much

[4] Saint Teresa wrote here in the margin of the Escorial MS.: 'Exclamations.'

[5] Ruth, i, 16: 'Quocumque enim perrexeris, pergam,'

[6] *Life*, xi, 15; xxii, 18.

harder His labours were than your own, however great you may fancy these to be and whatever pain they cause you. This will console you: you will go away comforted, seeing that they are but trifles compared with what our Lord bore.

7. Perhaps you will ask me, sisters, how you are to do this now, though if you had lived while Christ was on earth and had seen Him with your bodily eyes, you would willingly have done it and would have watched Him constantly. Do not believe this; if you will not use a little self-constraint now[7], in order to recollect yourselves and to picture our Lord in your mind (which may be done without danger and solely by a slight effort), much less would you have stood at the foot of the cross with the Magdalen, who had the risk of death before her eyes. What must have been the sufferings of the glorious Virgin and of this blessed saint! What threats, what evil words, what insolence, what shocks and pain! The rude populace they had to deal with were truly fiendish, being the devil's own instruments. Terrible must have been their ordeal, yet it was effaced by a still more bitter pain.[8] Therefore, sisters, do not imagine that you would have endured these heavy trials, seeing that you cannot bear the light ones you meet with now: practise patience with these, and you may receive greater crosses later on. You can believe what I say, for I am speaking from personal experience.

[7] 'Our good Jesus and His most blessed Mother are too good company to be left, and He is well pleased if we grieve at His pains, even though sometimes at the cost of our own comfort and pleasure.' (*Castle*, M. VI. vii, 16).

[8] Escorial, xliii. Continuation of the same subject. Commences to explain a devout and pleasant way of reciting the *Pater Noster*.

8. It would be very helpful if you wore a medal or some picture of our Lord that pleases you. Do not merely hang it round your neck never to look at it, but often speak to it: He will teach you what to say. If you can find words for other people, why can you not speak to God? Do not fancy that you are unable. I, at least, will not believe that you cannot do so if only you endeavour to accustom yourselves to it. Unless you do this, you will find nothing to say. When we never talk to people we become estranged from them and do not know how to address them: even if they are relations they seem like strangers, for kinsfolk and friends become lost to us if we keep aloof from them.

9. It is very helpful to read a book of devotion[9] in the vulgar tongue, so as to learn how to collect the thoughts and to pray well vocally, thus, little by little, enticing the soul by coaxing and persuasion, so that it may not take alarm. Be wary, for it has deserted its Lover many years ago, and needs very careful management to induce it to return to its home. We sinners have so accustomed ourselves and our thoughts to run after pleasure (or pain, as it might more fitly be called), that the poor soul no longer understands itself, and needs many stratagems to make it stay with its Bridegroom; yet unless we succeed in doing this, we shall accomplish nothing. Once again do I assure you that if you carefully practise what I have taught you—that is, if you consider in Whose company you are, and if you speak to your Saviour—your

[9] *Life*, iv, 13.

reward will be too great for me to describe even if I wished. Keep close beside this kind Master[10] and firmly resolve to learn all that He teaches you.[11] He will ensure your proving good scholars, and will never leave you unless you first desert Him. Meditate on the words those divine lips uttered: you will at once realize what love He bears you, and it is no small gain and joy for the pupil to feel sure of his Tutor's affection.

CHAPTER XXVII[1]

SPEAKS OF THE GREAT LOVE SHOWN US BY OUR LORD IN THE FIRST WORDS OF THE PATER NOSTER. HOW IMPORTANT IT IS THAT THOSE WHO SINCERELY DESIRE TO BE THE DAUGHTERS OF GOD SHOULD DESPISE ALL PRIDE OF BIRTH

1. 'Our Father Who art in heaven.' God our Father. 2. Thanking our Lord for having given Him to us as our Father. 3. Our dignity as children of God. 4. Contempt to be felt for aristocratic lineage. 5. Love for our heavenly Father.

'OUR FATHER WHO ART IN HEAVEN.'

1. O my God, how worthy art Thou to be the Father of such a Son, and how manifest it is that He is Thy Son indeed! Mayest Thou be for ever praised! Would not this great favour have come more suitably at the end of the prayer? From the

[10] *Life*, xii, 3, 4.

[11] A confessor of the Saint, who was extremely learned, one day asked what she did when she had finished her prayer. He supposed that she gave her thoughts to other matters, but she replied: 'Imagine a person so deeply in love that it is impossible for him to live apart from the object of his affection for a moment. Yet his love could not be compared with that I feel for our Lord, which prevents my quitting Him for an instant, either consoling myself with His presence, or speaking with Him or about Him.' (*Ribera*, bk. IV. x.)

[1] Valladolid edition, xxix; Escorial, xliv.

very first Thou dost fill our hands and dost grant us a grace so great that it would be well if the understanding could be absorbed so as to preoccupy the will, and make us unable to say another word. How appropriate, my daughters, would be perfect contemplation here! Well might the soul retreat into itself, the better to rise above self, so that this holy Son might teach us what the 'heaven' is like in which He tells us that His Father abides. Let us leave this world, daughters, for we ought not to hold this favour so cheap, after we have once realized its value, as to remain on earth any longer.

5. O Thou Son of God and Lord of mine! Why dost Thou give us so much with the very first word Thou speakest? Besides humbling Thyself to the dust by joining Thy petitions to our own and by making Thyself the Brother of such miserable wretches as ourselves, Thou dost give us, in Thy Father's name, all that can be given—Thou dost ask Him to make us His children, and Thy word cannot fail, but must perforce accomplish its object. Thus dost Thou bind Him to do Thy will which implies no slight obligation, for since He is our Father, He must bear with us however deeply we offend Him, if like the prodigal son, we return to Him. He must pardon us; console us in our trials; maintain us in a way that becomes Him Who must needs be a far better Father than any earthly parent, since all His attributes must be supreme in their perfection. More than this, He must make us brethren and co-heirs with Thee! Thy love for us, O Lord, and Thy humility remove

all obstacles: besides Thy having lived on earth clothed with a mortal body offers some reason for Thy caring for us, seeing that Thou dost share our nature. But remember that, as Thou hast told us, Thy Father dwells in heaven, therefore Thou shouldst guard His honour. Although Thou hast offered Thyself to suffer shame for our sake, yet leave Him free! Impose no such ties upon Him on behalf of any one so guilty as myself, who will most certainly requite Him ill. O good Jesus! how clearly Thou hast shown that Thou art One with Him, that Thy will is His, and His is Thine. What confession of Thy love for us could be more clear? Thou didst perplex the devil and hide from him that Thou wert the Son of God, but Thine ardent longing for our welfare made Thee set aside all else in order to grant us this sublimest favour. I wonder that the devil did not guess, from this word alone, Who Thou art, to the exclusion of any doubt. Who but Thyself could have bestowed it on us Lord? I see that like a dearly loved Son, Thou didst speak both for Thyself and for us, and through Thy power didst obtain that Thy petition made on earth should be granted in heaven. Blessed mayest Thou be for ever, Lord, Who dost so love to give that naught can stay Thy hand.[2]

3. Now, daughters, do you not consider Him a kind Master, for He begins by conferring on us this signal grace, in order to persuade us to learn what He is teaching us? Do you not think it would be well for us to efface from our minds the meaning of this prayer while we say it with our lips,

[2] Escorial editon, xlv. It is most important that those who sincerely wish to be daughters of God should ignore pride of birth,

lest our hearts should be rent in pieces at the very idea of such a love? Yet no one could say this who recognized the depths of this tenderness. What son could be found on the face of the earth who would not try to discover who his father was if the latter had been as good, as princely, and as powerful as our heavenly Father? If God were not such as He is, I should feel no surprise at our reluctance to be called His children. It is the way of the world for a son to feel ashamed of recognizing a parent in an inferior position. Such a thing cannot happen here, for, please God, none of us ever think of such things. Let the nun who comes of the highest family be the last to mention her father: we must all be equals here.

4. O blessed College of Christ! which, by His wish, ranked St. Peter the fisherman higher than St. Bartholomew,[3] who was a king's son. His Majesty foresaw how the world would wrangle over the question of who was formed of the finest clay—which is like disputing about whether clay is fittest for making bricks or a mud wall! Good God, what a misery this is! May He deliver you, sisters, as I trust He will, from such contentions, were they only in fun. When you notice anything of the sort in one of the nuns, you must at once apply some remedy. Let her dread lest she be a Judas among the Apostles. Rid yourselves, if possible, of such a bad companion; but if this cannot be done, impose on her penances until she understands that she is not fit to be even common clay.

[3] Some medieval writers thought the name Bartholomew was derived from the Chaldean word *Bar* (Son) and the name of Ptolemy, as though the Apostle had been a descendant of the Macedonian dynasty.

5. You have a good Father given you by the holy Jesus: let no other father be known here through any words of yours. Strive, daughters, to merit God's caresses; cast yourselves into His arms. You know that He will never send you from Him while you remain dutiful children. Who would not guard against losing such a Father? Ah, what a consolation this is! Still, rather than enlarge on the subject, I prefer to leave it to your own thoughts, for, however inconstant your imagination may be, between such a Son and such a Father the Holy Spirit must perforce be found. May He inflame your will and constrain you with most fervent love, since even your own great gain suffices not to urge you to it.

CHAPTER XXVIII[1]

DESCRIBES THE PRAYER OF RECOLLECTION AND LAYS DOWN RULES FOR PRACTISING IT. [ESCORIAL: BEGINS TO TEACH HOW TO RECOLLECT THE MIND.]

1. 'Who art in heaven.' Where this 'heaven' is. 2. How God makes His heaven in our soul. 3. It is false humility not to recognize this. 4. The prayer of recollection. 5. Its advantages. 6. Exterior signs of recollection. 7. Result of practising recollection. 8. How it helps our progress. 9. The interior palace. 10. How to treat our Divine Guest. 11. How He dilates our soul. 12. What He asks of us in return.

'WHO ART IN HEAVEN.'

1. Do you suppose it is of little consequence whether or not you know what this heaven is, and where you must seek your most holy Father? I assure you that it is most important for restless minds not only to know this but to realize it by

[1] Valladolid edition, xxx,; Escorial, xlvi.

experience, for it is a most efficient means of concentrating the thoughts, and of recollecting the soul. You know that God is everywhere, which is most true. Now, the place in which the king dwells[2] is called his court: so, wherever God dwells, there is heaven, and you may feel sure that all which is glorious is near His Majesty.

2. Remember what St. Augustine tells us—I think it comes in his *Meditations;* how he sought God in many places and at last found the Almighty within himself.[3] It is of no slight importance for a soul given to wandering thoughts to realize this truth[4] and to see that it has no need to go to heaven in order to speak to the eternal Father or to enjoy His company: nor is it requisite to raise the voice to address Him, for He hears every whisper however low. We are not forced to take wings to find Him, but have only to seek solitude and to look within ourselves. You need not be overwhelmed with confusion before so kind a Guest, but, with utter humility, talk to Him as to your Father: ask for what you want as from a father: tell Him your sorrows and beg Him for relief, realizing at the same time that you are unworthy to be called His daughter.

[2] *Castle*, M.I. ii, 8.

[3] This quotation is from a medieval book bearing the title *Soliloquia of St. Augustine*, which was translated into Spanish from the edition of Venice of 1512, and published, together with the *Meditations* and the *Manuale* (hence St. Teresa's mistake) at Valladolid in 1515 and again at Medina del Campo in 1553, and at Toledo in 1565. The passage alluded to occurs in chapter xxxi. St. Teresa quotes it also in her *Life* (xl, 10) and in the *Interior Castle*, M. IV. iii, 3, and St. John of the Cross quotes another passage from the same work in the *Ascent of Mount Carmel*, bk. I. v, 1.

[4] *Life*, xiv, 7, 8 ; xviii, 20.

3. Lay aside a cerain reticence which some people maintain towards Him under the impression that it is humility. Humility would not lead you to refuse a favour from the king, but would make you accept and take pleasure in it although you recognized how little it was your due. What humility! I receive in my house the Lord of heaven and earth Who comes to show me kindness and to talk to me, and because of my *humility*, I neither answer nor remain with Him, nor accept His gifts, but go away and leave Him alone! And though He allows me and even bids me to ask Him for wealth, yet through humility I remain in my poverty, and even permit Him to depart because He sees that I want resolution to speak to Him. Practise no such humility; my daughters, but address Him sometimes as a Father or as a Brother, or again as a Master or as your Bridegroom: sometimes in one way and sometimes in another, for He will teach you what He wishes you to do. Do not be foolish: remind Him that He has promised to be your Bridegroom, and treat Him as if He were. Be convinced of your need of realizing that God dwells within you, and that you may remain there with Him.[5]

4. Although only vocal, yet this kind of prayer rivets the thoughts much more quickly than any other kind, and has many advantages. It is called 'recollection', because by its means the soul collects together all the faculties and enters within itself to be with God. The divine Master thus comes

[5] Escorial edition, xlvii. Begins to explain the prayer of recollection.
[6] *Life*, xiv, 2, sqq. *Rel.* viii. 3, 23.

more speedily than He otherwise would to teach it and to grant the prayer of quiet. For, being retired within itself, the spirit can meditate on the Passion and can there picture in its thoughts the Son, and can offer Him to the Father without tiring the mind by journeying to find Him on Mount Calvary, or in the garden, or at the column.

5. Those who are able thus to enclose themselves within the little heaven of their souls where dwells the Creator of both heaven and earth, and who can accustom themselves not to look at anything nor to remain in any place which would preoccupy their exterior senses, may feel sure that they are travelling by an excellent way, and that they will certainly attain to drink of the water from the fountain, for they will journey far in a short time. They resemble a man who goes by sea, and who, if the weather is favourable, gets in a few days to the end of a voyage which would have taken far longer by land. These souls may be said to have already put out to sea, and though they have not quite lost sight of *terra firma*, still they do their best to get away from it by collecting their faculties.

6. If this recollection is genuine it is easily discerned, for it produces a certain effect that I cannot describe, but which will be recognized by those who know it from personal experience. The soul seems to rise from play—for it sees that earthly things are but toys—and therefore mounts to higher things. Like one who retires into a strong fortress to be out of danger, it withdraws the senses from outward things, so thoroughly despising them that involuntarily the eyes close so as to veil from the

sight what is visible, in order that the eyes of the soul may see more clearly. Those who practise this prayer almost always keep their eyes shut during it. This is an excellent custom for many reasons, because one thus forcibly prevents oneself from looking at earthly things. This restraint is only required when one first begins to practise this prayer: later on a strong effort would be needed to open the eyes. The soul appears to gather strength and to dominate itself at the expense of the body, which it leaves lonely and enfeebled and thereby gains a stronger empire over it.

7. At first these signs are not apparent, as the recollection, which may be more or less, is not very great. In the beginning it requires a painful effort, for the body claims its rights, not understanding that its rebellion is suicidal. Yet, by persevering in the habit for several days, and by controlling ourselves, the benefits that result will become clear. We shall find that when we begin to pray the bees will return to the hive and enter it to make the honey without any effort on our part, for our Lord is pleased to reward the soul and the will by this empire over the powers in return for the time spent in restraining them. Thus the mind only requires to make them a sign that it wishes to be recollected and the senses will immediately obey it and retire within themselves. Although afterwards they may wander again, still it is a great thing to have conquered them, for they go forth as captives and servants and cannot do the mischief they did before. When the will recalls them they return more quickly, until after they

have re-entered a number of times, our Lord is pleased that they should settle entirely in perfect contemplation.

8. Pay great attention to what I have said, for though it may seem obscure, yet any one who practises it will understand it. Since we can thus make the journey by sea, and it is imperative for us to lose no time over it, let us consider how to accustom ourselves to such a good habit. Souls are thereby delivered from many occasions of sin, and are more easily inflamed by the fire of divine love, for as they are near this fire, any little spark that reaches them will, with but a mild blast of the understanding, at once ignite them. Exterior hindrances being removed, the soul is alone with its God and is predisposed to take fire.

9. I wish you to understand this prayer thoroughly: as I told you, it is called the prayer of recollection.[7] Let us realize that we have within us a most splendid palace[8] built entirely of gold and precious stones—in short, one that is fit for so great a Lord—and that we are partly responsible for the condition of this building, because there is no structure so beautiful as a soul filled with virtues, and the more perfect these virtues are the more brilliantly do the jewels shine.[9] Within this palace dwells the mighty King Who has deigned to become your Father, and Who is seated on a throne of priceless value—by which I mean your heart.

10. At the first glance you may think that such

[7] Escorial, xlviii. Makes a comparison and suggests a way of accustoming the soul to retire within itself.

[8] *Castle*, M. I. i, 2, sqq. [9] *Castle*, M. II. i, 1-4.

a simile to explain this truth is far-fetched, yet it may prove very useful to you, for we women are not learned and must make use of every means in order to understand well that we have within us an incomparably greater treasure than anything we can see around us. Let us not fancy that the centre of our soul is empty: God grant that none but women may overlook this fact. If we took care to remember what Guest we have within us, I think it would be impossible for us to give ourselves up so much to worldly vanities and cares, for we should see how vile they are in comparison with the riches within us. What more do the brutes do than satisfy their hunger by seizing on whatever takes their fancy? Yet how different should we be from them, seeing that we are children of a heavenly Father! Perhaps you will laugh at me and say that this is obvious enough. You may be right, yet I took a long time to realize it. Although I knew that I possessed a soul, yet I did not appreciate its value, nor remember Who dwelt within it, because I had blinded my eyes with the vanities of this life. I think that, had I understood then as I do now, that so great a king resided in the little palace of my soul,[10] I should not have left Him alone so often, but should have stayed with Him sometimes and not have kept His dwelling-place in such disorder.

[10] 'Remember that the Word, the Son of God, together with the Father and the Holy Ghost, is hidden in essence and in presence in the inmost being of the soul. The soul therefore, that will find Him must go out from all things in will and affection, and enter into the profoundest recollection, and all things must be to it as if they existed not.... O thou soul, most beautiful of creatures, who so earnestly longest to know the place where thy Beloved is, that thou mayest seek Him and be united to Him! Thou art thyself that very tabernacle

11. How wonderful it is that He Who by His immensity could fill a thousand worlds should enclose Himself within so narrow a compass![11] Thus was He pleased to be contained within the bosom of His most holy Mother. He is Lord, therefore He is free to act, and loving us as He does, He accommodates Himself to our measure. At first, lest the soul should feel dismayed at seeing that a thing so petty as itself can contain One Who is infinite, He does not manifest Himself[12] until, by degrees, He has dilated it as far as is requisite for it to contain all that He intends[13] to infuse into it. I say that 'He is free to act', because He is able to enlarge this palace.

12. The chief point is that we should resolutely give Him our heart for His own and should empty it of everything else, that He may take out or put in whatever He pleases as if it were His own property. This is the condition He makes, and He is right in doing so: do not let us refuse it Him. Even in this life we find visitors very troublesome at times, when we cannot tell them to go away. As Christ does not force our will, He only takes what we give Him, but He does not give Himself entirely until He sees that we yield ourselves entirely to Him. This is an undoubted truth which I insist upon so often because of its great importance. Nor

where He dwells, the secret chamber of His retreat where He is hidden. Rejoice, therefore, and exult, because all thy good and all thy hope is so near thee as to be within thee; yea, rather rejoice that thou canst not be without it, for lo, "the kingdom of God is within you." (St. Luke xvii, 21).' St. John of the Cross, *Spiritual Canticle*, stanza i. 7, 8.

[11] *Life*, xviii. 17.

[12] *Castle*, M.VII. i, 9-12.

[13] *Castle*, M.IV. i, 5; ii, 5.

does He work within the soul to the same extent when it is not wholly given to Him—indeed, I cannot see how He could, for He likes all things to be done suitably. But, if this palace is crowded with common people and rubbish, how can it receive our Lord with all His court? It would be a great condescension on His part to stay even for a very short time amid such disorder. Do you think, daughters, that He is alone when He comes to us? Does not His Son say, 'Who art *in heaven*'? The courtiers of such a King do not leave Him in solitude: they throng round Him and pray for our welfare, for they are full of charity. Do not imagine that heaven is like this world, where, if a prince or prelate shows partiality for any one for some special reason or out of friendship, other people at once feel jealous and abuse the poor man who has never injured them, so that the favours he receives cost him dear.

CHAPTER XXIX[1]

CONTINUES THE INSTRUCTION ON THE PRAYER OF RECOLLECTION. THAT IT IS OF LITTLE CONSEQUENCE WHETHER OR NO THE PRIORESS LIKES US.

1. We should be indifferent to the partiality of the superior. 2. Human favour incompatible with divine consolations. 3. How to become recollected. 4. We must realize God's presence. 5. How recollection aids our vocal prayer. 5. Perseverance needed to acquire it.

1. FOR the love of God, sisters, do not wish to be the favourite of your Superior. Let each one do her duty, and if the Prioress is not pleased with her you may be sure our Lord will repay her and be satisfied with her. We did not come here to be rewarded in this life: let us keep our minds fixed on eternity and make no account of this world's matters, which do not even last our lifetime. To-day, another nun is the favourite—to-morrow, if she sees some greater virtue in you, the Superior will like you best—if not, it is of little consequence. Never give way to such thoughts which sometimes rise from some trifling matter and may worry you a great deal. Check them at once by reflecting that your 'kingdom is not of this world'[2] and that everything will come to an end, for there is nothing here that does not change.[3] But this is a poor remedy and an uncertain and imperfect one: it is best that you should be disliked and humbled and that you should wish to be so for the sake of that Lord Who

[1] Valladolid edition, xxxi; Escorial, continuation of xlviii.

[2] St. John xviii, 36: 'Regnum meum non est de hoc mundo.'

[3] Escorial edition, xlix. Continues the same subject. This chapter is very useful.

dwells within you. Turn your thoughts upon yourself and look within: there you will find your Master and your Bridegroom Who will never forsake you. The less consolation you receive from without, the more He will caress you. He is full of compassion, and never fails those who are afflicted and despised if they trust in Him alone. David tells us that he had 'never seen the just man forsaken':[4] and again, 'The Lord is nigh unto the afflicted.'[5] Either you believe this or you do not: if you believe it as sincerely as you ought, why are you anxious?

2. O my God! If only we really knew Thee, all things would be indifferent to us, for Thou givest in abundance to all who truly trust in Thee. Believe me, my friends, the grasp of this truth helps us immensely to see the deception of all worldly favours that prevent the soul from entering into itself. God have mercy on me! Who can make people understand this? Not I for certain, for although no one has better reason to say so than myself, yet I never realize it as I should do.

3. To return to my subject. Oh! if only I could describe how the soul holds intercourse with this Companion, the Holy of holies, with nothing to intrude on the solitude of itself and its Spouse whenever it seeks to retire within itself with its God into this 'heaven,' shutting the door against all the world. I say 'the soul seeks', because you must understand that this is not a supernatural state, but something which, with the grace of God, we can desire and obtain for ourselves. This

[4] Psalm xxxvi, 25: 'Et non vidi justum derelictum.'

[5] Psalm xxxiii, 19: 'Juxta est Dominus iis, qui tribulato sunt corde.'

'grace' is always implied whenever I say in this book that we are able to do anything, for without it we can do nothing—*nothing*—nor could we, by any strength of our own, think a single good thought.

4. This is not what is called silence of the powers; it is a recollection of the powers within the soul itself. There are several ways of acquiring the habit. Many books advise us to cast aside all other thoughts in order to approach God Who dwells in our souls: and they tell us that even in the midst of our occupations we should occasionally withdraw into ourselves, if only for a moment. It is always very profitable to remember Who resides within our hearts. All I desire is that we should realize to Whom our prayers are addressed,[6] and should remain in His presence and not turn our back on Him, as we appear to do if, while we are speaking to God, we occupy our thoughts with a thousand vanities. All this evil comes from our not really understanding that God is near us, but imagining that He is far away—and how very far away, if we must go to heaven to find Him! And dost Thou not deserve a glance from us, O Lord! since Thou art so near us? Unless the person we are speaking to looks at us, we think he is not listening: shall we then close our eyes so that we cannot see whether Thou dost attend to us or not? How could we tell whether our words were heard?

5. I want to teach you that, in order to accustom ourselves to quiet our mind with facility so that we may understand what we are saying and

[6] *Castle*, M. I. i, 9.

Whom we are addressing, we must withdraw our senses from outward things and keep them occupied within our souls. Then we shall possess heaven within us, since the King of heaven dwells there. Let us accustom ourselves to the fact that we need not call loudly to make God hear us: His Majesty will make us feel He is there. Thus we shall be able to recite, in great peace, such a prayer as the Pater Noster or any other that we select. We shall save ourselves a great deal of trouble, for God will aid us lest we grow weary. In return for the short time spent in forcing ourselves to keep near Him, He will make us understand by certain signs that He is listening.[7] Thus, if we have to recite the Pater Noster several times, He will show us that He heard us sufficiently the first time we said it, for He dearly loves to save us trouble. We need not repeat it more than once in a whole hour if we only apprehend that we are in His presence and know for what we are asking Him, and believe that He is willing to grant it, like a tender Father Who loves to be with us and to enjoy our company. He does not want us to make our head ache by much talking, and to those who do not know it He will teach this way of prayer. For the love of God, then, sisters, cultivate the habit of saying the Pater Noster with recollection; you will soon discover its advantages, for thus the soul is easily checked from losing self-control and the senses remain undisturbed, as I will explain to you. I beg of you to practise it although at first

[7] Escorial edition, 1. Explains the great advantages of this mode of prayer.

you may find it difficult, as it is harder for those unaccustomed to it. I assure you, however, that before long you will find that you need not tire yourselves by seeking the holy Father to Whom you pray, since He resides in your soul. For my part, I own that I never knew what it was to pray in peace until God taught me this way. The great benefits I have reaped from the habit of interior recollection have made me write about it here at such length. Perhaps all of you know this already: however, in the future some nun might not know: so you must not be annoyed at my having discussed it here.

6. To conclude, I advise whoever wishes to acquire this habit (which as I said we have the power to gain) not to grow tired of persevering in trying gradually to obtain the mastery over herself. This self-denial will profit any nun by making her senses serve her soul. If she wishes to talk, let her know that there is One within her to Whom she can speak: if she prefers to listen, let her realize that she can hearken to Him Who is nearer to her than all others. In short, let her be convinced that she may, if she likes, ever keep this holy companionship. Let her grieve when, for any length of time, she has deserted the Father of Whom she has such need. If possible, let her recollect herself often during the day in this way; if she is unable to do so, at least let her practise it occasionally. When accustomed to it, she will benefit greatly sooner or later; when once God has bestowed this grace on her, she would not exchange it for any earthly treasure. Nothing can be learnt without a certain amount of trouble. For the love of God, sisters,

reckon your time well spent in acquiring this habit. I know that, with His help, if you practise it for a year, or perhaps for only six months, you will gain it. Think what a short time that is for so great an advantage as laying this firm foundation, so that if our Lord wishes to raise you to a high degree of prayer He will find you prepared for it, since you keep close to Him. May His Majesty never allow us to withdraw from His Presence! Amen. Now we must learn what our good Master says next: how He begins to speak on our behalf to His most blessed Father, and what He asks, for we ought to understand this.

CHAPTER XXX[1]

THE IMPORTANCE OF UNDERSTANDING THE MEANING OF OUR PRAYERS. THE WORDS OF THE PATER NOSTER: 'HALLOWED BE THY NAME; THY KINGDOM COME.' HOW THESE APPLY TO THE PRAYER OF QUIET, OF WHICH THE EXPLANATION IS BEGUN.

1. 'Hallowed be Thy name.' Why our Lord mentioned our separate needs in the Pater Noster. 2. We must not make rash prayers. 3. 'Thy kingdom come.' Why this petition follows the last. 4. Of what the happiness of the heavenly kingdom consists. 5. This kingdom is in our souls. 6. The prayer of quiet. 7. How vocal prayer may end in divine union.

'HALLOWED BE THY NAME.'

1. Is there any one, however uncultured, who would not consider beforehand how to address a person of high rank of whom it was necessary to ask a favour? Would not one be careful to gratify

[1] Valladolid edition, xxxii; Escorial, li.

him, to avoid offending him, and to think over what one meant to petition for, and what use could be made of it, especially if the request were an important one, such as the good Jesus tells us to beg for? I think this point deserves serious consideration. Couldst Thou not, O my Lord! have included everything in one phrase, saying: 'Give us, Father, whatever we need'? For, as God knows all things, further words seem useless. O eternal Wisdom! This alone would have sufficed between Thee and Thy Father. Thus didst Thou address Him in the garden: Thou didst show Him Thy will and Thy dread, and didst submit Thyself to Him. But Thou knowest, O my God, that we are not as resigned as Thou wert to the will of Thy Father—there was need to name each thing we pray for, that we might decide whether it was what we wanted; if not, we would not ask it of Thee. Having free-will, we should not receive God's gift unless we had first chosen it, although it might be best for us—for we never think we are rich unless we see the money in our hands.

2. Alas, O God! what is it that paralyses our faith so that we cannot see how inevitably we shall some day be either punished or rewarded? This, daughters, is why you ought to understand what you beg for in the Pater Noster, so that if God bestows it you may not cast it back at Him. Always think first carefully over what you ask and whether it would be well for it to be granted. If not, do not make the petition but implore His Majesty to give you light, for we are both blind and fastidious: we do not relish the food that nourishes us but

prefer that which causes death—and what a death! full of horror and lasting to eternity.[2]

3. The good Jesus bids us say these words which ask that this kingdom may come in us—'Hallowed be Thy name; Thy kingdom come.' How great is the wisdom of our Master and our Spouse! It is well that we should all learn what we ask for when praying for this kingdom. His Majesty knew that, unless He enabled us to do so by giving us His kingdom here on earth, our natural defects would render us unfit either to hallow, praise, magnify, glorify, or extol the holy name of the eternal Father. The good Jesus therefore placed the two petitions close together. I will tell you what I understand about the matter, that you may realize what you are praying for, how eager we should be to gain it, and how we should strive to please Him Who can give it to us. If this subject does not please you, meditate on some other: God permits you to do so as long as you submit in all things to the teaching of the Church, as I always do myself. I will not give you this book until it has been read by competent judges: if it contains errors they come from ignorance and not from malice.

4. Among the many other joys, the principal happiness of heaven appears to me to consist in a disregard of all earthly things and in a peace and glory that dwell in a soul which rejoices in the bliss of its companions. It lives in perfect peace

[2] Escorial edition, lii. Comments on the words: 'Hallowed be Thy name; Thy kingdom come.' Commences the explanation of the prayer of quiet.

and feels supreme satisfaction in seeing that all those around it honour and praise God and bless His name, and in knowing that they never offend Him. In heaven every one loves Him; the soul cares for nothing but loving Him: it cannot cease to do so because it knows Him as He is. If only we really knew Him we should do the same in this world, although not so constantly and so perfectly as in heaven; yet very differently from what we do now.

5. You must imagine that I mean we must be angels in order to make this petition and to pray well vocally. This is what our divine Master wishes since He tells us to ask for so sublime a grace, for most certainly He would never order us to ask for impossibilities. And why should this be an impossibility for us during our exile here? Perhaps while we are voyaging by sea and are still on our journey, we shall not attain to the same perfection as do souls delivered from this prison, yet there are times when our Lord puts the weary travellers into a rest of the powers and a quietude of soul that show, by a foretaste, what those enjoy whom He brings to His kingdom. Souls to whom He gives in this world the 'kingdom' we ask for receive pledges encouraging them to trust confidently that they will one day enjoy for ever that happiness which on earth He only permits them to taste.

6. You would reproach me with speaking of contemplation, or it would be appropriate here, while writing of this petition, to treat of the beginning of pure contemplation, which is called the

'prayer of quiet'—yet I said I should only write about vocal prayer, and this might seem a contradiction. This I will not admit—for it would certainly be consistent with my promise. Excuse my mentioning the subject: as I said, I know that many people who practise vocal prayer are, without their knowing how, raised by God to a high state of contemplation. This is why I am most anxious that you should say your prayers well.

7. I knew a nun who could only make vocal prayer, yet, while keeping to this, she enjoyed all the rest as well. Unless she used oral prayer, her thoughts wandered to an unbearable extent—yet I wish we all made such mental prayer as she did! She spent two or three hours in reciting certain Pater Nosters and a few other prayers in honour of our Lord's Blood-sheddings. One day she came to me in great distress because she did not know how to make mental prayer nor could she contemplate, but was only able to pray orally. I questioned her and found that she enjoyed pure contemplation while saying the Pater Noster, and that occasionally God raised her to perfect union with Himself. This was evidenced by her conduct, for she lived so holy a life that I thank God for it, and I even envied her such vocal prayer. If this was the fact (as I assure you it was), let not any of you who are the foes of contemplatives feel sure that you run no risk of being raised to contemplation yourselves if you say your vocal prayers as well as you ought and keep a good conscience. This I felt bound to say: those who do not wish to know it need not read this part.

CHAPTER XXXI[1]

CONTINUES THE SAME SUBJECT AND DESCRIBES THE PRAYER OF QUIET. GIVES ADVICE TO SOULS IN THAT STATE. THIS CHAPTER IS VERY NOTEWORTHY.

1. The prayer of quiet is this 'kingdom.' 2. Its effects on soul and body. 3. How the soul then desires that God's name may be 'hallowed.' 4. A prolonged form of the prayer of quiet. 5. Advice respecting this prayer. 6. Distractions coming from the imagination. 7. Comparison of the babe and its mother. 8. Difference between the prayer of quiet and the prayer of union. 9. How to treat the wandering imagination. 10. Detachment required from souls in this state of prayer. 11. The divine predilection for such souls. 12. Vocal prayer a distraction during the prayer of quiet.

'THY KINGDOM COME.'

1. NEVERTHELESS, my daughters, I will try to tell you about the prayer of quiet as I have heard it explained or as our Lord has been pleased to make me understand it—perhaps in order that I might teach you. Here God seems to show us that He has heard our petition, and He begins to give us His kingdom in this world, so that we may truly 'hallow' and bless 'His name', and try to make others do the same. However, as I said, I have written elsewhere about the prayer of quiet,[2] so I will do little but touch on the subject here. This prayer is a supernatural state to which no effort of our own can raise us, because here the soul rests in peace—or rather, our Lord gives it peace by His presence, as He did to the just man Simeon. Thus all the faculties are calmed, and in some manner, in no way connected with the exterior senses, the spirit realizes that it is close to its God,

[1] Valladolid edition, xxxiii; Escorial, continuation of lii, and liii.

[2] *Life*, xiv., xv. *Concep.* iv. *Castle*, M. IV. i, 4, 5; ii, 3-8; iii, 7.

and that if it drew but a little nearer to Him, it would become one with Him by union. This is not because such a person sees Him either with the corporal or spiritual sight. Nor did the just Simeon see more outwardly of the glorious but poor Infant, and from the swaddling clothes that wrapped Him and the small number of attendants in the procession might rather have taken Him for a little pilgrim, the child of indigent parents, than for the Son of the heavenly Father. But the Babe Himself gave the old man light to recognize Him, as He enlightens the soul to recognize Him during the prayer of quiet. It cannot tell how it knows Him, yet it feels sure it is in that 'kingdom', or at least, near the King from Whom the kingdom is to come. So reverential is the awe felt by such a soul that it dares ask nothing of God.

2. This state resembles a swoon, both exterior and interior, so that the exterior man (or as I will call it 'the body', lest some simpleton among you may say she does not know what 'exterior' and 'interior' mean) does not wish to move, but rests like a traveller who, having nearly come to his journey's end, stops so that he may start again refreshed, for the strength of the soul is now double what it was. The body feels enjoyment while the spirit is supremely satisfied and so delighted at finding itself near the fountain that, before even tasting the water, its thirst is quenched and there seems nothing left to desire. The faculties are reluctant to stir;[3] all action seems to impede their loving God—yet they are not entirely lost, for

[3] *Life*, xv, 1.

they can and do realize, by peaceful contemplation, in Whose Presence they are. Two of them are free; the will alone is captive, and, if capable of feeling pain at this time, can only do so at the thought that it will regain its liberty. The mind, centres itself on one thing only and works but little, and the memory tries to remember nothing else, for both see that this is 'the one thing needful' and that anything else disturbs them. At such a time, people wish the body to remain motionless; they think its movement would destroy their repose, therefore they dare not stir. Speaking troubles them: they spend an hour in saying one Pater Noster: being very close to God, they know that He understands them by signs. They are in the palace and near their King, and they perceive that here on earth He is beginning to bestow on them His 'kingdom.'

3. At times they shed a few tears, not sadly but with extreme sweetness: their only wish is that the name of God may be 'hallowed'. They seem no more to belong to this world—they neither wish to look at nor to listen to aught but God: nothing troubles them, nor does it seem as if anything ever could do so again. In short, while the prayer of quiet lasts, the soul is so intoxicated with delight and joy that there no longer seems anything left to wish for, and it would gladly cry with St. Peter: 'Lord, let us build here three tabernacles'![4]

4. Occasionally during the prayer of quiet God bestows on the soul another grace that is difficult to understand by any one who has not experienced

[4] St. Matt. xvii, 4: 'Domine, . . . faciamus hic tria tabernacula.'

it. Any among you who have done so will recognize it at once and will be very glad to know what it is. I believe God often gives this favour with the other. When the quiet is great and lasts long I think the will must be held fast in some way, or such peace could not be protracted. Sometimes, although we cannot understand how, it lasts for one or two days. I am speaking here of souls raised to this degree of prayer.[5] They are conscious that their attention is not entirely given to whatever they may be doing, but that the chief factor —that is, the will—is wanting. I believe that it is united to God, leaving the other powers free to attend to His service. The latter are more apt than ever for this but are dull and at times even imbecile concerning worldly affairs. God grants a great favour to these souls, for the contemplative and active life are here combined. Thus the whole being serves Him, for the will, while rapt in contemplation, works without knowing how, and the other two powers share Martha's labour—thus Martha and Mary toil together.[6] I knew some one whom our Lord often raised to this state. She could not understand it, and questioned a great contemplative,[7] who told her that such a thing was quite possible and indeed had happened to himself. From the soul's feeling such entire satisfaction, I believe that during most of the time the

[5] St. Teresa, afraid of having betrayed what favours she had received, changes the pronoun to the third person. (*Œuvres.*)

[6] *Life*, xvii, 6. *Rel.* viii, 6. *Concep.* vii. *Castle*, M. VII. i, 14; iv, 17. *Way of Perf.* xvii, 4.

[7] St. Teresa wrote on the margin of the Toledo edition that the contemplative was Father Francisco Borgia, Duke of Gandia. The *Book of the Life*, xxiv, 4, gives an account of her friendship with him.

prayer of quiet lasts, the will must be united to Him Who alone can satisfy it.

5. Perhaps it would be well to give some advice to those to whom God, solely out of His beneficence, has granted this prayer. This I know has been the case with some among you. Firstly, souls feel this joy, and though they do not know where it came from and see that they could not gain it for themselves, yet they are tempted to imagine they can retain it, and even try to do so by holding their breath. This is absurd—we cannot make the day break nor can we stop night from coming on. This prayer is no work of ours: it is supernatural and utterly beyond our control. The surest way to prolong it is to recognize that we can neither diminish nor add to it, and, unworthy as we are, we can but receive this grace with thanksgiving—and this, not by daring to utter many words, but like the publican by merely raising our eyes.

6. It is well to seek solitude so as to give place to our Lord and to allow Him to do His work. We may occasionally make a gentle aspiration, as one blows a candle that is going out in order to rekindle it, though if it had been burning brightly our breath would only have extinguished it. I think we should ignite it gently, for by straining our minds to compose long sentences the will might be disturbed. Pay great attention to the following piece of advice. You will often find that you cannot aid yourselves with either of the other powers: while the soul is immersed in peace the wandering mind or the imagination (I do not

know which it is) meanwhile is so distracted that it seems to take no part in what is passing in the house, but to be merely lodging in it as a stranger. Being unhappy at home, it looks for some other dwelling, not knowing how to enjoy this repose. Perhaps this only happens in my case, and other people do not suffer in the same way.[8] Sometimes —I am only speaking of myself—I long to die, so hopeless is it to attempt to control my thoughts. At other times the mind seems settled at home and stays with the will. When the three faculties concur this state resembles heaven. It may be compared to a loving married couple who are happy together and who both wish for the same things, but a bad husband makes his wife very wretched.

7. Mark well what I say, for it is most important. When the will enjoys this quiet, it should take no more notice of the understanding (or imagination) than it would of an idiot. If it tries to compel the imagination to keep it company, it will perforce be preoccupied and disturbed and in a state of painful struggle: thus, instead of profiting, the soul will lose what God was giving it without its having made any effort. Think well over the comparison which I am about to make— our Lord suggested it to me in this very state of prayer and it explains my meaning very clearly.[9] The soul is here like a babe at the breast of its mother, who to please it, feeds it without its

[8] *Castle*, M. IV. i, 8-13. *Life*, xv, 10; xxx, 19.

[9] St. Teresa wrote on the margin of the Valladolid edition: 'This comparison explains how it is possible to love without knowing that one loves, nor what one loves: a most difficult matter to comprehend.

moving its lips.[10] Thus it is now, for the soul loves without using the understanding. Our Lord wishes it to realize, without reasoning about the matter, that it is in His company. He desires that it should drink the milk He gives and enjoy its sweetness while acknowledging that it is receiving a divine favour, and that it should delight in its own happiness. He does not require the soul to know *how* it enjoys this, nor *what* it is enjoying, but to forget itself. He Who is beside it will care for its highest interests. Any effort made to constrain the mind to take part in what is passing will result in failure and the soul will be forced to lose the milk —that is, the divine nourishment.

8. The prayer of quiet differs from that of union,[11] in which the spirit is entirely united to God. In the latter, the soul does not even swallow the nourishment which without its knowledge God Himself places within it. During the former prayer He appears to wish the soul to work a little, although with so much ease as hardly to be conscious of any labour. My meaning will be clear to any one who has enjoyed this degree of prayer if she reads this attentively: what I say is important, although to others it may seem only jargon. In this state the mind disturbs the soul, which is not the case when there is union of the three faculties. Their Creator then suspends them, the delight He bestows on them keeping them occupied without their being able to understand why. Therefore during this prayer of union, which is a peaceful and supreme content of the will together

[10] *Concep.* iv, 6. *Castle*, M. IV. iii, 9. [11] *Life*, xvii, 5, 6.

with a feeling of repose, the soul cannot decide with certainty what it enjoys, although recognizing the immense difference between this and all earthly pleasures. To possess the whole world with all its delights would not bring such happiness to the interior of the will, for, as it appears to me, all the joys of this life only reach the exterior of the will, or its rind as we may call it.

9. When any of you find yourselves in the high state of the prayer of quiet—which as I said is manifestly supernatural—if the mind, or to speak more clearly, the imagination, wanders about after the greatest nonsense in the world, laugh at it, treat it as a lunatic, and maintain your own peace.[12] Thoughts will come and go, but here the will is mistress and recalls them without your troubling yourselves in the matter. If you try to control them by force you will lose your power over them which comes from the divine nourishment within you, and neither the one nor the other will gain but both will be losers. As the proverb says: 'Grasp at too much and you will catch nothing,'[13] and this seems the case here. Experience will bring my meaning home to you; without it, what I have told you may well seem superfluous and obscure. However, a very little acquaintance with it will make my words clear: they may help your soul, and you will thank God for having enabled

[12] Everybody is not so distressed and assaulted by these weaknesses as I have been for many years. . . . The thing is inevitable, therefore do not let it disturb or distress you, but let the mill clack on while we grind our wheat; that is, let us continue to work with our will and intellect. (*Castle*, M. IV. i, 12).

[13] The Spanish proverb says; *Quien mucho abarca, poco aprieta*—too large a load is most of it dropped.

me to explain the matter. We need a great deal of experience to understand this until we have read about it: afterwards we easily comprehend it. To conclude with, it may be affirmed that when the soul is raised to this prayer the Father has granted its request and His 'kingdom' has 'come' to it on earth.

10. O holy prayer, wherein unwittingly we crave so great a good! What a blessed petition to make! This, sisters, is the reason I want us to say the Pater Noster and other prayers with care and to think about what we ask for in them. Most certainly, when once God has shown us this favour, we ought to forget all worldly things, for the Lord of the whole earth has come and cast them forth. I do not mean that all who have enjoyed the prayer of quiet must necessarily be detached from everything in this world; but I wish them to know what they ought to be, and to try to mortify themselves in every way, otherwise they will stop here. They should not ask for so precious a gift as if it were worthless, and if God grants it them, let them not throw it back at Him.

11. God shows, by bestowing these pledges on the soul, that He designs it for great things. The fault will be its own if it does not make great progress. However, if He sees that after He has set within it the kingdom of heaven it returns to this world, not only will He desist from revealing to it the mysteries of His kingdom, but He will only show it the former favour at rare intervals and for a short time. I may be mistaken, but I have both seen and known that this occurs. I

believe that the reason why so many persons fail to become thoroughly spiritual[14] is that they do not worthily respond by their actions to this signal grace by preparing themselves to receive it again. They withdraw from our Lord's hands their will which He considered His property: as they centre their affections on base things, He seeks other souls whose love for Him is so fervent that He can grant them even more sublime favours. Still, He does not altogether deprive the former persons of what He gave them, provided they keep a good conscience.

12. There are many souls (and I was among their number) whom God moves to devotion and visits with holy inspirations and light[15] to know the worthlessness of all earthly things, and on whom He finally bestows His kingdom in this prayer of quiet. Yet these souls close their ears against Him because they prefer to speak and to hurry through a number of vocal prayers as if a task has been set them to say a certain amount every day. Thus when our Lord puts His kingdom into their possession by means of the prayer of quiet and interior peace, they will not accept it, but think they can do better by reciting prayers which distract their attention. Do not imitate them, my sisters, but be attentive when God gives you this grace; think what a priceless treasure you would lose, and be assured that you had far better say one petition of the Pater Noster from time to time than repeat the whole prayer mechanically and hurriedly over and over again. He to Whom

[14] *Castle*, M. IV. ii, 7; M. V. ii, 4, 5; iv, 2, 9.
[15] *Castle*, M. IV. ii, 6, 7.

you speak is very near you—He cannot fail to hear, and I believe that in this way we truly praise and 'hallow' His name.[16] Now that you are the inmates of His house, you glorify Him with stronger love and desire; indeed, it seems as if you could not choose but serve Him. I advise you to be very careful about this, as it is of the utmost importance.

CHAPTER XXXII[1]

EXPLAINS THE WORDS OF THE PATER NOSTER: 'THY WILL BE DONE ON EARTH AS IT IS IN HEAVEN.' HOW MUCH IS EFFECTED BY UTTERING THESE WORDS WITH ATTENTION, AND HOW RICHLY GOD REWARDS US FOR IT.

1. 'Thy will be done.' God requires us to give Him our will in return for all He has given us. 2. His grace enables us to do so. 3. To shrink from crosses on account of our weakness is false humility. 4. An act of resignation. 5. The vow of obedience. 6. The will of God means suffering for us. 7. The vow of obedience is the jewel that nuns offer Him. 8. Perfect contemplation impossible without entire resignation of our will to God. 9. An offering of the will. 10. God's kingdom given us in return for the gift of our own will. 11. God gives us His will. 12. Humility the path to contemplation.

'THY WILL BE DONE ON EARTH AS IT IS IN HEAVEN.'

1. So great is the gift that our good Master has asked for us and has taught us to beg for ourselves, that it includes all we can desire in this life. He has done us the immense favour of making us His

[16] Directly novices entered the convent, St. Tesesa made them leave off vocal prayers and similar devotions, which they had practised in the world. She told the novice-mistresses to guide them by the way of mental prayer and the practice of the presence of God. (Deposition of Maria de San Francisco. Fuente, Vol. VI. 311, Note 22. See also *Visit.* 28).

[1] Valladolid edition, xxxiv; Escorial, liv.

brethren: let us now learn what Christ offers God on our behalf and what He wishes us to give His Father in return. We must first see what our Lord requests of us, for it is only right that we should do Him some service in acknowledgment of such supreme blessings. O good Jesus! whilst demanding so much for us, how little dost Thou give in return—how little, I mean, on our part—for it is as nothing compared with the debt we owe this mighty Monarch. And yet, my Lord, Thou hast not left us without means of repaying Him, for we give all we can if when we say the words, 'I wish that as Thy will is done in heaven so it may be done on earth,' we yield Him our wills.[2]

2. Thou hast done well, O our good Master! in making this petition come last, so that we may be able to accomplish what thou dost promise for us here. For truly, O Lord! hadst Thou not done so our task would have seemed hopeless; yet, since Thy Father bestows His kingdom on us at Thy prayer, I know that we can fulfil Thy promise by giving what Thou didst offer in our name. For since my 'earth' is now made 'heaven' it is possible for Thy will to be done in me; otherwise, in 'earth' so barren and so wretched, I know not how it could have come to pass. For Thou askest so great a thing.

3. I wish you, daughters, to realize its importance. I am amused at the thought of people fearing to ask for crosses from God. Some say it would be a want of humility to pray for crosses. I have met with other people who, without even

[2] *Life*, xx, 30. *Castle*, M. V. iii, 3. *Found.* v, 10.

this pretext, have not the courage to beg for the sufferings they think would be sent at once. Persons who refrain, out of humility, from demanding them, believe that they would not be able to bear such trials. For my part, I believe that He Who gives the love that longs for such a hard way of proving its sincerity would also give love enough to suffer. I would ask souls who will not sue for the crosses they fancy would be sent them immediately, whether they know what they are asking for when they beg that the will of God may be done in them? Do they simply repeat the words in imitation of other people? This, my daughters, would be exceedingly wrong. The good Jesus is here our Ambassador, Who at no small cost to Himself seeks to mediate for us with His Father, and it would be unfair for us to refuse to give what He pledges on our behalf— it would be better that we should never proffer it. I will put the case in a different way. Inevitably the will of God must be done—whether we wish it or no, it will prevail both in heaven and earth. Then take my advice; trust what I say and make a virtue of necessity.

4. O my God! well is it for me that Thou didst not leave such a wretch as myself at liberty to fulfil or to frustrate Thy will! What should I have done had it depended upon me whether Thy will should be done in heaven or on earth? Yet, although it is not purged from all self-seeking, freely do I yield my will to Thee, for experience has taught me what I gain by resigning my own will to Thine.[3] Mayest Thou be blessed for ever, and may

[3] *Foundations*, Prologue 1, 2; v, 6, 7.

all creation praise Thee: may Thy name be evermore glorified!

5. O my friends, what benefits this brings us! What do we not lose by withholding from God that which we offer Him in the Pater Noster! Before explaining all its advantages, I will show you all that you are offering here, lest you might afterwards say that you had been cheated and inveigled into it without understanding it. Do not copy certain nuns who make their vows but never fulfil them, pleading that they did not know what they undertook when they made their profession. This may well have been the case, for words are easy but deeds are hard, and if any one thought there was no difference between them, she was much mistaken. We can promise lightly enough to give up our will to somebody else, but when it comes to the test we shall find it the most difficult thing in the world to do thoroughly.[4] By means of a long probation, you should make persons who enter here clearly understand that they are bound to give *deeds* as well as *words*. Superiors are not always so strict, because they see our weakness; sometimes they treat both weak and strong in the same way. But God does not do this: He knows what each can bear, and when He finds a valiant soul He accomplishes His will in it.

6. I wish to remind you what is the will of God, so that you may know with Whom you have to deal, as the saying goes, and may realize what the good Jesus is offering to the Father on your

[4] Sister Dorotea de la Cruz says that whenever any of her daughters asked the Saint how to advance in virtue, she answered: 'By perfect obedience to the Rule.' (Fuente, vol. VI. 282, Note 3.)

behalf. Know that when you say: 'Thy will be done' you are begging that God's will may be carried out in you,[5] for it is *this*, and nothing else, for which you ask. You need not fear that He will give you riches, or pleasures, or great honours, or any earthly good—His love for you is not so lukewarm—He places a higher value on your gift and wishes to reward you generously, since He has given you His kingdom even in this life. Would you like to see how He treats those who make this petition unreservedly? Ask His glorious Son, Who in the garden uttered it truthfully and resolutely. See whether the will of God was not accomplished in the trials, the sufferings, the insults, and the persecutions sent Him, until at last His life was ended on the cross.[6] Thus you see, daughters, what God gave to Him He loved best: this shows what His will means. These are His gifts in this world, and He grants them in proportion to His affection for us. To souls He cherishes most He gives more—and fewer to those less dear to Him, according to their courage and the love He sees they bear Him. For fervent love can

[5] Although perforce we satisfy our obligation to avoid sin, yet we fall far short of what must be done in order to obtain perfect conformity to the will of God. What do you think, my daughters, is His will? That we may become quite perfect and so be made one with Him and with His Father, as He prayed we might be.... There is no need for us to receive any special gifts from God in order to arrive at conformity with His will; He has done enough by giving us His Son to teach us the way.... Our Lord asks but two things of us: love for Him and for our neighbour; these are what we must strive to obtain. Let us try to do His will perfectly; then we shall be united to Him. (*Castle*, M. V. iii, 7).

[6] Escorial edition, lv. That religious are bound to fulfil their vows by their actions.

suffer much for Him, while tepidity will endure but little. For my part, I believe that our love is the measure of the cross we can bear.[7]

7. Then, sisters, if you have this love, think of what you are doing: let not the promises you made to so great a God be only words of empty compliment, but force yourselves to suffer whatever God wishes. Any other way of yielding Him our will is like offering some one a jewel, begging him to accept it, and holding it fast when he puts out his hand to take it. It is shameful to trifle thus with One Who has done so much for us. Were there no other reason, it would be wrong to mock Him thus, again and again, whenever we repeat the Pater Noster. Let us give Him once for all the gem we have so often proffered Him—although He first gave us what we now tender to His Father. Ah, how well does Jesus understand us! He does not surrender our will to God in our name until we have already been amply repaid for this trivial service. This shows us what great benefits it will obtain for us from His Father, Who begins to recompense us for it in this life, as I will explain to you later on. People who live in the world do much if they sincerely resolve to submit their will to God, but *you*, daughters, must both say and act, must both vow and fulfil your vows, as indeed religious may truly be said to do.[8] Yet sometimes,

[7] The Saint was never impatient at her trials, but used to say: 'Let us bear this persecution and suffering, my daughters, for they come with our Lord's permission.' (Deposition of Mother Mary of St. Joseph. Fuente, vol. VI. 284. Note 11.)

[8] While Father Jerome Gracian was staying at Veas with St. Teresa he bade her ask our Lord whether she should make a foundation first

not only do we offer God our jewel, but we actually put it into His hand—then we turn round and take it back again. We are so generous at first, and so miserly afterwards, that it would almost have been better to have shown more caution in giving.

8. My whole aim in writing this book has been to incite us to yield ourselves entirely to our Creator,[9] to submit our will to His, and to detach ourselves from all created things. As you already understand how important this is I will say no more on the subject, but will explain to you why our good Master makes us say this petition. He well knows how we shall benefit by accomplishing the promise made to His eternal Father. In a very short time we shall find ourselves at the end of our journey and shall drink of the fountain of living water of which I spoke.[10] But unless we resign and conform our will entirely to the Divine will, we shall never obtain that water. This is the perfect contemplation that you wished me to write about. Here, as I have shown you, we can do nothing on our part. Here we neither

at Seville or Madrid. The answer was: 'At Madrid'. The Father Visitor replied: 'I, however, am of opinion that it should be at Seville.' The Saint made no answer, and immediately began to prepare to go there. Two or three days later Father Gracian asked her why she had obeyed him, who was only guided by reasons of prudence, rather than our Lord, although she had made a vow always to do what was most perfect. She said she could not be so sure of any revelation as she was of her Superior's command being the will of God, for she might be mistaken in revelations, but of this there could be no mistake. The Father ordered her to consult our Lord again: she was told that she had done well in obeying, and was to go to Seville. (*Yepes*, bk. II. xxvii).

[9] *Rel.* v, 3.

[10] *Way of Perf.* xix, 4.

work nor plan for ourselves, nor is it necessary, for everything, except the prayer 'Thy will be done,' would only hinder and disturb us.

9. In every way and in every matter, do Thy will in me, O Lord! as Thou pleasest. If Thou desirest to give me crosses, grant me strength and let them come: if Thou wouldst send me persecutions, shame, poverty, illness—I stand ready, nor will I turn away from them, O my Father! I have no right to flee from them, since Thy Son has offered Thee my will with the rest in the name of us all. Let Thy kingdom come to me as Thy Son has asked of Thee, so that I may fulfil Thy will. Dispose of me as of Thine own, according as Thou willest.

10. What power, sisters, lies in this gift of the will! Made with full determination, it is able to draw the Almighty to become one with our baseness and to transform us into Himself, thus uniting the creature with its Creator. Are you not well repaid? See how good your Master is! He knows how to gain His Father's good-will and teaches us how to do the same.[11] The more resolute we are and the more clearly our actions testify that ours are no empty vows, the closer does God draw us to Him. He raises us far above all earthly things and even above ourselves, that He may prepare us to receive heavenly favours. Even in this life He rewards us unceasingly for this service which He values exceedingly.

11. While we do not know for what more we

[11] Escorial edition, lvi. What God gives to souls that have abandoned themselves to His will.

could ask, His Majesty never wearies of giving us fresh favours. Not contented with having united such a soul to Himself, He begins to caress it and reveals His secrets to it. He is pleased at its understanding what it has gained and that it knows something of what He has in store for it. He deprives such a person of her exterior senses[12] lest they should disturb her. This produces what is called 'rapture.' His friendship with her becomes so intimate that not only does He restore her will to her but He gives her His own as well. For having made a close friend of her, God is pleased to take the command with her 'by turns', as we may say, and just as she obeys His commands, so He in return does what she asks of Him,[13] only in a far more complete manner, for being almighty He can do what He wills and He always wills to do this, while the poor soul cannot carry out all His wishes, however strong its desire may be. Neither has it power to do anything unless the grace is first given it, and yet it grows richer although the more it serves God the heavier grows its debt. It often becomes weary of being subject to so many drawbacks, obstacles, and bonds while imprisoned in the flesh, for it longs to pay God something of what it owes Him. This is very foolish, for when we have done all we can, what repayment can we make Him, since He has given us all we possess except self-knowledge?

12. The one thing which by the grace of God we can do is to utterly resign our will to His; all

[12] *Castle*, M. VI. iv, 17. *Rel.* viii, 8. *Life*, xx. 23, 29. *Concep.* vi.
[13] *Rel.* ix. 25.

else only hinders the soul that He has raised to this state: humility alone can help us here, and that not a humility won by means of our intellect but one gained by a pure intuition of the truth by which we perceive, in an instant, our own nothingness and the greatness of God with greater clearness than we could have learnt in many years by the use of our reason. But as I have already explained in another book[14] what contemplation is and how the soul should conduct itself in that state, and have described in detail the spirit's experiences and the knowledge it gains of the Divinity, I will only allude to it here, so that you may learn how to recite the Pater Noster. One piece of advice I will give you, however—do not fancy that any efforts or actions of your own can raise you to contemplation, for you would be mistaken; they would only cool any devotion you already felt—but with the simplicity and humility which obtain all things you must simply say: 'Thy will be done'.

[14] *Life*. xviii, sqq. *Rel.* viii, 8.

CHAPTER XXXIII[1]

HOW NEEDFUL IT IS FOR US THAT GOD SHOULD GRANT OUR DEMAND IN THE PATER NOSTER: 'GIVE US THIS DAY OUR DAILY BREAD.'

1. 'Give us this day our daily bread.' Why this 'Bread' is given us. 2. Without It we could not do God's will. 3. Our Lord asked It for us. 4. Reasons why Christ remains in the Blessed Sacrament. 5. Address to God the Father respecting It. 6. The Saint beseeches Him to protect the Blessed Sacrament from insults. 7. Humility shown by Jesus in this petition. 8. Appeal to the Father.

'GIVE US THIS DAY OUR DAILY BREAD.'

1. OUR good Jesus understood how difficult a thing He had promised on our behalf, for we are frail by nature and often succeed in persuading ourselves that we do not know what is the will of God. We are weak and He is merciful; thus He saw that some remedy was needed, for by no means ought we to desist from giving what He offered for us, since in this consists our highest good although it is a most difficult task for us to fulfil. For instance, if a rich man is told that he ought to moderate his table so that those who are dying of hunger may have bread to eat, he will find a thousand excuses for not understanding this better than he chooses. If you say to a scandal-monger that he is bound to love his neighbour as himself, he will lose all patience and nothing will convince him of the truth.

2. Declare to a religious who is accustomed to liberty and self-indulgence that he ought to give

[1] Valladolid edition, xxxv; Escorial, lvii.

a good example; that when he says, 'Thy will be done,' it is his duty to observe these words not only by tongue but by deed; that he has sworn and promised to do the will of God, and God's will is that he should perform his vows: represent to such a person that if he gives scandal, although he may not absolutely break his vows yet he infringes on them greatly—that he has taken a vow of poverty which he must in no way evade, for this is the will of God—yet you will never be able to bring such a man even to wish to do what is right. What, then, would have happened if our Lord had not done the principal part of our work for us by means of the remedy He has given us? Surely there would have been very few who would have fulfilled the promise He made in our name when He said to the Father, 'Thy will be done.' May He vouchsafe to grant that many may do so, even now!

3. Seeing our needs, the good Jesus found a most wonderful way by which to prove His excessive love for us—in His own and in His brethren's name He made this petition: 'Give us this day our daily bread, O Lord!'[2] For the love of God, daughters, let us realize the meaning of these words: our spiritual life depends on our not disregarding them.

4. Reckon as of little value whatever you may have given to God in comparison with this rich reward. It appears to me, although I submit my opinion to a higher judgment, that though the good Jesus knew what an advantage it would be

[2] Escorial edition, lviii. Treats of the great mercy shown us by the eternal Father in allowing His Son to remain with us in the most holy Sacrament.

for us to yield to His Father what He had offered on our behalf, yet He recognized the obstacles to our keeping our promise that come from our human nature, its tendency to degradation, and our want of love and courage. He saw that there was need to aid and encourage us, and this, not once for all, but day by day, therefore He determined to remain among us.

This being an immense grace, He wished it to come from the hand of His eternal Father, although, They both being One, He knew that whatever He did on earth God would hold good and ratify in heaven since His will and His Father's are identical. Yet, such is the humility of the good Jesus as man, that He appeared to ask leave for this favour although He realized how His Father loved and delighted in Him. Our Lord understood that we ask far more in this petition than in the rest, because He foresaw the death to which men would put Him and the shame and insults He would suffer.

5. O my God! what father could be found who, having given us his son, and such a son, would, after we had so ill-used him, have allowed him to remain among us to endure fresh wrongs? No such father could be found, save Thy Father, O Lord! Well didst Thou know of Whom Thou wast asking this boon. Ah! what excess of love in both the Father and the Son! I am not so amazed at the good Jesus; having already said: 'Thy will be done', for the sake of His word He was bound to accomplish it. I know that He is not like us, but as He recognized that He fulfilled His Father's

will by loving us as Himself, He sought how, although at His own cost, He might do this most perfectly. But why, O eternal Father! didst Thou consent to this? How couldst Thou see Thy Son daily in such wicked hands, after Thou hadst already permitted it once? Thou didst witness how they treated Him: how couldst Thou have the heart to see Him thus affronted day by day?[3] How many insults are being offered Him this very day in this most holy Sacrament! How often must His Father watch Him in the hands of His foes! What profanations are committed by the heretics!

6. O eternal Sovereign![4] How canst Thou then consent to such a request? How canst Thou permit such a thing? Yield not to His love which for the sake of fulfilling Thy will and of succouring us would lead Him to endure being hacked into a thousand pieces every day. It is for *Thee* to look to it, my God, since Thy Son is reckless what He suffers. Why must every good thing come to us

[3] I went to say Mass at her convent at Medina del Campo and was given a strongly perfumed towel when I washed my fingers. I thoughtlessly took offence at it, and told the holy Mother afterwards that she should order such an abuse to be stopped in her communities, for though I thought the corporals and altar-linen ought to be scented, it did not seem right to me that towels for toilet purposes should be so. She answered me with charming grace, saying: 'Now, you must not be annoyed, for the nuns learnt this defect from me. When I remember how our Lord reproached the Pharisee who had invited Him as a guest for not showing Him more attentions, I wish everything, from the threshold of the church-door, to be saturated with orange-flower water.' I was ashamed of my hastiness and set myself to look closely at everything relating nearly or remotely to the Blessed Sacrament. For this reason, her friars and nuns have grown so careful in the matter that the altars in their churches are more cleanly kept than in any part of the world of which I know.' (From a letter of Yepes to Fray Luis de Leon. Fuente, vol. VI. 139, Note 53, 54.)

[4] Escorial, lix. A petition to the Father.

only at *His* cost? How is it that He is mute and knows not how to speak for Himself, but only pleads for *us?* Shall no one intercede for this most meek and loving Lamb? Give *me* the right, Lord, to be His advocate, since Thou hast deigned to leave Him in our power and He submits His will to Thee thus utterly and gives Himself so lovingly to us.

7. In this petition alone does Christ repeat His own words: first He prays: 'Give us our daily bread', and then He says: 'Give us it this day, O Lord'.[5] He puts us in the first place when appealing to His Father, as much as to say that now, having once for all given us this gift, it is our own and He will not take it away from us until the end of the world, but will leave it for our succour every day. Let this win your hearts, my daughters, to love your Bridegroom, for though no slave in the world willingly acknowledges his bondage, yet the good Jesus seems to consider it an honour.

8. O eternal Father, how unspeakable is this humility! What treasure will suffice to purchase Thy Son for us? How to sell Him we know—that was done for thirty pieces of silver, but no riches will enable us to buy Him. Being made one with us by that portion of His nature which He had assumed, and being Master of His own will, He reminds His Father that, since His manhood is His own, He has the right to bestow it upon us. Therefore He says: '*Our* bread'; making no distinction between Himself and us, but ranking

[5] The wording of the Lord's Prayer in Spanish is: 'El pan nuestro de cada dia dánosle hoy'—literally 'Our daily bread, give us it to-day.'

us with Himself, so that as He daily joins His prayer with ours we may obtain from God that for which we ask.

CHAPTER XXXIV[1]

CONTINUES THE SAME SUBJECT. CONTAINS VERY USEFUL ADVICE FOR THOSE WHO HAVE RECEIVED HOLY COMMUNION. AN EXPLANATION OF THE WORD 'DAILY'.

1. What 'daily bread' means. 2. What 'this day' signifies. 3. The 'bread' of bodily sustenance. 4. For which we must trust to God. 5. As the servant trusts his master for maintenance. 6. And must only ask Him for the 'heavenly' bread. 7. Christ our food and medicine. 8. St. Teresa's Communions. 9. Why Christ remains hidden in the Holy Eucharist. 10. The time after Holy Communion. 11. Holy Communion.

1. THE good Jesus, having resolved to give Himself to us, asks His Father to allow Him to remain with us 'daily', which appears to mean 'for ever'. Yet, while writing this, I have been wondering why, having said 'daily', He should add, 'this day'. I tell you of my foolish thoughts so that, if they really are absurd, you may see what a simpleton I am—as indeed I must be, to dare to discuss such matters. Yet, as we are to think over what we are praying for, let us consider what this petition means, so that we may fulfil its obligations reasonably and may thank our Lord for taking so much trouble to teach us. I believe that 'daily' means that we may enjoy His presence while we dwell in this world, where He remains with us and we receive Him as our Food, and in heaven also, if we profit by His company here. His sole object in abiding

[1] Valladolid edition, xxxvi; Escorial, lx.

with us is to aid, to incite, to strengthen us to do the will of God which we have asked may be 'done' in us.

2. The term 'this day,' seems to mean the one day, and no more, during which this mortal life lasts—and indeed it is but a single day for the unfortunate wretches who condemn themselves to forfeit our Lord's presence in the next world. He has done all that He could to aid them, as His own children, while they lived on earth, dwelling with them and strengthening them, and if they are overcome He will not be to blame, for He never ceased to encourage them until the end of the fray. Lost souls will have no excuse to make for themselves, nor will they be able to accuse Christ's Father of depriving them of this Bread in their direst need. Therefore Jesus covenants with His Father that, since the world only lasts 'one day', He may be allowed to spend it in our service. As God has given Him to us and has sent Him on earth of His own free-will, it is incredible that He would deprive us of His Son when most we want Him, for the insults men offer Him will endure but for a single day. Our Lord respects the obligation He has contracted by offering our will in conjunction with His own, which binds Him to aid us to fulfil this promise by every means in His power; He is not willing to desert us, but desires to remain with us for the greater glory of His friends and the confusion of His enemies. He prays for nothing new when He says 'this day', for since His Majesty has given this food and manna for the children of men once for all, we can obtain it whenever we

please: we shall never die of famine except by our own fault, for the soul that receives the Blessed Sacrament will find in it whatever solace and help it requires. There is neither need, nor cross, nor persecution that cannot easily be borne when we once begin to share and to love those our Lord bore and to keep them ever in our hearts.

3. As regards the other bread—I mean bodily nourishment and wants—I neither wish you to remind God of them nor to remember them yourselves. Keep your thoughts as guarded as if you were raised to the heights of contemplation where one no more thinks of food than if one had already quitted this world. Would our Lord have laid such stress on our asking for our *meals?* It would not seem to me becoming either for Him or for us. He is here teaching us 'to fix our affections on things above'[2] and to pray that we may enjoy the first-fruits of them here: would He, then, bid us concern ourselves about anything so base as asking God for our sustenance? He knows perfectly well that, if we once began to concern ourselves about the needs of our bodies, we should soon forget the needs of our souls. Besides, who would carry prudence to such an excess? We are satisfied with little and we do not beg for much; the more men give the more the heavenly water appears to fail us. Let those of you, daughters, who are most anxious about our necessities, ask for this.

4. Join our Lord, then, in praying to His Father to let you have your Bridegroom 'this day', that

[2] Coloss. iii. 1: 'Quæ sursum sunt quærite.'

you may never be without Him in this world—your joy will be tempered by His remaining hidden beneath the accidents of bread and wine, which is a torture to those who can find no love or consolation elsewhere. Beg Him not to fail you but to give you grace to receive Him worthily. Since you have completely abandoned yourselves into the hands of God, have no care for any other bread but this: I mean while you are at prayer and are asking Him for other things of far greater importance, for there are times when you ought to work to gain your living,[3] although without feeling undue anxiety about it. Never trouble your mind about such matters, but while your body labours (for you ought to support yourselves) let your soul be at peace. As I have fully explained to you,[4] these cares should be left to your Bridegroom Who will always provide for you. Never fear that He will fail you, if you do not fail to keep your promise of resigning yourselves to the will of God. As for me, daughters, I assure you that if I deliberately broke this pledge, as I have often done before, I would neither ask Him to give me bread nor any other food: let Him leave me to die of hunger! For why should I seek to live, if every day I am making eternal death more inevitable?[5]

[3] 'Our holy Mother was very anxious that her nuns should not be idle. She was always busy herself, although her health was very delicate, and even when she went to the parlour she took her task of work with her.' (Deposition of Guiomar del Sacramento. Fuente, vol. VI. 320, Note 11.)

[4] *Way of Perf.* ii, 1, 6.

[5] Escorial, lxi. Continues the same subject; a comparison is given. This chapter is very useful for those who have received Holy Communion.

5. *A comparison.* If then you have truly surrendered yourselves to God, as you say, abandon all care of yourselves, for He cares for you and will always do so. We may be compared to a servant who enters into service with a householder: the domestic is obliged to do all he can to please his master and the master is bound to maintain the servant while employing him in his house, unless prevented by poverty from feeding either himself or his dependents. Here the case differs, for our Master is and always will be rich and powerful. It would seem very strange if the servant went to his employer every day to ask for his meals, knowing perfectly well that without this he would be fed and cared for. It would be waste of time, and his master might tell him to look after his own work, for if he worried himself about other people's business he would do his own badly.

6. Then, sisters, let who will demand this earthly bread. Let us speak to the purpose and beseech the Father to give us grace so to prepare ourselves for the reception of this sacred and heavenly food that, although our bodily eyes cannot rejoice in looking on Jesus, hidden as He is beneath the sacramental veils, yet He may reveal Himself to the sight of our soul and may teach us that this Bread is a special kind of nutriment, which contains in itself sweetness and joy, and sustains our life. Inadvertently, we shall often desire and pray for earthly things, but we need not purposely recall such matters to our minds. Our miserable tendency to whatever is base and low may often excite these thoughts against our will, but let us not deliberately ask for any gifts

except those I have recommended to you, for if we obtain these we obtain all the rest.

7. Do you not know that this most holy Sacrament is a most beneficial food even for our body and a powerful remedy for its diseases? I am sure that it is. I am acquainted with a person subject to severe illnesses which often cause her acute pain; she was freed from them instantaneously by this Bread,[6] and remained in perfect health. This often occurs, and people are cured of visible maladies which I do not think could be counterfeit. The miracles worked by this most holy Bread on those who receive it worthily are so well recognized that I will not say much about those which happened to the person I mentioned, although I know all about them and am sure of their truth. But our Lord had given her so lively a faith and devotion that when she heard people say that they wished they had lived while Christ, our only Good, dwelt in the world, she used to smile to herself, thinking that, while He so undoubtedly remains among us in the Blessed Sacrament, we have nothing left to desire.

8. Although she was far from perfect, yet I know that for many years my friend endeavoured so to strengthen her faith that whenever she received Holy Communion, at which time, as she believed, our Lord entered her poor little dwelling, she might as far as possible withdraw her mind from all earthly things and enter into herself with Him. She strove to control her senses in order that they might comprehend the grace she was

[6] *Life*, xxx, 16.

enjoying, or rather, that they might not prevent her soul from enjoying it. She imagined herself at the feet of our Lord and wept with Magdalen as if she had really seen Him in the house of the Pharisee. Even if she felt no devotion, faith told her that it was well for her to be there, and she continued conversing with Him. For unless we choose to be obtuse and to blind ourselves to the fact, we cannot suppose that Christ's presence here is only an image of our imagination, as when we think of Him on the cross or in any other phases of His Passion. These happened in the past, but He is here with us at the present moment in very truth: we need not go far to seek Him, for we know that our good Jesus remains with us until the accidents of bread have been consumed by our natural heat. Let us not lose this golden opportunity but let us stay in His company.

9. If, while Jesus lived in the world, the mere touch of His garments healed the sick, who can doubt that when He is dwelling in the very centre of our being He will work miracles on us[7] if we

[7] Saint Teresa felt an unspeakable joy, when founding a fresh convent, at the thought that there would be one more church in which the Blessed Sacrament would be reserved (see *Life*, xxxvi, 5). It was this that gave her strength to bear all the hardships of the journey and the other labours which she had to go through. While she was at St. Joseph's at Avila she was often enraptured after communicating and could not leave the little Communion grille, but had to be removed by the nuns. While she was at Toledo she went into an ecstasy after receiving the Blessed Sacrament. The sacristan, not suspecting what had happened, used great force to make the holy Mother sit down, even pulling her by both hands, but she remained leaning against the wall in a rapture, and was as immovable as a stone until she came to herself. She was seen to rise several feet in the air in the choir of St. Joseph's, Avila, after having communicated. (*Ribera*, bk. IV, xii.)

have a living faith in Him? And will He not grant our petitions while He is our guest? His Majesty is not a bad Paymaster for a good inn. Are you grieved at not seeing Him with your bodily eyes? That would not be expedient for us here. It would be a different matter, now that He is glorified, from what it was when He lived in the world. Human nature would be too weak to bear it. The world would exist no longer and no one would remain in it, for when men had once seen eternal Truth they would perceive that all we value on earth is but a lie and a mockery. And if His sublime glory could be seen, how could such a sinful wretch as I am dare to draw thus near to Him after my many offences? Beneath the accidents of bread, He is accessible—if the King disguises Himself, there does not seem to be the same need for ceremonies and court etiquette; indeed He appears to have waived His claim to them by appearing *incognito.* Who otherwise would venture to approach Him thus tepidly, unworthily, and laden with imperfections? Indeed, we know not what we ask; but He in His wisdom understands far better than we do. When He sees that it would profit a soul, He reveals Himself to it; although unseen by the bodily eyes, He manifests Himself to it by vivid interior intuitions and by other means.

10. Take pleasure in remaining in His society: do not lose this most precious time, for this hour is of the utmost value to the soul, and the good Jesus desires you to spend it with Him; take great care, daughters, not to waste it. If obedience calls

you, try to leave your soul with our Lord, Who is your Master; although you may not understand how, He will continue to teach you. But if you allow your thoughts to wander at once to other matters and you show no more care or reverence for Him Who dwells within you than if you had not received Holy Communion, how can He make Himself known to you? You have no one to blame for this but yourself. This is the time for our Master to instruct, and for us to listen. I do not assert that you must use no vocal prayers, for you would say I was speaking of contemplation. If our Lord does not raise you to this, recite the Pater Noster, but take care to remember how truly you are in the company of Him Who taught it you: kiss His feet for having done so and beseech Him not to leave you. If you are accustomed to ask for graces from Christ while looking at His picture, would it not be foolish, at this time, to turn away from Him Who is now with you in person, and to look at His image? It would be the same thing as if, when a friend we dearly loved came to visit us, we refused to talk to him and would only speak to his portrait. Do you know when the gazing on a representation of Christ is a good and holy practice in which I take great pleasure? It is when our Lord is absent and makes us feel His loss by aridities. It is a great joy to look at an image of our Lady or of any Saint for whom we have a devotion. How much more so when the likeness is that of Christ, Who has given us such cause to love Him? To gaze on His picture rouses the soul to fervour.[8] And I should like to see His image wherever I turned my eyes. What can we look on that is better or more delightful than Him Who loves us so tenderly and Who comprises in Himself all good things? Unhappy heretics who have forfeited this consolation[9] and support, as well as many others![10]

11. When you have received our Lord, since He really dwells within you, try to shut the eyes of your body and to open those of your soul; look into your heart. I have told you, and shall tell you, again and again: if you do this whenever you go to Holy Communion—I do not mean once or twice, but every time you communicate—and if you strive to keep your conscience clear so that you may frequently enjoy this grace, His coming will not be so hidden but that, in many a way, He will reveal Himself to you in proportion to the desire you have of seeing Him. Indeed, if your

[8] One of the reasons why St. Teresa was so fond of images was her ardent desire of seeing God and His saints. It was delightful to hear the loving tender words with which she would address a picture of our Lord or His holy Mother while holding it in her hands; her soul seemed melted with devotion. (Ribera, bk. IV, x.)

[9] *Rel.* v. 5.

[10] Mother Mary of St. Joseph says: 'Our holy Mother told her nuns to show great reverence to images, not by means of rich decorations and embellishments, but consistently with poverty by keeping them in good order, for they are great aids to charity and the love of God. I saw an account in her handwriting of a revelation our Lord made to her, ordering that her daughters should frequently pay reverence to images. He said, "My Christian people, daughter, must now, more than ever, run counter to the heretics, who in these days have specially set themselves to pull down churches and to destroy images."' (Fuente, vol. VI. 259). See also St. John of the Cross, *Ascent of Mount Carmel*, bk. III. xiv; xxxvi.

longing for Him is very vehement,[11] He may disclose Himself entirely to you.[12] But if we care nothing for Him Whom we have received in such intimate union, but either go to seek Him elsewhere or busy ourselves about other and lower matters, what would we have Him do? Must He drag us by force to look at Him and to stay with Him because He wishes to manifest Himself to us? No! for men did not treat Him too well when He showed Himself visibly among them and told them Who He was—few indeed of them believed Him. He has done us a great grace by teaching us that He is present in the Blessed Sacrament. But He will not show Himself openly or reveal His glories or bestow His treasures, save on souls which prove that they ardently desire Him, for these are His real friends. But let not the soul which is not of their number, which offends Him and approaches to receive Him without having prepared itself to the best of its ability—let not that soul importune Him to reveal Himself to it. Scarcely is the hour over which has been spent in fulfilling the precepts of the Church, when such a person leaves her own home and tries to drive Christ out of it, or if she does enter into herself it is only to engage in worldly thoughts in the very presence of Jesus. Indeed, what with other interests, business, and the cares of this life, she seems to make all possible haste to prevent our Lord from taking possession of her house!

[11] *Life*, xxxix, 31, 32.

[12] *Life*, xvi, 3; xviii, 10, 18; xxxviii, 24. *Rel.* iii, 6, 7, 19; iv, 4, 5; ix, 12, 13, 20, 26.

CHAPTER XXXV[1]

CONTINUES THE FOREGOING SUBJECT. CONTAINS AN APPEAL TO THE ETERNAL FATHER. OF THE RECOLLECTION WHICH SHOULD BE PRACTISED AFTER HOLY COMMUNION.

1. Spiritual Communion. 2. Difficulties of acquiring the habit of recollection. 3. A prayer that the Blessed Sacrament may be honoured. 4. And that outrages against It may be stopped. 5. An offering of propitiation.

1. ALTHOUGH I had already written about it while explaining the prayer of recollection, yet because of its great importance I have spoken here at length of the need of our retiring into our own souls to be alone with God. When you hear Mass, but do not go to Holy Communion, you may make an act of Spiritual Communion, which is exceedingly profitable. Recollect yourselves in the same manner: this impresses a deep love for our Lord on our minds; for if we prepare our souls to receive Him, He never fails, in many ways unknown to us, to give us His grace. It is as if we approached a large fire—if we kept at a distance from it and covered our hands, we should hardly feel its heat although we should be warmer than without it. But if we approach this fire (which is our Lord), with the intention of expelling the cold, the case is quite different, for if the soul is thus well-disposed and perseveres for some time, it retains its warmth for several hours and any small spark which flew out would at once ignite it.

2. It is of such immense advantage for us to

[1] Valladolid edition, xxxvii; Escorial, lxii.

cultivate the habit of recollection that you must not be surprised at my mentioning it very frequently. Do not be disturbed if you cannot succeed at first; perhaps the devil may be filling your heart with repugnance and trouble because he sees what loss he would suffer by your acquiring this habit. Though he may try to make you believe that you could practise greater devotion in other ways, do not be dissuaded from this: our Lord thus tests your love for Him. Remember, there are few souls that keep beside Him or follow Him in His trials.[2] Let us suffer something for Him—He will repay us. Only think! there are people who not only do not like to be with Him, but who drive Him from their houses with rudeness and insults; therefore we ought to endure some discomfort in order to show that we wish to see Him. Although, in many places, men leave Him by Himself, or treat Him badly, yet He endures all this, and will continue to endure it for the sake of finding but one single soul that will receive Him with affection and bear Him loving company. Let this soul be *yours*, for if none were to be found, the eternal Father would justly refuse to allow Him to remain with us. Yet He loves Christ's friends so well, and is so kind a Master that, knowing it is the will of His holy Son, He will not dissuade Him from this praiseworthy deed in which He so generously proves His love for His Father by finding this wonderful way of testifying His affection for us and of aiding us to bear our trials.

3. Since, O our Father Who art in heaven!

[2] *Imitation*, bk. II. xi, 1.

Thou dost will and ratify this act (for by no means wouldst Thou deny us so great a boon,) there must be some one to plead the cause of Thy Son, as He will never defend Himself. Let that part be ours: daring as the task may be for us unworthy creatures, yet let us rely on our Lord's command that we should pray. In obedience to this decree I beg of you, daughters, to join me in asking of our holy Father, in the name of the good Jesus, that, seeing how He has done all that could be done in granting this great gift to sinners, He would mercifully prevent our Lord's being so ill-treated. Since His blessed Son has left us so powerful a means as the sacrifice of the Mass, by which we can repeatedly offer Him up, let us implore God that this precious oblation may prevent the spread of the terrible wickedness and sacrileges committed among the Lutherans against the most Blessed Sacrament. It seems as if the end of the world must have come, for they demolish the churches, massacre numbers of priests, and abolish the Sacraments. Even many Christians behave so irreverently in church that they seem sometimes to have gone there more for the purpose of offending our Lord than of worshipping Him. Why do such things happen, O Lord God? Either let the world come to an end, or stop these dreadful crimes, for, wicked as we are, they are more than our hearts can bear. I beseech Thee, O eternal Father! to extinguish this conflagration, since it is in Thy power to do so.

4. Behold, Thy Son remains on earth with us: in deference to Him, stop these foul and abominable

outrages, for one so pure and beautiful as He ought not to dwell amid such pollution. We do not ask this for ourselves, O God! we do not deserve it—grant it for the sake of Thy Son. We dare not beg that He should stay with us no longer, for Thou hast consented to His prayer that for 'to-day', that is, as long as the world lasts, Thou wouldst leave Him with us. Without His presence, what would become of us? Everything would go to wrack and ruin, for if aught can propitiate Thee it is this Hostage which we hold. As some redress must be found for these wrongs, may it please Thee to supply it, for Thou canst do so if Thou wilt.

5. O my God! would that my fervent importunity and the signal services rendered Thee gave me the right to beg of Thee so great a favour in return, for never dost Thou leave a just claim unrewarded. But I have done nothing of the kind. Indeed, perchance it is *I* who have provoked Thee and brought about these evils in punishment for my sins. What then can I do, O my Creator! but offer Thee this most holy Bread, thus rendering Thee back Thine own gift, beseeching Thee, by the merits of Thy Son, to grant this boon which, in so many ways, He has earned from Thee? Do Thou, O God! calm the sea and no longer permit the ship of the Church to be tossed in this tempest. Save us, O Lord, for we perish![3]

[3] St. Matt. viii, 25: 'Domine, salva nos, perimus.'

CHAPTER XXXVI[1]

ON THE WORDS 'FORGIVE US OUR TRESPASSES.'

1. 'Forgive us our trespasses.' On forgiving injuries. 2. Forgiveness of others a debt we owe to God. 3. False and true honour. 4. Honour in religious houses. 5. Humility obtains true honour, while pride forfeits it. 6. The merits of mutual forgiveness. 7. Forgiveness of injuries a mark of true contemplatives. 8. Humility and patience of contemplatives. 9. Union always accompanied by forgiveness and longsuffering, though in a less degree than in contemplatives. 10. The divine example. 11. The prayer of contemplation is not genuine unless it produces these two virtues.

'FORGIVE US OUR TRESPASSES AS WE FORGIVE THEM THAT TRESPASS AGAINST US.'

1. OUR kind Master sees that, unless the fault be our own, this heavenly Bread renders all things easy to us and that we are now capable of fulfilling our promise to the Father of allowing His will to be done in us. Therefore, continuing to teach us the prayer He says: 'Forgive us our debts, as we forgive our debtors.' Notice, daughters, He does not say, 'as we *are about* to forgive our debtors', because we are to understand that we must have already done this before we beg for so great a gift [as this Bread] and the surrender of our own will to that of God. Therefore Christ's words are: 'as we forgive our debtors.' Whoever wishes to be able to say to God in all sincerity: 'Thy will be done', must have forgiven others beforehand, at least in intention.

2. Now we see why the saints rejoiced in injuries

[1] Valladolid edition, xxxviii; Escorial, lxiii.

and persecutions, for thereby they had some payment to offer God when they made this petition. Otherwise, what could such poor sinners as myself do, who have so little to forgive and so much to be forgiven? We ought to think over this very seriously, sisters; it is so grave and so important a matter that God should pardon us miserable creatures our sins which merit eternal fire, that we must pardon all offences committed against us,[2] which are not really affronts nor anything at all. For, how is it possible to wrong, either by word or deed, such a one as I am, who in simple justice deserve to be treated unkindly in this world and tortured by the devils in the next?[3] Thus it is, O my God! that I have no other gift to offer Thee whereby I might plead that Thou shouldst remit my debts. Thy Son must forgive me, for no one has done me any real injustice, therefore I have nothing to pardon in return.[4] Accept my wish to pardon others, O my God! for I believe that I could forgive my neighbour anything since Thou dost pardon me, or that I might fulfil Thy will unreservedly—yet, when it comes to the test, if I were unjustly accused, I know not what I might do. But in Thine eyes I am so guilty that all the evil men could say of me would fall far short of the truth,

[2] *Life*, xxi, 12. *Way of Perf.* xii, 8, 9; xiii, 1-4. *Concep.* ii, 15, 16, 32, 33.

[3] *Excl.* xiii, 3. *Rel.* i, 28. *Life*, xxxi, 13.

[4] Mother Isabel de Jesus, once said to the Saint: 'Mother, how can you bear their saying such things about a nun?' (people were speaking very ill about her at the time). She replied: They have good reason for it. I am surprised at their not flogging me. What do you suppose I care for their words? No music could be sweeter to my ears.' (Fuente, vol. VI. 306. Note, 7. Deposition of Damiana de Jesus).

although those who see not all which Thou knowest might think that I had been injured. Therefore, O my Father! Thou must indeed forgive me *freely*, which demands from Thee *mercy*. All praise is due to Thee for bearing patiently with one so poor as I am. When Thy most blessed Son promised Thee this repayment from other men, He left out my name because I am utterly destitute. But, O my God! are there not other souls which, like mine, have never grasped this truth? If there are, I beg them in Thy name to remember it, and to ignore the trifling matters which they call affronts, lest, in their care for points of honour, they resemble children building houses out of straw.

3. Ah, my sisters, would that we realized what such 'honour' means, by which true honour is forfeited! I am not speaking about what we are at the present moment: it would indeed be shameful if we did not recognize this. I apply it to myself in the days when I prided myself on my honour, as is the custom of the world, without knowing what the word really meant.[5] Oh! how ashamed I feel at recalling what used to annoy me then, although I was not a person accustomed to stand on ceremony. Still, I did not realize where the essential point of honour lay, for I neither knew nor cared for real honour, which is of some use because it benefits the soul. How truly has some one said: 'Honour and profit do not go together'! I do not know whether he applied this meaning to it, still, quoting his words as they stand, the soul's

[5] *Life*, ii, 4.

profit and what men call honour can never agree. The perversity of the world is most astonishing: thank God for taking us out of it! May He always keep its spirit as far from this house as it is now! Heaven defend us from monasteries where the inmates are sensitive as to their fancied rights: they will never pay much honour to God there.[6]

4. What can be more absurd than for religious to stand upon their dignity on such petty points that I am absolutely surprised at them! You know nothing about such things, sisters: I will tell you so that you may be on your guard. The devil has not forgotten us—he has invented honours in religious houses—he has settled the laws by which the dwellers rise and fall in dignity (as men do in the world), and they are jealous of their honour in surprisingly petty matters. Learned men must observe a certain order in their studies which I cannot understand: he who has read theology must not descend to read philosophy. This is a point of honour which consists in advancing and in not retrograding. If obedience obliged any one to do the contrary, he would secretly take it as an affront and would find others to take his part and say that he had been ill-used: the devil would easily find reasons, even from the holy Scriptures, by which he would appear to prove this. Even among nuns, she who has been Prioress must not afterwards fill any lower office: deference must be shown to the first in rank and she takes care we do not forget it; at times this even seems a merit because the Rule enjoins it. The thing is absurd, and enough to

[6] Escorial edition, lxiv. Denounces superfluous honours.

make one laugh—or rather *weep*, and with better cause than can be told. I know the Rule does not forbid me to be humble: the regulation is made to maintain order, but I ought not to be so careful of my dignity as to insist on this point's being obeyed as strictly as the rest. And perhaps I keep those injunctions very slackly, while I will give up no jot or tittle of this one. Let others see to what concerns my rank and let me take no notice of it. The fact is, we are bent on rising higher although we shall never mount to heaven by this path, and we will not dream of descending.[7]

5. O my Lord! art Thou not our Pattern and our Master? Indeed Thou art. And in what did Thine honour consist, O ever honoured Master and King? Didst Thou lose it in being humbled even unto death? No, Lord, Thou didst thereby gain it and didst win graces for us all. Therefore, sisters, how far we shall err from the right path if we follow this way, for it leads us wrong from the very beginning. May He grant that no soul may be lost through observing these miserable points of etiquette without realizing in what true honour consists. At last we come to believe that we have done a great thing when we forgive some trifle which was neither an affront nor an injury nor anything of the sort, nor gave us any just cause for resentment. Then afterwards, as if we had done

[7] So far was the Saint from caring for honours that not only did she wish to leave Avila because she was held there in high esteem, and retire with her dowry to another house of the Order far away where she would be unknown (*Life*, xxxi. 16), but she also wanted to become a lay sister so as to do the meanest and hardest work. She would have executed this design had she not been prevented by authority. (Ribera, bk. IV. xv.)

some virtuous action, we petition God to forgive us because we have forgiven others. Give us grace O Lord! to know that we do not understand what we are saying, and that all such souls come to Him as empty-handed as I do myself. Grant this for the sake of Thy loving mercy. Indeed, O Lord! I see nothing that I can offer worthy to obtain from Thee so great a gift, for all earthly things perish, but hell is eternal: yet I plead to Thee for souls who think that others are always injuring and insulting them.

6. What value God places on our loving and keeping peace with one another! For when once we have given Him our will we have given Him the right to it, and this we cannot do without love. See, sisters, what need there is for us to love and to agree with each other. The good Jesus places it before anything else. He does not mention the many things we gave Him on one single occasion, nor does He offer them in our name to His Father. He might have said: 'Forgive us because of our many penances, or prayers, or fasts, or because we have left all for Thee and love Thee fervently, and have suffered for Thee and long to suffer more.' He never says: 'Because we would lay down our lives for Thee', or recounts the many other things the soul does for God when it loves Him and gives Him its will. He only pleads: 'As we forgive our debtors'. Perhaps this was because He knew of our attachment to this miserable 'honour', so that we will overlook no slight upon it. This being the most difficult thing for us to overcome, our Lord put it in the first place, so that, after

having asked such sublime graces for us, He offers this for our repayment.[8]

7.[9] Notice, sisters, that Christ says, 'As we have forgiven our debtors,' to show that it is a thing we have already done, as I said. Be sure of this—when a soul, after receiving some of the special favours in prayer which I have described and after having been raised to perfect contemplation, does not come away with a firm determination to forgive others, and if occasion offers, does not actually pardon any injury, serious as it may be—unless these fruits are left in the soul, the graces never came from God but were illusions and delights caused by the devil to make such a person think herself holy and therefore worthy of greater honour. I am not speaking of the trifles people call injuries, for these do not affect a soul that God raises to so high a prayer, nor does it care whether it is highly esteemed or no. I am wrong in saying that it does not care, for honour troubles it far more than contempt, and it dislikes rest much more than toil. The good Jesus, knowing that these results remain in the soul that has reached this state of prayer, assures His Father that we forgive our debtors, for when God has really given His kingdom to a person she no longer wishes for any kingdom in this world: she understands that this is the way to reign in a far higher manner, experience having taught her what benefit accrues from it and that the soul makes rapid progress through suffering for God. Only in very exceptional cases does He bestow

[8] Escorial edition, lxv. Treats of the effects left by perfect prayer.

[9] St. Teresa wrote against this paragraph on the margin of the original manuscript: 'Effects produced by the good Spirit.'

sublime favours on souls which have not willingly borne many severe trials for His sake, because, as I have already told you in this book, contemplatives have heavy crosses to bear,[10] so our Lord chooses hearts which have been thoroughly tested.

8. You must know, sisters, that such souls, having learnt the worth of all created things, do not pay much heed to any transitory matter—if they experience a first movement of pain at some serious injury or suffering, they have hardly felt it before reason comes to their aid, and, as it were, erects the standard of faith for them and overthrows their pain by the joy of seeing that God has given them an opportunity of gaining, in one day, more graces and lasting rewards than they could have earned for themselves in ten years by any self-sought labours undertaken for Him. From what I have been told by many contemplatives, I believe this is very usual: they prize afflictions as other people prize gold and jewels, knowing that sorrows will make them rich. Such souls have no self-esteem —they are glad that their faults should be known[11] and reveal them to anyone who they know feels esteem for them.[12] It is the same as regards their parentage: they recognize that it will avail them nothing in the eternal kingdom. If they felt any pleasure in being of noble birth, it would only be when it enabled them to render God greater service.

[10] *Way of Perf.* xviii, 1.

[11] A devout person, while talking to our holy Mother said: 'Well, Mother, you may be a saint, but you don't seem one to me.' St. Teresa was delighted, and answered: 'God reward you for those words. You tell the truth, and you know what I really am.' (Deposition of Damiana de Jesus. Fuente, vol. VI. 305. Notes 5, 6.)

[12] *Life*, xxxi, 17.

If they are not well-born, they are distressed when people over-rate them, and, if they take no pleasure in undeceiving their friends, at any rate they feel no reluctance to doing so. This must be because the souls on whom God has bestowed such great humility and love for Him so entirely forget themselves in all that concerns rendering Him greater service that they cannot believe any one can be troubled by certain annoyances which they themselves do not resent as injuries.

9. These last mentioned effects are proper to persons who have arrived at a high degree of perfection,[13] to whom our Lord often grants the favour of uniting them to Himself by sublime contemplation. But the first degree of this virtue, that is, a firm resolution to bear injuries and the suffering of them although they wound one, is obtained in a very short time by the soul to whom God grants the grace of union. If these effects are not found, and are not greatly increased by this prayer, we must conclude that this was no divine favour but a delusion of the devil sent to increase our self-esteem. The soul may possibly be lacking in this strength when God first bestows these favours on it, but if He continues doing so it will soon gain vigour, if not in the other virtues, at least in this of forgiving injuries.

10. I cannot believe that one who has approached so near to the Source of all mercy, which has shown the soul what it really is and all that God has pardoned it, would not instantly and

[13] *Castle*, M. VI. viii, 5. *Life*, xix, 2.

willingly forgive, and be at peace, and remain well-affected towards any one who has offended her. For the divine kindness and mercy shown her prove the immense love felt for her by the Almighty, and she is overjoyed at having an opportunity of showing love in return.

11. I repeat that I know a number of people on whom our Lord has bestowed supernatural favours, such as the prayer or contemplation I have described, and, although they have other faults and imperfections, yet I never saw one who was unforgiving, nor do I think such a thing possible if these really were divine graces. If any one receives very sublime favours, let her notice whether the right effects increase with them: if these are not found, there is cause for great fear. Let no one fancy that such feelings were graces from God, for He always enriches the souls He visits. This is certain, for although the grace or consolation may pass away quickly, it is detected later on by the benefits it has left in the soul. The good Jesus is well aware of this and therefore deliberately assures His Father that we forgive our debtors.

CHAPTER XXXVII[1]

OF THE BEAUTIES OF THE PATER NOSTER AND THE GREAT CONSOLATION IT BRINGS US.

1. All perfection and contemplation comprised in the Pater Noster. 2. It is suited to every one. 3. The reward of efforts made for God. 4. 'Lead us not into temptation.'

1. THE sublime perfection of this evangelical prayer is marvellous and we ought to thank God fervently for it. So admirably is it composed by the good Master that everybody may apply its meaning to his own wants. I am astonished at finding all perfection and contemplation comprised in it,[2] so that there seems to be no need to study any other writings. For here our Lord has unfolded to us mental prayer from its very beginning, through the prayer of quiet and union up to the most high and perfect contemplation. Therefore, if I had not already written about it elsewhere, and also for the reason that I dare not enlarge upon it as the results would only be exasperating, I could, were I able to express myself, write a large book on prayer based upon this solid foundation. Our Lord here shows us, as you have seen, the effects of prayer and contemplation when they are divine graces.

[1] Valladolid edition, xxxix: Escorial, continuation of lxv.

[2] Blessed Angela de Foligno said: 'I recited the "Our Father" with so much contrition and recollection, pronouncing every word, that, though I was plunged in great anguish by the thought of my sins, I yet received immense consolation and tasted something of the bliss God grants His beloved. I have never found a better way for realizing His mercy than by saying the prayer which Jesus Himself taught us.' (*Miniature Lives of the Saints*, by Rev. H. S. Bowden).

2. I have sometimes wondered why His Majesty did not speak more clearly on such sublime subjects, so that we might all understand His meaning: then I reflected that perhaps Christ left the meaning obscure because this prayer was meant for all men, and thus each one might ask for what he wanted and might feel happy in the idea that he was using the words in their right sense. Blessed be His Name to endless ages, Amen! I implore the Father, for His Son's sake, to remit all my debts and grievous sins, for there is neither cause nor person that requires forgiveness from me. Every day I have fresh need for pardon, and may He grant me the grace of having something to offer Him every day in compensation for my own offences. Contemplatives, and very devout people who seek no earthly goods, may ask for the heavenly favours which, by the great mercy of God, can be enjoyed while we still live in this world. The good Jesus has here taught us a most celestial prayer by which He seeks that we may resemble the angels while still in exile here, if we strive with all our might to conform our actions to the petitions we make—in short, if we do our best to be the children of such a Father and fit brethren of such a Brother. As I said, if His Majesty sees that our works conform to our words, He will not fail to grant our prayers, to establish His kingdom within us, and to aid us with supernatural graces such as the prayer of quiet, perfect contemplation, and the other favours with which God rewards our small efforts. People who live in the world do right in conforming to the

duties of their state, and may hereby ask for the bread that they require to maintain their households. This is right and just, as it is for them to pray for whatever else they need. But, let them notice that the two things—yielding up our will and forgiving others, apply to everybody. It is true that there are degrees in the way of carrying them out—perfect souls resign their will perfectly and pardon wrongs with the perfection I described,[3] while as for us, sisters—well—we do our best, and our Lord receives all we offer Him. We can neither do nor gain much for ourselves, but as it is all we can do, God is sure to help us, since His Son begs Him to do so. Christ seems to have made a sort of agreement on our behalf with His eternal Father, as if He had said: 'Lord, if Thou doest this, My brethren shall do that.'

3. It is certain that He will never fail on His part and Oh, what a Paymaster He is, and how boundless are His rewards! It is possible, daughters, that, as He sees that there is no duplicity about us but that we shall fulfil our promises, some day when we say this prayer He will leave us rich. Never practise any evasion with Him, for His Majesty is greatly pleased if we are sincere with Him. We can never succeed in deceiving Him, because He knows all things. Do not say one thing and mean another: if we treat Him with truth and candour, He will always give us more than we ask for. Our kind Master knows that

[3] Although the administrator of the archdiocese was strongly opposed to the foundation at Toledo, St. Teresa always spoke well of him and told the nuns to pray specially for him. (Deposition of Maria de San Francisco. Fuente, vol. VI. 310, Note, 10.)

those who tend to great perfection will by reciting this prayer reach to a high degree by means of the graces the eternal Father will bestow on them, and that perfect souls, or those who are on the road to become perfect, have already trodden the world beneath their feet, at which the Sovereign of the universe is well pleased. These souls, from the effects they discover in themselves, may feel a strong hope that His Majesty is contented with them, and, inebriated with these delights, they would not willingly remember the present world nor that they have any enemies. O eternal Wisdom! O great Teacher! What a boon it is, daughters, to have such a good Master, Who is wise and prudent and Who wards off all dangers! This is all that a devout soul could desire, for it means perfect safety.

4. No words can exaggerate the importance of this. Our Lord saw that it was necessary to arouse such souls, and to remind them that they had enemies, and that there is even greater danger in their growing careless: He knew that they have more urgent need than others of help from the eternal Father because they would fall from a greater height. That they might also be guarded from being unwittingly deceived, He offered this petition, so necessary for us all while we live in the exile of this world: 'LEAD US NOT INTO TEMPTATION, BUT DELIVER US FROM EVIL, LORD'.

CHAPTER XXXVIII[1]

TREATS OF THE URGENT NEED THERE IS OF BEGGING THE ETERNAL FATHER TO GRANT US THE PETITION, 'LEAD US NOT INTO TEMPTATION, BUT DELIVER US FROM EVIL.' ENUMERATES AND EXPLAINS SOME TEMPTATIONS WHICH COME FROM THE DEVIL.

1. By temptation is meant, not sufferings, but the snares of the devil. 2. Wiles of the evil one. 3. Humility our safeguard. 4. Fallacious virtues. 5. Their danger for ourselves and others. 6. Our virtues are unstable. 7. Humility is our safeguard. 8. Fictitious patience. 9. Imaginary poverty of spirit. 10. True and fancied poverty of spirit. 11. Religious poverty and care for the future. 12. The guard we must keep against deceptive virtues.

'AND LEAD US NOT INTO TEMPTATION, BUT DELIVER US FROM EVIL. AMEN.'

1. We must now think of and interpret these words as applying to sublime matters, since we are here praying for such graces. I feel convinced that souls which have arrived at this degree of perfection in prayer do not ask God to deliver them from trials or temptations, nor from persecutions and combats.[2] This is another unmistakable and noteworthy effect, showing that the contemplation and favours given to such people come from the Holy Ghost and are not illusions, for, as I said just now, these souls wish for and demand such troubles and love them instead of hating them. They are like soldiers — the more they fight, the

[1] Valladolid edition, xl; Escorial, lxvi.

[2] *Castle*, M. VI. iv, 19; M. VII. iii, 4. *Excl.* xiv. 3. *Life*, xl. 27.

better they like it, for thus they hope for a richer booty. When there is no war they live on their pay, but they know they will not grow rich on that. Believe me, sisters, the battle never comes soon enough for the soldiers of Christ. I allude to contemplatives and people who practise prayer. They have little fear of open enemies, knowing them well already and being aware that such foes have little power against the strength given them by God through which they always gain the victory and come forth from the fray with great spoils and riches, so that they never beat a retreat. The foes they really dread—and it is well that they should dread them and should always pray God that they may be delivered from them—are those treacherous antagonists the devils, who transform themselves into angels of light. They come in disguise and do not let us find them out until they have wrought great harm to the soul. They suck our very life-blood and destroy our virtues, whilst we unwittingly are surrounded by temptations.

2. Let us constantly beg of God, daughters, in the Pater Noster, to deliver us, that we may not be deluded by their temptations, but that we may detect their poison and that light may not be withdrawn from us. What good cause has our kind Master to teach us to ask for this and to demand it Himself on our behalf! Consider in how many ways the evil spirits injure us. You must not suppose that it is only by persuading us that the sweetness and consolations they give us come from God.[3] This seems to me the least harm they can do: it

[3] *Castle*, M. V. iv, 7. *Life*, xxv, 15, 16.

may even help some souls who, lured by the devotion they feel, will spend more time in prayer. Not knowing that the devil has a hand in it, they continually praise our Lord for having granted them favours which they did not deserve: they feel bound to serve Him more fervently and strive to prepare themselves to receive still further graces, supposing that these have come from His hand.

3. Always try to be humble, sisters; believe that you are unworthy of these gifts and do not seek them. I am convinced that in this way the evil one loses many a soul which he thought to have ruined, and that our Lord draws good out of the harm the fiend meant to work us, for His Majesty looks at our intention, which is to serve and please Him by keeping in His presence in prayer, and He is ever faithful. But we must be cautious, lest the enemy make a breach in our humility by vainglory: and we must beg God to preserve us from this. Then you need not fear, daughters, that He will allow any one but Himself to console you for long.

4. The evil one may secretly injure us seriously by making us believe that we have virtues which we do not possess—this is most pestilent.[4] In consolations and favours we seem only recipients and therefore feel the more strictly bound to serve God: but this delusion makes us think that we render Him some gift and service which He is called upon to repay. By degrees, this damages us greatly, for while on the one hand it weakens our humility, on the other, we neglect to acquire

[4] *Castle*, M. V. iii. 9, 10.

the virtue we believe that we already own. Suspecting no evil (for we think we are safe), we fall into a ditch from which we cannot get out. For although there does not always appear to have been any evident mortal sin which would certainly drag us to hell, yet we are lamed, so that we cannot travel on the road I began to speak of (and which I have not forgotten). For how can any one walk when he is plunged into a deep ditch? it would be the death of him—and it is fortunate if it does not reach down to hell. He can never make progress and in any case can do nothing but harm to himself and others. As long as the ditch remains, many travelling by the same road may fall into it, but if the man climbed out and filled it up with earth it could cause no damage to him or any one else.

5. I assure you this is a very dangerous temptation. I have had great experience of it, so that I can explain the matter, although not as well as I could wish. What remedy is there for it, sisters? That which our Master has taught us seems to me the best—to pray and to beseech the eternal Father not to suffer us to fall into temptation.

6. There is another temptation. When God gives us some virtue, we must understand that it is only a loan and that He may take it away again, as indeed often happens, not without a wise providence. Have you never found this out yourselves, sisters? I certainly have. Sometimes I fancy that I am very detached, as I really am when it comes to the trial. Yet at another time I discover that I am so attached to things which I should perhaps have laughed at the day before, that I hardly

know myself. Again, I feel such courage that there is nothing I should fear to do in God's service, and I find, when it comes to the proof, that I am brave sometimes—yet, next day, I should not venture to kill an ant for Him if I met with any opposition. Sometimes I care nothing if people talk or complain of me; and indeed very often it has even given me pleasure. Yet there are occasions when a single word disturbs me and I long to leave this world, for everything in it disgusts me. I am not the only person to whom this happens, for I have noticed it in people better than myself, and I know that it is a fact.

7. If this be the case, who can say that he possesses any virtue, or that he is rich, when at the time he most needs these goods he finds himself destitute of them? No, sisters; let us think we are poor, and not run into debts which we have no money to pay. Our wealth must come from elsewhere, and we never know when our Lord will leave us, without any aid from Him, in the prison of the miseries of human nature. If others think we are good because He shows us mercy or honour, they will find our virtues are only lent us and will look as foolish as we shall. The truth is that if we serve God with a lowly heart, He will succour us at length in our needs. But if we are not really humble, He will let us slip at every step,[5] as they say, and He thus shows great kindness, for He does so to make us value His grace and thoroughly to realize that we possess nothing which we have not received.

[5] *Castle*, M. III. ii, 2, 3.

8. Now, let me counsel you upon another point. The devil makes us believe that we own some virtue—patience, for instance—because we make frequent resolutions and acts of suffering for God. It seems to us that we really should endure trials for Him: Satan helps to convince us of it, and so we are very much pleased with ourselves. Yet I advise you to place no faith in such virtues: we ought never to think we know more than the name of a virtue or imagine that God has bestowed it on us until it has been put to the test. For perhaps, at the first word that annoys you, your patience will collapse. Praise God when you have much to try you, for He is beginning to teach you patience: force yourselves to be meek, for He thus gives you a sign that He wishes to be repaid for His gift, which must be looked upon as a loan, as I said.

9. Again, the evil one makes us fancy that we are very poor in spirit—and he has some reason for this because we have made a vow of poverty with our lips, as is even done by some people in the world who practise prayer. I say, 'with our lips', for if we really understood, in the depths of our heart, what we promise and have even already vowed, the devil could not deceive us about it as he does—perhaps for twenty years, or perhaps for a whole life-time—but we should discover how we are imposing upon every one else as well as ourselves. We are in the habit of saying that we want nothing and do not care for anything, yet directly something is offered us, even though it is superfluous, our poverty of spirit disappears—and much

good do our professions of poverty seem to have done us! A person who has taken this vow and who thinks that she really is poor in spirit, says to herself: 'I do not want anything, but I keep this because I cannot do without it; we must live, in order to serve God, and He wishes us to maintain our bodies.' The demon, disguised as an angel of light, persuades her that she needs a thousand other things, for all this is right in itself. Thus he leads her to imagine that she possesses the virtue of poverty of spirit, and that everything is accomplished.

10. Let us now come to the time of trial—for we can only test ourselves by watching our actions narrowly—and we shall soon detect signs of the devil's deceptions. For instance, let us suppose that a man possesses a larger income than he needs—I mean, than is really necessary for him, and he keeps three valets when he could manage with one. When he is sued for some part of his estate, or one of his poor tenants does not pay his rent, this person is as disturbed and worried as if his living depended on it.[6] He will tell you that he cannot lose his property through neglecting it, and at once pleads this excuse. I do not say that he should neglect his business—on the contrary, he ought to attend to it; then, if it succeeds, very well; if not, never mind! One who is poor at heart cares so little for such affairs that though, for certain reasons, he attends to them, yet they give him no trouble because he never thinks he will come to want—if he should, it would not grieve him because

[6] *Concep.* ii, 11, 12. *Castle*, M. III. ii, 4, 5. *Letters*, vol. II. no. 161. To Don Lorenzo de Cepeda, Jan. 2, 1577. *Life*, xi, 3.

he considers such things secondary matters and not the main point. His thoughts are fixed on higher objects, and he only constrains himself to attend to temporal cares against his will.[7]

11. A monk (or a nun) who is really poor, or at least who ought to be, possesses nothing, sometimes because there is nothing to possess: but if anything is offered this religious as a gift, it would be strange if he thought it superfluous, for he always likes to keep something in reserve. If he can have a habit of fine material, he does not ask for a coarse one. He always has some little thing that he can pawn or sell, if only a few books,[8] for if he fell ill he would want better food than usual. Sinner as I am! Is this the vow you made to forget yourself and to leave everything to God, whatever might happen? If you are to provide for the future, it would harass you far less to hold a settled income. Though this may be done without sin, yet it is well for us to recognize these imperfections, that we may see how far short we are of possessing poverty of spirit and that we may ask our Lord to give it us. If we think we have this virtue we shall grow careless, and, worse still, we shall be deceived on the point.

12. The same sort of thing happens as regards

[7] Escorial edition, lvii. Continues the same subject. A caution about false humility produced by the devil.

[8] This was written before the stringent reforms of the Council of Trent were introduced in the Spanish provinces of the Carmelite Order (1567). The old Constitutions, dating back from the beginning of the fourteenth century, allowed, for instance, a scholar at a university, in case of urgent need, to sell his books—of greater value then than now—in order to provide for himself. B. Zimmerman, *Monumenta historica Carmelitana*, vol. I. p. 149. (Lerins, 1907).

humility. We fancy we do not wish for honour and that we are indifferent to everything of the kind — yet, let any one offer us the slightest affront, and our feelings and behaviour will at once betray that we are not humble.[9] Besides, if any opportunity occurs of augmenting our dignity (like the poor religious I have just spoken of), for the sake of a greater good we do not reject it. And God grant we may not seek such honour. We are so accustomed to saying that we want nothing and are indifferent to everything (which we really believe is the truth), that at last the very habit of asserting it convinces us of its truth more strongly. It is wise to be on our guard against this temptation as well as the others I mentioned. Indeed, there are many we must be watchful about if we wish to detect them, for when God gives us any solid virtue, it is a well-known fact that it brings all the others in its train. But I warn you again always to fear deception even when you believe that you possess such virtue. A truly humble soul mistrusts its own good qualities: it believes in them more readily and values them more highly when it finds them in another.

[9] *Castle*, M. III. ii, 6

CHAPTER XXXIX[1]

CONTINUES THE SAME SUBJECT. A DESCRIPTION OF DIFFERENT KINDS OF TEMPTATIONS AND OF THE MEANS OF FREEING THE SOUL FROM THEM.

1. How Satan discourages the soul. 2. Difference between humility and discouragement. 3. How to resist this temptation. 4. Indiscreet penances. 5. Temptations to presumption. 6. Humility during divine consolations. 7. A prayer against temptation. 8. How prayer protects us from the devil's snares.

1. BEWARE daughters, of a certain kind of humility suggested by the devil which is accompanied by great anxiety about the gravity of our past sins.[2] He disturbs souls in many ways by this means, until at last he stops them from receiving Holy Communion by doubts as to whether they are in a fit state for it, and such thoughts as: 'Am I worthy of it? Am I in a good disposition? I am unfit to live in a religious community.' The evil one thus hinders Christians from prayer, and when they communicate, the time during which they ought to be obtaining graces is spent in wondering whether they are well prepared or no. Things come to such a pass that Satan makes the soul believe that God has forsaken it on account of its sins, so that it almost doubts His mercy. Everything such a person says seems to her on the verge of evil, and all her actions appear fruitless, however good in themselves. She becomes discouraged, thinking that she can do nothing right, for what is good in others she fancies is wrong in herself.

[1] Valladolid edition, xli; Escorial, continuation of lxvii.

[2] *Life*, x. 4; xxiii. 3, 45. *Castle*, M. I. ii 11.

2. Pay great attention, daughters, to what I am about to say. At one time it may be humility and a virtue to think ourselves thus sinful, and at another time it is a most dangerous temptation. I know this, for I have passed through this state myself. However deep humility may be, it neither disquiets, wearies, nor disturbs the soul, but is peaceful, sweet and serene. Although the sight of our wickedness grieves us and proves to us that we deserve to be in hell and that in justice all mankind should hate us, so that we hardly dare to beg for mercy, yet if it is a right humility this pain is accompanied by suavity, content, and joy, and we do not wish to be without it; indeed, it ought to be prized since it results in self-knowledge. It dilates, instead of troubling or depressing the soul, making it more capable of serving God. The other sorrow which distresses the mind renders it uneasy, completely subverting it and causing great pain, so that there is no possibility of calming the thoughts. You may feel certain that this is a temptation and not humility, with which it has no connection. I believe that this is a plot of the devil to make us think we are lowly, and at the same time to lead us to distrust God.

3. If you are ever in this state, turn your thoughts, as far as possible, from your own misery and meditate on the mercy of God, His love for us, and all that He suffered for our sake. If this depression is a temptation you will be unable to do even this, or to calm your mind and fix it on any other subject except that which wearies you still more; it will be much if you even recognize that it is a temptation.

4. A thing of the same kind occurs when we perform indiscreet penances in order to make ourselves think we have greater sorrow for sin than others, and to feel that we are doing something. If we conceal our mortifications from our confessor or Prioress, or are annoyed at being forbidden to practise them,[3] and disobey the order, this is clearly a temptation. Strive to obey, even though you find it harder, for this is far more perfect. This advice applies to every case and you must take special care to remember it.[4]

5. Another very treacherous temptation is a feeling of confidence that we shall never relapse into our former faults or care for worldly pleasures again. We say to ourselves: 'Now I know what the world is, that all it contains passes away, and I care more for divine things.' This temptation is the most dangerous of all, especially at the beginning of the religious life, for such souls, feeling that they are safe, do not guard themselves against occasions of sin. Unforeseen obstacles arise in their path and God grant they may not fall lower than ever before, and if they fall, that they may rise again: this the devil, seeing the harm they may do him and the good they may do their neighbours, will use every means in his power to prevent.

6. Whatever consolations and signs of love our Lord may give you, avoid all occasions of evil and never feel safe against a relapse. Be sure to mention these favours and graces to some one who is able to counsel you: hide nothing from him. Always

[3] *Castle*, M. I. ii. 19. *Rel.* iii 12.

[4] Escorial, lxviii. Continues the same subject and gives counsel about temptations.

begin and finish your prayer with the thought of your own nothingness, however sublime your contemplation may be, and even though our Lord may impart Himself to you and offer you proofs of His love. If this contemplation comes from God, you will often find yourselves unconsciously doing this, for such prayer produces humility and leaves us with a greater knowledge of our own unworthiness. Be cautious and consult some one who understands such matters,[5] for the devil attacks us at these times in various ways. I will say no more here, as there are many books which give advice about it: I have written this because I have had much experience on the subject which has given me a great deal of trouble. Still, nothing that can be said will make us perfectly secure, because we cannot understand ourselves.

7. What, O eternal Father! can we do, except have recourse to Thee and beg Thee not to permit our enemies to lead us into temptation? Let open assaults come, and with Thine aid we can defend ourselves; but how can we detect these subtle snares? O my God! never must we cease to beg Thy help. Give us some safeguard against surprise and show us how to understand ourselves and to feel secure. Thou knowest how few are the souls that follow the way of prayer—and if they must live thus beset with fears, their number will diminish.

8. How strange it seems! One would think the devil never tempted any one who did not pray! The world is more horrified at one person who aims at perfection falling into some deception than

[5] *Castle* M. VI. iii, 18; ix, 10. *Life*, xxvi, 4.

at witnessing the crimes and errors of a hundred thousand souls on the road to hell, about whom there can be no question as to whether they are saints or sinners, for any one can see, a thousand leagues off, that Satan has them in his clutches. Still, the world is right, for the devil entraps so very few who say the Pater Noster with devotion, that when he succeeds men are startled and wonder at it as at something strange and unheard of. For as a rule, people think little of every-day sights but anything new or uncommon strikes them with surprise. The evil spirits too incite them to take scandal at this, for a single soul that reaches perfection snatches many others from their hands. And the thing itself is so strange that no wonder men marvel at it, for unless they have themselves to blame, souls travel far more safely by this way than by any other—just as those who watch the bull-fight behind the barrier do not run the same risk as others who expose themselves to the animal's horns. I heard some one make this comparison and it seems most appropriate. Do not be afraid, sisters, to walk in these paths—for there are many kinds of prayer; some minds profit by one sort and some by another,[6] as I told you. The way is a safe one: you will be freed more quickly from temptation if you are near our Lord than if you were far off. Beg and entreat this of Him, as you do every day in the Pater Noster.

[6] *Way of Perf.* xvii.

CHAPTER XL[1]

HOW, BY ALWAYS LIVING IN THE LOVE AND FEAR OF GOD, WE SHALL BE SAFE AMONG THESE TEMPTATIONS. TREATS OF FEAR.

1. Divine love and holy fear are our safeguards. 2. The love and fear of God are unmistakably shown. 3. Temptations experienced by contemplatives. 4. Apprehensions raised in their souls by Satan. 5. Weakness of human compared with divine love. 6. Signs of love for God. 7. The death of one who loves God. 8. Contrasted with that of a sinner.

1. GIVE us, O our good Master! some safeguard against surprise in this most dangerous warfare. The weapons which we may use, daughters, and which His Majesty has given us, are love and fear. Take this advice: it is not mine but your Teacher's. Try to keep them by you on your journey. Love will quicken your footsteps and fear will make you look where you set your foot down, lest you should trip against the many stumbling-blocks on that road by which all men must pass in this life. Thus armed, you will be secure from pitfalls.

2. You will ask me: 'Can I tell whether I possess these two very, *very* great virtues?' You are right, for there can be no absolutely certain proof of this; if we were sure we possessed charity, we should be sure we were in a state of grace. But, sisters, there are some signs which are at once apparent, and which, as they say, the blind can see. There is no secret about them; although you may not wish to hear them, they cry aloud, for few souls have these virtues in perfection: therefore

[1] Valladolid edition, xl; Escorial, lxix.

they call the more for notice. The love and fear of God need not advertise themselves! They are two strong fortresses from whence war is waged on the world and the devils. The soul that truly loves God loves all good, seeks all good, protects all good, praises all good, joins itself to good men, helps and defends them, and embraces all the virtues: it only loves what is true and worth loving. Do you think it possible that any one who loves God cares, or can care, for vanities, or riches, or worldly things, or pleasures, and honours? Neither can such a soul quarrel nor feel envy, for it aims at nothing save pleasing its Beloved. It dies with longing for His love and gives its life in striving how to please Him better. But a *hidden* love indeed! as if a real love for God could possibly be hidden! Look at St. Paul or the Magdalen—in three days *he* found he was sick with love,[2] but *she* knew it the first day. And how sure they were of it! A love for God may be great or small and shows itself according to its strength. If it is weak it is little seen, and if it is strong it appears more clearly; but small or great, love for God can never be concealed.

3. The illusions and temptations the devil plots against contemplatives are numerous.[3] Such souls love fervently or they would not be contemplatives, and this is plainly shown in many ways, for a large fire throws a bright and clear flame. If they are wanting in love, let them be apprehensive and think they have good cause for fear: they should try to find out what is amiss and pray fervently.

[2] Acts, ix, 19, 20.

[3] *Castle*, M. IV. iii, 10.

They must be very humble and must ask God not to lead them into temptation, into which I fear they will fall if they have not this token. But if they are lowly and try to find out the truth—if they submit to their confessor and are frank and outspoken with him,[4] then—God is faithful. Let them feel assured that, if there is neither malice nor pride in them, the devil will gain them life by the means whereby he sought to kill them. There is no need for fear while they keep to the guidance of the Church; but Satan's bug-bears and deceits will soon be found out.

4. But if you feel the love for God I have described besides the fear of which I am about to speak, you may feel happy and at peace. In order to disturb the soul and to prevent its enjoying these great graces, the evil one will himself suggest, and will make other people arouse in you a thousand false fears,[5] for if he cannot win you for himself at least he will try to snatch something from you and to cause some loss to souls who might have benefited greatly by believing that the favours shown to such a miserable wretch came from God: he will also suggest that it is impossible for such things to be, for now-a-days we sometimes seem to forget His mercies in the past.[6]

5. Do you fancy that the devil wins but little through these fears? No, indeed, he gains immensely. He thus harms us in two well-known manners as well as in many other ways. First, he frightens those who listen to him from practising

[4] *Castle*, M. VI. ix, 10. [5] *Castle*, M. VI. ix, 8.
[6] Escorial edition, lxx. Treats of the love of God.

prayer by making them dread deception: secondly, he deters many others from devoting themselves to God as they were inclined to do when witnessing the immense goodness which leads Him to communicate Himself so fully to sinners. Such souls think He would console them in the same way and long that He should. They are right in this: I know certain persons who thus encouraged have given themselves to prayer and in a short time have become thorough contemplatives, receiving great graces from God. Thank Him warmly when you see any one among you favoured in this way, knowing that she feels this fervent love for Him. But you must not imagine that she is safe: rather you must aid her the more with your prayers, for no one can be free from danger while living involved in the perils of this tempestuous sea.

6. You will be sure to discover this love immediately: indeed I do not know how it could be concealed. They say it is impossible to hide a human love for some poor foolish man or woman, but that the more we strive to conceal it, the more clearly it is seen—although a thing so base, felt for a mere worm undeserving of any regard, does not merit the name of love, being founded upon nothingness: indeed I loathe to make the comparison. Then, could a love so strong, so just, ever growing while it lives, which never discovers any cause why it should cease, but finds as many reasons for its being as does the love of God, built as it is on the firm foundation of a love which is returned—can such a love as this be hidden? And that it is returned we cannot doubt, for the bitter

sorrows, the trials, and blood-shedding which cost our Lord His life were known to men and prove His love beyond all question. In short, a love for God is *real* love and merits its name, and the vanities of this world should be looked upon as thieves that would steal it from us.

7. O God! what a vast contrast between the one love and the other must be felt by the soul that has tried them both! May His Majesty give us grace to prove it before He takes us from this life! What a boon it will be, at the hour of death when we are going we know not where, to think that we are to be judged by Him Whom we have loved above all things[7] with an ardour that has crushed self-love. We may feel safe concerning the acquittal of our debts: we shall not be going into a foreign country but into our fatherland, for it belongs to Him Whom we love so dearly and Who loves us in return. For this affection excels all earthly fondness, because if we love Him we are assured of His love for us.

8. Oh, my daughters! think of what we gain by this love! What, then, do we lose for the want of it which delivers us into the hands of the tempter—into hands so cruel—hands which are the foes of all good and the friends of every evil thing! What will become of the poor soul which has just passed through the pains and anguish of death, when it falls at once into the clutches of Satan? What a frightful fate! How it is torn and lacerated as it sinks to hell! What a brood of different kinds of serpents swarm around it! How appalling is

[7] *Excl.* iii. 4; x. 5.

the place and what a miserable reception! A self-indulgent person, such as are most of those who are lost, can hardly bear to pass the night in a bad inn, yet here he will lodge for ever, *for ever*, to endless ages! What do you suppose will be the feelings of this unhappy soul? Let us not look for luxuries, daughters: we are well enough off here—it is only one night in a bad inn—thank God! Let us force ourselves to do penance in this life. How sweet death will be to her who has expiated all her sins and who needs no purgatory! She may begin to enjoy glory even in this world, and will fear nothing, but will be in perfect peace. Although we should not attain to this, sisters, let us beg God, that, if we must suffer pain after death, it may be where it can be endured willingly with the hope of deliverance, and where we shall forfeit neither His friendship nor His grace; and may He grant them to us in this life, so that we may not fall into temptation unknowingly. Let us praise the Lord, and persevere in begging Him to keep us and all sinners in His hands, and not to lead us into these hidden temptations.

CHAPTER XLI[1]

TREATS OF THE FEAR OF GOD, AND THAT WE OUGHT TO AVOID VENIAL SINS.

1. Fallacy of human affection. 2. Holy fear. 3. Inadvertent and deliberate sin. 4. How to obtain holy fear. 5. Our conduct when we possess it. 6. We must not repel others by our manners. 7. Disadvantages of being over-strict. 8. We must show cordiality to others. 9. Exhortations.

1. HAVE I enlarged on this subject? Not half so much as I should like, for it is delightful to talk about the love of God—what will it be, then, to possess it? Do Thou O Lord! bestow it on me: suffer me not to depart from this life until I care for nothing which it contains, and know what it is to love nought but Thee. Let me no longer say that I love anything else nor give the name of love to what is nothingness, since all earthly things are false, for if the foundation shifts, how can the building stand? I do not know why we should feel surprised at people's saying, 'This man has treated me ungratefully'; 'That person does not love me'. I laugh to myself when I hear such speeches. How else should he treat them, or why should any one love them? This will show you what the world is, for such love brings its own punishment with it, and the reason that you are tortured is that your will keenly resents your employing it in such child's-play.

2. Now let us think about the fear of God, although I regret saying nothing about the love of this world, for through my own fault I have learnt

[1] Valladolid edition, xliii; Escorial, lxxi.

what it is, and I should like to make you understand it so that you might always keep free from it. However, I cannot do so as I should be leaving my subject. The fear of God is easily recognized by its possessor and by those around her, although at first it is not strong enough to be perceived by every one, but develops gradually. I except the case of certain persons, on whom, as I said, our Lord bestows such great favours that, in a short time,[2] they become rich in virtues and are raised to a high degree of prayer. In their case this fear of God becomes at once apparent, otherwise it increases daily by degrees. This, and the love of God, are more plainly seen as they attain perfection, although the former virtue may soon be detected because whoever owns it forsakes sin and its occasions and gives up bad company: there are also other signs of it. But when souls such as those above mentioned are raised to contemplation, both their love and fear of God are very evident even in their outward conduct. Whoever watches such persons narrowly will find that they are never careless, for God upholds them, so that, whatever they might gain by it, they would not willingly commit a venial fault—as for mortal sin, they dread it like fire. These are the illusions of which, sisters, I wish you to stand in fear. You should beg God that temptation may not be strong enough to overcome you, but that He will give you the power to conquer it, for it can do you little or no harm while you keep a good conscience. This is the important matter; this is the fear which I hope we shall never lose: this must be our defence.

[2] *Way of Perf.* xvi, 4, 6. *Concep.* v, 3.

3. Oh, if we have not offended God, how easy it is for us to control the minions and slaves of hell![3] We must all serve Him in the end, whether we will or no—the devils by force and we with alacrity. So that, if we are pleasing to Him, they will be kept within bounds and will be unable to harm us, however they may tempt and lay their snares for us; in fact, they will only leave us with more merit. Remember this caution and advice; it is most important for you not to neglect it until you have such a fixed determination not to offend God that you would rather forfeit a thousand lives than commit a mortal sin. You must also be extremely vigilant about venial faults, so that you would rather suffer persecution from the whole human race than fall into this offence. I am speaking about misdeeds that are committed with full consent and are deliberate, for who does not constantly lapse into inadvertent errors? But there is one advertency which is very deliberate and another so sudden that to commit the sin and to know it seem one and the same thing and we hardly realize what we are about, though yet, to a certain extent, we are aware of it. But from wilfully committing any sin, however trivial, may God deliver us! I cannot think how we could dare to set ourselves against so great a Sovereign in however small a matter, though no offence against such majesty can be called small, because we know that He is watching us. Such a fault seems to me thoroughly premeditated.[4] It is as if we said: 'Lord, although this displeases Thee,

[3] *Life*, xxxi, 10.
[4] *Concep.* ii, 27.

yet I shall do it. I know that Thou seest it and art angered at it: this I know: but I would rather follow my own fancies and desires than Thy will.' Is such a misdeed as this a little one? I think not; I think it is very, very serious.

4. For the love of God, sisters, always be as careful in this matter as, thank Him, you are at present. Much depends upon your cultivating the habit of watchfulness. If you wish to gain this fear, it is important for you constantly to bear in mind how heinous a thing it is to offend God. This is a vital matter, especially if we can thus graft this virtue strongly in our souls. Until we possess it, we must act cautiously, keeping aloof from all places and persons that do not draw us to God. We must be careful to break our own will in whatever we do; we must take care that our words are edifying, and must avoid places where the conversation is irreligious.

5. Great pains are required in order to root this holy fear deeply in the soul, although, when a genuine love is felt for God, He soon gives it on seeing its firm determination not to commit even a venial sin for the sake of any created thing and that not to avoid a thousand deaths would it offend Him[5] although, in spite of this, such a one may fall into defects, for we are weak and cannot trust ourselves. The firmer are our resolutions, the less ought we to confide in our own strength, for all our confidence must rest on God. When we find that we have this fixed resolve we need not be so timid and strict with ourselves, for our

[5] *Castle*, M. VI. i, 21; M. VII. iv, 3. *Life*, xxiv, 1, 3.

Lord and the good habits we have formed will aid us not to offend Him. We may now act with a holy liberty and may associate with any one we meet. We may even prefer to be with the worldly, for, though before we felt this genuine fear of God they would have proved a poison destructive to our soul, yet now, when we see the contrast there is between us, their company will often strengthen our good resolutions and make us love God better and thank Him for having delivered us from danger. If, in the past, you fostered their weaknesses, now you will help them by forcing them to restrain themselves in your presence, for they will pay you this compliment unasked,

6. I often wonder why it is—and thank God for it—that the presence of a religiously minded person, even though he is silent, frequently stops profanity.[6] I suppose it must be the same as in human fellowship: people are careful not to speak ill of one absent before those whom they know to be intimate with him. Since such a person as I speak of is in a state of grace, this must cause him

[6] St. Teresa's influence over the irreligious is shown by an incident which occured when she was on her way to make the foundation at Seville. She and the nuns were in the same field with some disorderly soldiers and other men who began to quarrel violently with one another. They drew their arms and began to fight. The terrified sisters ran to their Mother as chickens take refuge beneath their parent's wings. The Saint said to the combatants: 'My brothers, remember that you are in the presence of God, Who is to be your Judge.' Struck with horror at her words, the men ceased their conflict and took to flight. (Ribera's *Life of St. Teresa,* bk. IV. xxi.)

When on her foundations, the holy Mother sometimes employed mule-drivers who were given to swearing and bad language, from which they always abstained out of respect for her when she was present. They often said that nothing on earth gave them so much pleasure as listening to her conversation. (*Ibid.* bk. II. xviii.)

to be respected, however low his station may be, and men will not give him the pain that they know an offence against God would cause him. To tell the truth, I do not know the reason, but it is generally the case. Do not be too rigid in conduct; for the soul to grow timorous will be a great hindrance in every way and may sometimes lead to scruples which cripple it both as regards itself and others. If things do not reach so far as this, still, though such a person may go on satisfactorily as regards herself, souls will not be drawn to God by her when they see her anxiety and distress. Human nature is frightened and oppressed at such a sight, and for fear of falling into the same uncomfortable state, even forfeits the reward of following in her footsteps, although clearly her way is the best.

7. Another drawback is that we shall think others imperfect because they do not follow the same path as ourselves, but perhaps with greater sanctity talk with freedom and without constraint for the sake of benefiting others. If they maintain an innocent cheerfulness, we think it is dissipation. This is especially the case with ignorant people like ourselves who do not understand what subjects it is wrong to speak about. It is a bad frame of mind to be in, being very dangerous and a source of continual temptation, because it injures our neighbour. It is very wrong to suppose that because they are not so scrupulous, people cannot be as good as ourselves. Another disadvantage is that, in cases when it is our duty and our right to speak, we dare not do so lest we should offend

God, or we speak well of what we ought to hate.[7]

8. As far as you can without offending God, try to be genial and to behave in such a way with those you have to deal with that they may take pleasure in your conversation and may wish to imitate your life and manners, instead of being frightened and deterred from virtue.[8] This is an important matter for nuns: the more holy they are, the more cordial they ought to be with their sisters. Although you may be pained because their conversation is not what you could wish, still, never keep aloof from them, for thus you will help them and win their love. We ought to strive our best to be sociable and to humour and please those with whom we talk, especially when they are our sisters.

9. Try to realize, sisters, that God does not care for such trifling matters as you suppose, and do not let these things alarm your soul and damp your courage, or you will lose greatly by it. Keep a pure intention and a firm resolve not to offend God, as I said, but do not trammel your soul, for instead of advancing in sanctity you would contract a number of imperfections which the devil would bring about in other ways, and you would not help others as you might have done. You see that with

[7] Escorial edition, lxxii. Against scruples. An explanation of the words, 'Deliver us from evil.'

[8] St. Teresa was of the sweetest disposition, so peaceful and pleasant that every one who had to deal with her felt attracted by her, and loved and sought her company. She detested the rude and disagreeable manners of some religious people, which make both themselves and perfection hateful to others. She often used to exclaim: 'God deliver me from sour-faced Saints'. (From Father Gracian's declaration, Fuente, vol. VI. 370, Note 4.)

these two things—the love and the fear of God—we can travel peacefully along the road without imagining that at every step we see some ditch to fall into. If we fancy this, we shall never get to the end of our journey, yet fear must always lead the way. Do not grow careless: we must never feel perfectly safe in this life. To do so would be most dangerous, as we cannot be absolutely sure whether we really possess this holy fear and love.

Our Lord took pity on us because we dwell amidst such uncertainty and are beset by many temptations and dangers; therefore, at the end of this prayer our Master asks for us and teaches us to ask for ourselves, 'BUT DELIVER US FROM EVIL. AMEN.'

CHAPTER XLII[1]

TREATS OF THE FINAL WORDS OF THE PATER NOSTER: 'BUT DELIVER US FROM EVIL. AMEN.'

1. 'Deliver us from evil.' What this evil is. 2. The evils of this life. 3. A prayer for deliverance from them. 4. Contemplatives long for heaven. 5. Contrast between earth and heaven. 6. Necessity of both vocal and mental prayer. 7. That our Lord has helped St. Teresa to write this book through the Pater Noster. 8. Conclusion.

'BUT DELIVER US FROM EVIL. AMEN.'

1. I THINK the good Jesus might well have made this prayer for Himself, for we see, by His speech to His Apostles, how weary He was of this life. 'With desire have I desired to eat this Pasch with you.'[2] As this was to be the last supper He ever

[1] Valladolid edition, xliv; Escorial, continuation of lxxii.

[2] St. Luke xxii, 15: 'Desiderio desideravi hoc Pascha manducare vobiscum.'

ate, these words prove how tired He was of living. Yet, nowadays, people of a hundred years old, far from being sick of existence, want to live longer! But we do not dwell in such misery, sufferings, and poverty as did His Majesty. What was His whole life but a continuous death, for His bitter Passion was always before His eyes?[3] Yet this was the least of His sorrows compared with witnessing the sins committed against His Father and the multitude of souls that are lost. For if this is a cruel torment to a heart filled with charity,[4] what must it have been to the boundless and supreme charity of our Lord? Well might He implore His Father to deliver Him from so many evils and trials and to place Him in peace in His kingdom, of which He was the rightful Heir.

2. *Amen.* I think that as 'Amen' is used at the end of all prayers, so our Lord means by it

[3] What must have been the feelings of our Lord Jesus Christ—and what must His life have been? For all things were present before His eyes, and He was the constant witness of the great offences committed against His Father. I believe without doubt that this pained Him far more than His sacred Passion. There He found the end of all His trials, with the consolation of gaining our salvation through His death, and of proving how He loved His Father by suffering for Him, which allayed His agony . . . Yet I think the constant sight of the many sins committed against God and of the numberless souls on their way to hell must have caused Him such anguish that, had He not been more than man, one day of such torment would have destroyed not only His life, but many more lives, if they had been His. (*Castle*, M. V. ii, 13.)

[4] 'St. Teresa delighted in reading the lives of the saints, but nothing so excited her devotion as the history of those who had converted many souls. Indeed, this moved her far more than the sufferings of the martyrs. She would cry to God, imploring Him to listen to her prayers since prayer was her only resource, and begging Him to allow her to rescue at least one soul from among the many victims of the devil.' (*Ribera*, bk. IV. xi.)

re, that we may be delivered from all evil for ver. It would be hopeless, sisters, to suppose hat while we are on earth we can be freed from numberless temptations, imperfections, and even sins, since Holy Scripture says: 'If we say that we have no sin, we deceive ourselves.'[5] This is the truth. Then, if we flee from bodily evils and sufferings—and who is without many a trial of the sort?—is it not right to ask to be delivered from the ills of the soul? Still, we must recognize that it is impossible for us to be delivered from every corporal evil or from imperfections and faults in God's service. I am not speaking of the saints—they 'can do all things in Christ',[6] as St. Paul said, but of sinners like myself. When I see how engulfed I am in my own weakness, tepidity, want of mortification, and other faults, I feel the need of asking God for some redress. As for you, daughters, pray for what you think best: I shall never be free from these evils in this life and so I beg to be delivered from them in eternity. What good do we possess on earth, where we are destitute of all good and absent from our Lord? Deliver me, O God! from this deadly nightmare; deliver me from the many labours, the frequent anguish, the numberless vicissitudes, the multitude of duties that devolve upon us in this world: from the many, many, *many* things that harrass and that weary me, and that would weary any reader of this book were I to enumerate them. Life is made

[5] I St. John i, 8: 'Si dixerimus quoniam peccatum non habemus, ipsi nos seducimus.'

[6] Phil. iv, 13: 'Omnia possum in eo qui me confortat.'

unbearable[7] by the loathing I feel at having led so bad a life and at the sight of its unworthiness even now, considering my indebtedness.

3. Therefore I beg of God to deliver me for ever from all evil since I cannot pay the score I owe, but, perhaps, only plunge deeper into debt each day. O God! Unbearable are the uncertainties as to whether I love Thee or whether my desires are pleasing to Thee. My Lord and my God! Deliver me from all evil and vouchsafe to take me to where all good things are to be found. What do souls look for here, after Thou hast shown them in some degree the nothingness of this world, or when they have learnt it by experience, and have a lively faith in what the eternal Father is keeping in store for us because His Son asked Him to bestow it on us and has bidden us beg it for ourselves?

4. An ardent and constant desire for heaven is a sure sign in contemplatives that the favours they receive come from God and that their contemplation is genuine, for He is drawing their souls to Him. So let those who possess it value it highly. But let nobody suppose that *I* ask for heaven for this reason—it is only because my life has been so wicked that I am afraid of living any longer—besides, I am tired of bearing so many crosses. But souls which receive divine favours may well desire to be where they will no longer taste of them by sips. Now that they know something of the grandeurs of God, they long to see them

[7] *Castle*, M. VI. xi, 9; M. VII. iii, 14. *Excl.* vi; xii, 2; xiv. Poems 2. 3 and 4 on the words 'I die because I do not die.' (Minor Works of St. Teresa.)

in entirety: they do not wish to dwell amidst so many obstacles to their enjoyment of this supreme good, but pine to be where the Sun of righteousness never sets. All earthly things henceforth seem dim to them. I cannot understand how they can live another hour—at all events, no one can ever feel content to do so who has once begun to delight in God and who has partaken of His kingdom here, so as no longer to do her own will but that of her King.

5. Oh, how different must be that life where one no longer pines for death! What a contrast in the bent of our wills to God's will! He wills that we should love the truth, while we prefer falsehood; He wishes us to love what is eternal—but we follow what is fleeting; He would have us care for the noble and sublime—we only value base and earthly things; He wills that we should rest on what is safe, while we seek danger. All things are vanity, my daughters, save to ask God to deliver us from these dangers for ever and to preserve us from all evil. Although our wish for this may not be perfect, yet let us force ourselves to make the petition. What does it matter if we pray for great things—we are asking it of One Who is all-powerful? It would be an insult to ask a great emperor for a farthing. But to make sure of obtaining our request, let us leave the choice of the gift to the will of God,[8] since we have already yielded our will to Him. May His Name be for ever blessed both in heaven and earth, and let His will be ever done in me! Amen.[9]

[8] *Excl.* xvi.

[9] Escorial edition, lxxiii. In which the book is concluded.

6. Now you see, my friends, that to make vocal prayer with perfection is to consider and to realize to Whom it is offered, who it is that makes it, and what is asked for. Do not be disheartened if people tell you that it is wrong to use any but vocal prayer. Read over very carefully all that I have written and beg God to teach you anything about the subject that you cannot understand. Nobody can hinder you from vocal prayer nor force you to say the Pater Noster hurriedly and thoughtlessly. If any one tries to prevent your prayer or advises you to give it up, do not trust what he says but look upon him as a false prophet. In these times you cannot listen to everybody: if to-day some one tells you that you have nothing to fear, there is no knowing what he may say to-morrow. I meant to have explained how you should say the Ave Maria, but having enlarged my book so much, I must leave it. To know how to recite the Pater Noster well will show you how to say any other prayer.

7. Now let us finish the journey which I have described. See, sisters, what trouble our Lord has saved me by teaching both you and myself 'the way' I began to describe to you, by showing me how much we ask for when we say this evangelical prayer. May He be for ever praised, for assuredly the idea never entered my mind that it contained such sublime secrets. As you have seen, it comprises the whole spiritual life from the very beginning until God absorbs the soul into Himself and gives it to drink freely of the fountain of living water[10] which I told you was to be found at the end of

[10] *Way of Perf.* xix, 4.

the pilgrimage. To speak the truth, after having gone through this prayer, I cannot find any more to say. Our Lord seems to have wished to teach us what great consolation it contains. It is most useful for those who cannot read: if they understood it, they might gather from it much spiritual instruction and solace. If other books are taken from us, no one can deprive us of this which came from the lips of the very Truth Who cannot err. And since, as I said, we recite the Pater Noster very often during the day, let us take delight in it, and let us strive to learn humility from the way in which our good Master prays, besides all the other things I have explained to you.

8. Beg of Him to pardon me for having dared to speak about such high matters. His Majesty knows well that I should never have had the courage nor would my mind have been capable of it, unless He had taught me what to say. Now, sisters, I think our Lord does not wish me to continue, though I intended writing more. Our Lord has taught both you and me the way I have described in the book which, as I have said, I have written (the *Life*). I have told you how to journey to this fount of living water and what the soul feels when it is attained: how God satiates the spirit, deprives it of all thirst for earthly things, and strengthens it in His service. That book will be a great help to those who feel called to such a state and will give them much light. Ask for it, for the Father-Master, Father Dominic Bañez, who is my confessor, has it; I shall also give him this before showing it to you; should he think

that you would be benefited by having it, and also give you the former, I should feel happy at having afforded you any comfort. If this work is unworthy of being read, you must take the will for the deed, as I have done my best to obey your request. I think that I have been well repaid for the pains it has cost me, as I have not had to study what to write because our Lord has taught me the secrets of this evangelical prayer, which have greatly consoled me.

Blessed and praised be God, from Whom comes all the good that we either speak, or think, or do! Amen.

JESUS.

HERE ENDS
THE WAY OF PERFECTION
TRANSLATED AND PRINTED BY THE
BENEDICTINES OF STANBROOK
A. D. MCMXXV

INDEX

Visits to the Blessed Sacrament. *St. Alphonsus* 5.00
Moments Divine—Before the Blessed Sacrament. *Reuter* 10.00
Miraculous Images of Our Lady. *Cruz* 21.50
Miraculous Images of Our Lord. *Cruz* 16.50
Raised from the Dead. *Fr. Hebert* 18.50
Love and Service of God, Infinite Love. *Mother Louise Margaret* 15.00
Life and Work of Mother Louise Margaret. *Fr. O'Connell* 15.00
Autobiography of St. Margaret Mary 7.50
Thoughts and Sayings of St. Margaret Mary 6.00
The Voice of the Saints. *Comp. by Francis Johnston* 8.00
The 12 Steps to Holiness and Salvation. *St. Alphonsus* 9.00
The Rosary and the Crisis of Faith. *Cirrincione & Nelson* 2.00
Sin and Its Consequences. *Cardinal Manning* 9.00
St. Francis of Paola. *Simi & Segreti* 9.00
Dialogue of St. Catherine of Siena. *Transl. Algar Thorold* 12.50
Catholic Answer to Jehovah's Witnesses. *D'Angelo* 13.50
Twelve Promises of the Sacred Heart. (100 cards) 5.00
Life of St. Aloysius Gonzaga. *Fr. Meschler* 13.00
The Love of Mary. *D. Roberto* 9.00
Begone Satan. *Fr. Vogl* 4.00
The Prophets and Our Times. *Fr. R. G. Culleton* 15.00
St. Therese, The Little Flower. *John Beevers* 7.50
St. Joseph of Copertino. *Fr. Angelo Pastrovicchi* 8.00
Mary, The Second Eve. *Cardinal Newman* 4.00
Devotion to Infant Jesus of Prague. *Booklet* 1.50
Reign of Christ the King in Public & Private Life. *Davies* 2.00
The Wonder of Guadalupe. *Francis Johnston* 9.00
Apologetics. *Msgr. Paul Glenn* 12.50
Baltimore Catechism No. 1 . . . . 5.00
Baltimore Catechism No. 2 . . . . 7.00
Baltimore Catechism No. 3 . . . . 11.00
An Explanation of the Baltimore Catechism. *Fr. Kinkead* 18.00
Bethlehem. *Fr. Faber* 20.00
Bible History. *Schuster* 16.50
Blessed Eucharist. *Fr. Mueller* 10.00
Catholic Catechism. *Fr. Faerber* 9.00
The Devil. *Fr. Delaporte* 8.50
Dogmatic Theology for the Laity. *Fr. Premm* 21.50
Evidence of Satan in the Modern World. *Cristiani* 14.00
Fifteen Promises of Mary. (100 cards) 5.00
Life of Anne Catherine Emmerich. 2 vols. *Schmoeger* 48.00
Life of the Blessed Virgin Mary. *Emmerich* 18.00
Manual of Practical Devotion to St. Joseph. *Patrignani* 17.50
Prayer to St. Michael. (100 leaflets) 5.00
Prayerbook of Favorite Litanies. *Fr. Hebert* 12.50
Preparation for Death. (Abridged). *St. Alphonsus* 12.00
Purgatory Explained. *Schouppe* 16.50
Purgatory Explained. (pocket, unabr.). *Schouppe* 12.00
Fundamentals of Catholic Dogma. *Ludwig Ott* 27.50
Spiritual Conferences. *Faber* 18.00
Trustful Surrender to Divine Providence. *Bl. Claude* 7.00
Wife, Mother and Mystic. *Bessieres* 10.00
The Agony of Jesus. *Padre Pio* 3.00

Prices subject to change.

Seven Capital Sins. *Benedictine Sisters* ... 3.00
Confession—Its Fruitful Practice. *Ben. Srs.* ... 3.00
Sermons of the Curé of Ars. *Vianney* ... 15.00
St. Antony of the Desert. *St. Athanasius* ... 7.00
Is It a Saint's Name? *Fr. William Dunne* ... 3.00
St. Pius V—His Life, Times, Miracles. *Anderson* ... 7.00
Who Is Therese Neumann? *Fr. Charles Carty* ... 3.50
Martyrs of the Coliseum. *Fr. O'Reilly* ... 21.00
Way of the Cross. *St. Alphonsus Liguori* ... 1.50
Way of the Cross. *Franciscan version* ... 1.50
How Christ Said the First Mass. *Fr. Meagher* ... 21.00
Too Busy for God? Think Again! *D'Angelo* ... 7.00
St. Bernadette Soubirous. *Trochu* ... 21.00
Pope Pius VII. *Anderson* ... 16.50
Treatise on the Love of God. 1 Vol. *de Sales. Mackey, Trans.* ... 27.50
Confession Quizzes. *Radio Replies Press* ... 2.50
St. Philip Neri. *Fr. V. J. Matthews* ... 7.50
St. Louise de Marillac. *Sr. Vincent Regnault* ... 7.50
The Old World and America. *Rev. Philip Furlong* ... 21.00
Prophecy for Today. *Edward Connor* ... 7.50
The Book of Infinite Love. *Mother de la Touche* ... 7.50
Chats with Converts. *Fr. M. D. Forrest* ... 13.50
The Church Teaches. *Church Documents* ... 18.00
Conversation with Christ. *Peter T. Rohrbach* ... 12.50
Purgatory and Heaven. *J. P. Arendzen* ... 6.00
Liberalism Is a Sin. *Sarda y Salvany* ... 9.00
Spiritual Legacy of Sr. Mary of the Trinity. *van den Broek* ... 13.00
The Creator and the Creature. *Fr. Frederick Faber* ... 17.50
Radio Replies. 3 Vols. *Frs. Rumble and Carty* ... 48.00
Convert's Catechism of Catholic Doctrine. *Fr. Geiermann* ... 5.00
Incarnation, Birth, Infancy of Jesus Christ. *St. Alphonsus* ... 13.50
Light and Peace. *Fr. R. P. Quadrupani* ... 8.00
Dogmatic Canons & Decrees of Trent, Vat. I. *Documents* ... 11.00
The Evolution Hoax Exposed. *A. N. Field* ... 9.00
The Primitive Church. *Fr. D. I. Lanslots* ... 12.50
The Priest, the Man of God. *St. Joseph Cafasso* ... 16.00
Blessed Sacrament. *Fr. Frederick Faber* ... 20.00
Christ Denied. *Fr. Paul Wickens* ... 3.50
New Regulations on Indulgences. *Fr. Winfrid Herbst* ... 3.00
A Tour of the Summa. *Msgr. Paul Glenn* ... 22.50
Latin Grammar. *Scanlon and Scanlon* ... 18.00
A Brief Life of Christ. *Fr. Rumble* ... 3.50
Marriage Quizzes. *Radio Replies Press* ... 2.50
True Church Quizzes. *Radio Replies Press* ... 2.50
The Secret of the Rosary. *St. Louis De Montfort* ... 5.00
Mary, Mother of the Church. *Church Documents* ... 5.00
The Sacred Heart and the Priesthood. *de la Touche* ... 10.00
Revelations of St. Bridget. *St. Bridget of Sweden* ... 4.50
Magnificent Prayers. *St. Bridget of Sweden* ... 2.00
The Happiness of Heaven. *Fr. J. Boudreau* ... 10.00
St. Catherine Labouré of the Miraculous Medal. *Dirvin* ... 16.50
The Glories of Mary. *St. Alphonsus Liguori* ... 21.00
The Three Ways of the Spiritual Life. *Garrigou-Lagrange, O.P.* ... 7.00

Prices subject to change.

St. Vincent Ferrer. *Fr. Pradel, O.P.* . . . 9.00
The Life of Father De Smet. *Fr. Laveille, S.J.* . . . 18.00
Glories of Divine Grace. *Fr. Matthias Scheeben* . . . 18.00
Holy Eucharist— Our All. *Fr. Lukas Etlin* . . . 3.00
Hail Holy Queen (from *Glories of Mary*). *St. Alphonsus* . . . 9.00
Novena of Holy Communions. *Lovasik* . . . 2.50
Brief Catechism for Adults. *Cogan* . . . 12.50
The Cath. Religion—Illus./Expl. for Child, Adult, Convert. *Burbach* . . . 12.50
Eucharistic Miracles. *Joan Carroll Cruz* . . . 16.50
The Incorruptibles. *Joan Carroll Cruz* . . . 16.50
Secular Saints: 250 Lay Men, Women & Children. PB. *Cruz* . . . 35.00
Pope St. Pius X. *F. A. Forbes* . . . 11.00
St. Alphonsus Liguori. *Frs. Miller and Aubin* . . . 18.00
Self-Abandonment to Divine Providence. *Fr. de Caussade, S.J.* . . . 22.50
The Song of Songs—A Mystical Exposition. *Fr. Arintero, O.P.* . . . 21.50
Prophecy for Today. *Edward Connor* . . . 7.50
Saint Michael and the Angels. *Approved Sources* . . . 9.00
Dolorous Passion of Our Lord. *Anne C. Emmerich* . . . 18.00
Modern Saints—Their Lives & Faces, Book I. *Ann Ball* . . . 21.00
Modern Saints—Their Lives & Faces, Book II. *Ann Ball* . . . 23.00
Our Lady of Fatima's Peace Plan from Heaven. *Booklet* . . . 1.00
Divine Favors Granted to St. Joseph. *Père Binet* . . . 7.50
St. Joseph Cafasso—Priest of the Gallows. *St. John Bosco* . . . 6.00
Catechism of the Council of Trent. *McHugh/Callan* . . . 27.50
The Foot of the Cross. *Fr. Faber* . . . 18.00
The Rosary in Action. *John Johnson* . . . 12.00
Padre Pio—The Stigmatist. *Fr. Charles Carty* . . . 16.50
Why Squander Illness? *Frs. Rumble & Carty* . . . 4.00
The Sacred Heart and the Priesthood. *de la Touche* . . . 10.00
Fatima—The Great Sign. *Francis Johnston* . . . 12.00
Heliotropium—Conformity of Human Will to Divine. *Drexelius* . . . 15.00
Charity for the Suffering Souls. *Fr. John Nageleisen* . . . 18.00
Devotion to the Sacred Heart of Jesus. *Verheylezoon* . . . 16.50
Who Is Padre Pio? *Radio Replies Press* . . . 3.00
The Stigmata and Modern Science. *Fr. Charles Carty* . . . 2.50
St. Anthony—The Wonder Worker of Padua. *Stoddard* . . . 7.00
The Precious Blood. *Fr. Faber* . . . 16.50
The Holy Shroud & Four Visions. *Fr. O'Connell* . . . 3.50
Clean Love in Courtship. *Fr. Lawrence Lovasik* . . . 4.50
The Secret of the Rosary. *St. Louis De Montfort* . . . 5.00
The History of Antichrist. *Rev. P. Huchede* . . . 4.00
St. Catherine of Siena. *Alice Curtayne* . . . 16.50
Where We Got the Bible. *Fr. Henry Graham* . . . 8.00
Hidden Treasure—Holy Mass. *St. Leonard* . . . 7.50
Imitation of the Sacred Heart of Jesus. *Fr. Arnoudt* . . . 18.50
The Life & Glories of St. Joseph. *Edward Thompson* . . . 16.50
Père Lamy. *Biver* . . . 15.00
Humility of Heart. *Fr. Cajetan da Bergamo* . . . 9.00
The Curé D'Ars. *Abbé Francis Trochu* . . . 24.00
Love, Peace and Joy. (St. Gertrude). *Prévot* . . . 8.00

At your Bookdealer or direct from the Publisher.
Toll-Free 1-800-437-5876 ***Fax 815-226-7770***

Prices subject to change.

NOTES

NOTES

NOTES